Honoring

TROY C. CRENSHAW
LORRAINE SHERLEY
RUTH SPEER ANGELL

This book says to three living voices that we and their thousands of students have heard them gladly, and that through this volume we intend that they should know of our gratitude and deep regard. None of us would trade a living voice for a book, yet books can almost make voices immortal, and such is the hope with this volume.

James M. Moudy, Chancellor
Texas Christian University

STUDIES IN

LITERATURE

a Festschrift

TEXAS CHRISTIAN UNIVERSITY PRESS

FORT WORTH

PREFACE

I doubt that Miss Sherley, Mr. Crenshaw, and Mrs. Angell would expect credit for being Sherley, Crenshaw, and Angell. They are the same accident of nature, in a way, that you and I are, that Milton was and the man who sweeps the stair.

But knowing them we are thankful. And if thanking them does not suffice, let us thank God. Yes, I think that we may give credit there. However such things are managed, these three and a few thousand students and you and I came together. And out of that conglomeration TCU was and is. Propinquity sometimes is all.

In the nighttime heavens, were each of us a star, I doubt that three unassuming English teachers would aspire to displace the names of Betelgeuse, Rigel, and Bellatrix with Sherley, Crenshaw, and Angell. But the rest of us might fix them in an appropriate constellation—something winsome, like the Pleiades, say—where we should know that we could always find them, fixed in their suitable place in the sky, making a happy configuration. We shall go right on going oh! and ah! at the shooting star, we might try to read our newspapers by the inconstant moon. But there, in the West in Texas in April, just as they ought to be, are clustered modestly, with others who teach and learn, these three who make fetchingly a cynosure.

Each of them has had his essential nature, with its preferences and prejudices. Each of them has subjugated it to the disciplined will, harking with the inner ear to voices he sought to recognize. And each of them upon the warp that God gave him has worked persistently his deliberate design.

Some names spell themselves. In time and place—in the mid-third of the twentieth century at TCU in Fort Worth—the letters found their sequence in the ordered years. And History, musing affectionately upon the scenes in Reed, will say again the names through all the days, Sherley, Crenshaw, and Angell.

James Newcomer

Vice Chancellor for Academic Affairs

Texas Christian University

ACKNOWLEDGMENTS

This volume includes three essays originally published elsewhere. The editor and the TCU Press are grateful to *Speculum* and the Mediaeval Academy of America for "John of Angoulême and His Chaucer Manuscript," by Michael Martin Crow; to *Drama Critique* for "*Everyman:* The Way to Life," by Jim Corder; to *Critique: studies in modern fiction* for "Nature and Grace in Caroline Gordon," by Louise Cowan. Each of these essays has been slightly revised for the present printing.

EDITOR'S NOTE

This book is purposed to honor three members of the Department of English of Texas Christian University who by their careers have honored the profession of teaching and the community of learning. The coincidence of the retirements from TCU in the spring of 1971 of Troy C. Crenshaw, Lorraine Sherley, and Ruth Speer Angell has occasioned the gathering of these essays in an academic interest of each of the three. Professor Crenshaw, who came to TCU in 1948 as Chairman of the Department of English, is identified with courses in medieval literature. Lorraine Sherley, who recently received an honorary doctorate from TCU, which is her alma mater and in which she taught for more than four decades, is associated with courses in Renaissance literature. Since coming to TCU in 1937, Professor Angell has been noted for courses in American literature.

Knowing their professional distinctions and their generous service to Texas Christian University and to the Department of English, we—former students, colleagues, and friends—are grateful and have made this book as token of our esteem and affection.

Betsy Feagan Colquitt

Department of English

Texas Christian University

Contents

STUDIES IN

Medieval

LITERATURE

The Polylithic Romance: With Pages

of Illustrations*

Alan M. F. Gunn

The extraordinary complexity, the multifaceted guises and significations of such genres of medieval literature as the allegory and the dream vision and of their chief exemplars have long been recognized. Within recent years, it has also been increasingly sensed that the medieval romance and its more notable exemplars exhibit a comparable degree of complexity in form, a similar multivalence in meaning. The "critical point" in the developing awareness of such complexity is signaled in Morton Bloomfield's 1961 study of *Sir Gawain and the Green Knight*. He there suggested "that romance is not a simple genre but a highly complex one and that there are many varieties of romance. . . . There are comic as well as serious, religious as well as amorous, psychological as well as objective, episodic as well as tightly organized, romances. The romance genre is by no means a unified monolithic type."[1]

"Much more needs to be done on this matter," Professor Bloomfield then rightly observed. Certainly it needs to be emphasized that the complexity of the medieval romance is not only a matter of the range and variety of its types and sub-types: it is also one of the balancing and the simultaneous development of its sub-genres in a single narrative or cycle of narratives. Furthermore, it may involve the blending or cross-breeding of the romance with such other literary genres and modes as those of the epic, the dream vision, the *fabliau,* the pastoral, allegory, and drama both tragic and comic in mode. The romance has its ancestry in myth and legend, and is inclined to unite with such exogamous, non-literary forms as chronicle and history and discourse on theological, philosophical, ethical, or scientific themes. A single romance may be at once comic and serious, potentially or even ultimately tragic; amorous in theme and yet profoundly religious or philosophical; successful in its representation of inner psychological reality and of external circumstance and appurtenance. Neither the genre nor the individual romance is a monolith.

This does not mean, however, that the individual romance need lack unity. Monolithic or polylithic, the "tightly-organized" romances, such as those of Chrétien, Chaucer, and the *Gawain* poet, and many of the so-called "episodic" romances, are shaped by and exhibit what Northrop Frye has termed "the underlying tonality of a work of fiction."[2] (This may indeed appear to be the overlying or major tonality.) The most frequently encountered or at least most familiar tonality of medieval romance is what after abundant precedent may be called the "chivalric romance." It has been succinctly described by Lady Bercilak: "In the records of chivalry the two things chiefly praised are true love and the lore of knightly warfare."[3] The description does not, to be sure, quite fit the poet's account of her dealings and her lord's with Sir Gawain. Yet that love and martial deeds are in varying degrees and proportions major themes of the romances of the age of chivalry can hardly be denied.

In the "taxonomy" of the medieval romance which I am here tentatively proposing, the chivalric romance must head the roster as its most characteristic if not always dominant tonality, as its partially if not totally inclusive form. With equal justice, it may be termed its culminating form, the "high romance" acclaimed by poets and lovers of later times. For the other varieties, types, subtypes, and sub-genres, the order of listing is hardly a genetic one or even roughly chronological. Yet it may suggest as it moves on from the "proto-romance" through to the "counter-romance" something of the movement from the myth and faërie and legend of the pre-Chrétien era through Chrétien's "high romance" to the first flights of irony and parody in Jean de Meun and in Chaucer and beyond to the apotheosis of these modes in Cervantes. Such a movement is close to if not identical with that which Northrop Frye has graphed from myth and marvel and legend through romance and comedy to the modes of tragedy and irony. Frye argues for a cyclic turning or returning from irony to myth.[4] If, for the medieval romance, we round out the circuit as we should with Chaucer and Malory, we find ourselves moving on through tragedy and sometimes through irony to the neomythical modes of the close of *Troilus* and the *Canterbury Tales* and of the Grail quest or of Arthur's departure for Avalon.

Quite clearly also the "taxonomy" here offered does not constitute a logical schema. It joins without distinction categories of content, origin, theme, structure, mode, tone, and purpose.[5] It may indeed be part of the complexity and multivalence of the dominant genre of the Middle Ages that it should resist logical categorizing and classification.

Primary or at least Partly Inclusive Genre: the Chivalric
   Romance: a tale of the deeds of knights, of their valorous
   exploits in honor of the ladies they loved, and of their marvelous adventures and quests. (Key concepts: knights, exploits, ladies, love, marvels, adventures, quests.) Cf. *Sir Gawain
   and the Green Knight,* verses 1512-1519, as translated by
   M. R. Ridley: "[For] in all the records of chivalry the two
   things chiefly praised are true love and the lore of knightly
   warfare. And the tale of their striving in honor of their
   loves is the title and the theme of the stories of the deeds
   of all true knights. For their true loves they have ventured
   their lives, and endured long days of woe, and then avenged
   themselves by their valor, and ended their sorrows, and
   brought happiness to their ladies in their bowers by their
   proven prowess."[6] (Quoted by permission of the publisher,
   Kaye & Ward Ltd., London, England.)
Proto-romances: narratives of love and adventure transitional
   between the heroic tales and sagas of the Northern and Celtic
   peoples and the *chansons de geste* on the one hand and the
   fully developed chivalric romance on the other. *Havelok, King
   Horn,* early versions of the Tristan legend, many of the
   Breton lays, Wace's *Roman de Brut,* Layamon's *Brut.*
   1. Cyclic Romances:
      a. Matter of Britain: Arthurian romances
      b. Matter of France: Charlemagne romances
      c. Matter of (Greece) and Rome: Trojan and Theban
         romances, romances of Alexander and Aeneas
      d. Matter of England: *Havelok, King Horn, Athelston*
   2. Breton Lays: brief narratives of love and faërie derived
      from tales recounted by Breton *conteurs:* lays of Marie de
      France; *Sir Orfeo, Lai le Freine, Sir Launfal, Franklin's Tale*
      (an imitation of a Breton lay?)
   3. Romances of Wonder, Faërie, the Marvelous, and the
      Supernatural: Breton lays, legends of begetting and passing
      of Arthur, legends of Merlin, *Sir Gawain and the Green
      Knight, Wife of Bath's Tale,* Grail romances
   4. Historical (or Legendary) Romances: all romances of Troy,
      Thebes, Alexander, Arthur, Charlemagne, Crusades; also
      Havelok, Athelston, King Horn
   5. Amorous Romances:
      a. of young love: *Aucassin and Nicolete*

    b. of illicit love: Tristan and Lancelot romances, *Troilus and Criseyde*

    c. of love and marriage: *Erec, Ywain; Sir Orfeo, Book of the Duchess, Knight's Tale, Franklin's Tale*, Malory's tale of Gareth

    d. of fraternal love: *Amis and Amiloun, Athelston, Knight's Tale* (in conflict with courtly love)

6. *The* High Romance: the "chivalric romance" in its culminating form: romances composed by Chrétien de Troyes; Malory's tale of Gareth

7. Episodic Romances: French prose Arthuriana; work of Malory (?)

8. "Tightly Organized" Romances: *Cligès, Erec, Ywain; Sir Orfeo, Havelok, Sir Gawain and the Green Knight, Troilus and Criseyde*

9. Comic Romances: *Cligès, Erec, Ywain; Sir Orfeo, Sir Launfal, Sir Gawain and the Green Knight, Knight's Tale, Franklin's Tale*, Malory's tale of Gareth

10. Tragic Romances: Tristan and Lancelot romances, *Troilus and Criseyde*, Malory's tale of Balin; the death of Arthur as recounted by alliterative and stanzaic poets and by Malory

11. Elegiac Romances: *Book of the Duchess*, close of the work of Malory

12. Dream-Vision Romances: *Roman de la Rose* (especially part composed by Guillaume de Lorris); *Book of the Duchess, Parlement of Foules*

13. Allegorical Romances: *Roman de la Rose* and romances of Machaut *et al.* in the *Rose* tradition; *Parlement of Foules*

14. Philosophical Romances: *Roman de la Rose;*[7] *Troilus and Criseyde, Parlement of Foules, Knight's Tale*

15. Psychological Romances: romances of Chrétien de Troyes, *Roman de la Rose* and other dream-vision poems; *Troilus and Criseyde*

16. "Educational" Romances (i. e., youth's *l'enfances*, initiation, "growing-up"): Chrétien's *Perceval, Roman de la Rose; Troilus and Criseyde* (?), *Knight's Tale, Sir Gawain and the Green Knight*

17. Problem Romances: romances of Chrétien de Troyes, *Roman de la Rose; Parlement of Foules, Knight's Tale, Wife of Bath's Tale, Franklin's Tale, Troilus and Criseyde* (?)

18. Christian Romances: romances of Charlemagne and of the Crusades, Grail quest romances; *Sir Gawain and the Green Knight*
19. Quasi-Realistic Romances: *Knight's Tale, Troilus and Criseyde* (?)
20. Popular Romances: *Guy of Warwick, Bevis of Hampton*
21., 22., 23., *et al.*

Counter-Romances (the Anti-romance or the Romance Parodied): *Miller's Tale, Sir Thopas;* in later time *Don Quixote*

Whatever challenges specialists may direct to specific designations or illustrations in the foregoing roster, not many, I believe, are likely to take issue today with Professor Bloomfield's view and mine that "there are many varieties of romance." The thesis may appear too obvious, hardly an occasion for surprise, for emphasis, or for extended demonstration. Its proof has indeed already been provided by multiple studies of the sub-types and of the cyclic or individual romances here cited. Whether patent truism or still arguable thesis, certain of its implications and corollaries call for further soundings and elaboration. For one, it is manifest that neither the genre as an inclusive entity nor any of its sub-genres nor any at least of the more notable exemplars of the genre exhibits simplicity and purity of type, mode, purpose. A single romance such as *Troilus and Criseyde,* as we shall see, can be justly described as at once historical, amorous, tightly organized, chivalric, comic, elegiac, tragic, pathetic, philosophical, psychological; perhaps also as allegorical, problematic, ironic, quasi-realistic, myth-oriented. Its particular sub-genre, if it can be said to belong to one, has been cross-bred with other sub-genres and with forms and genres beyond the boundaries of romance or even of those of imaginative literature. For the medieval romance as the dominant genre of its time tended to absorb allied or competing genres and also to encompass, to exogamously seize upon and embrace as it were, modes and forms and themes usually reserved to quasi or non-literary forms of discourse. In such advances beyond its own domain, it resembles the dominant genres of earlier and later periods, such as the epic, the drama, and the novel.

As a class, as a genre, the medieval romance is therefore justly described as "polylithic." The major, the more representative exemplars of the genre are also, it is my contention, so to be designated. We find in such exemplars an extraordinary complexity and variety in content, structure, theme, mode, style, tone, and purpose. As J. A. Burrow has observed, Northrop Frye has provided both the theoretical and the descriptive account of such complexity: "[Frye] says, no one mode will have exclusive rights either in a given period or in a given individual work, 'for while one mode constitutes the underlying tonality of a work of fiction, any or all of the other four may be simultaneously present. Much of our sense of the subtlety of great literature comes from this modal counterpoint.' "[8]

Examples of the polylithic nature of individual or cyclic romances of the Middle Ages are presented not only by the Arthurian narratives, as Ferdinand Lot and Eugène Vinaver have demonstrated,[9] and by those of Chaucer and the *Gawain* poet which we shall shortly examine, but by many long viewed as naively simplistic, as wholly monolithic. Quite recently, Judith Weiss has pointed to the subtle design and thematic richness of such a supposedly simple romance as *Havelok the Dane*.[10] The Breton lay achieves a comparable complexity in *Sir Orfeo*.[11] A hybrid form such as that of the *Nun's Priest's Tale*, with its cross-breeding of the beast fable with the mock epic, the *fabliau*, the chivalric romance, and the *exemplum*, may exhibit an even more remarkable involution of form and style and substance.

I break no fresh ground here and refrain from doing so quite deliberately. For the simultaneous presence of multiple tonalities, genres, modes, and the corresponding appropriate styles can be most quickly and clearly apprehended through an examination of works of recognized merit, long familiar to the student, the complexity in design and multivalence in meaning of which have been attested to by critics and scholars of quite divergent schools. Such works are Chaucer's *Troilus* and *Knight's Tale* and their contemporary, *Sir Gawain and the Green Knight*.

The further "pages of illustrations" here offered are intended to exhibit the internal complexity of these romances. Text citations have been omitted in the analyses of Chaucer's poems lest it be suggested that the indicated sub-genres and modes appear only in isolated passages when they may be pervasive throughout all or a major portion of the work. Such an economy of statement may serve also as a challenge to the reader to provide relevant citations and to develop in his own mind justifications or refutations of my summary headings.

Modes and Aspects of *Troilus and Criseyde*

Primary or Dominant Modes (or Tonalities): Mode of Romance/
Tragic Mode: i.e., a "Tragic Romance," of fortune, destiny,
character, or circumstance; and a "Romantic Tragedy" of
courtly love, or of passionate love of man and woman, *et al.*

Means of Development:

Narrative: of love story; of quasi-historical fiction; of epic
themes; *exempla* of Fortune's reversals, destinal and stellar
influences, love's folly, *et al.*

Dramatic in episodes, scenes, dialogue, total structure and
development: at various times and under various aspects
suggestive of five-act Shakespearean tragedy, medieval tragedy
(cf. the *Monk's Tale*), drama of intrigue, sentimental comedy,
musical, soldier's tragedy, tragedy of excessive reflection, *et al.*

Stylistic Modes: epic, exalted (or high style), rhetorical, lyrical,
proto-operatic, cultivated colloquial, dramatic, vocative (in
poet-narrator's direct addresses to his audience), aphoristic
or proverbial, hortatory and homiletic, ironic, blended,
bathetic, liturgical, *et al.*

Moods of Feeling, Attitude, Atmosphere: heroic, tragic, romantic, sentimental (books I, II), pathetic (book V), comic
(as in comedy of manners, comedy of intrigue, sentimental
comedy, celestial comedy, *et al.*), humorous (in modern
sense), ambiguous, ironic, realistic, analytic, nostalgic, re-
flective, personal and apologetic (as in poet-narrator's
digressive addresses to his audience), devout (in expressions of piety of adherent of religion of love or of pagan
or Christian faith), *et al.*

Thematic and Interpretative Modes: destinal, erotic, political,
martial, psychological, philosophical, astrological-scientific,
cosmic, religious (in expression of concepts of religions of
love, of Olympic pantheon, and of Christian faith), *et al.*

Plot, Aspects and Characteristic of:

Organic, with cause-and-effect relationship of deeds and
events; sequential, with events recounted in linear-temporal
order; dilative, with much amplification of major episodes
and themes; simplistic, in absence of sub-plot or of episodes
not related to main narrative;

Dramatic, with major episodes developed in dramatic scenes;
at once dramatic and simplistic, with action consisting of

limited number of major events, moving forward as in a Shakespearean tragedy from point of initial impulse through rising action to pivotal action or highest point of hero's fortunes to tragic crisis to falling action to fallacious hopes to final catastrophic discovery and death of hero to reconciliation through account in postlude of hero's celestial bliss;

Cyclic, wheel-like, W-shaped in movement and design, with clearly marked rise and fall and rise and fall (reversals) of hero's fortunes;[12]

Developed through intrigue, with Pandarus in fourfold role of playwright, director, stage manager, and actor, as he maneuvers love suit toward its culmination;

Zodiacal, seasonal, diurnal in patterning through matching (and organic nexus) of events of love story with revolutions of the heavenly bodies and the progression of the seasons and of day and night;[13] cosmic-meteorological in nexus of stars and resultant weather with climax of plot; et al.

Characterization, Methods of: explicit and descriptive; dramatic (through words and actions of characters); analytic as in direct comments of poet-narrator, soliloquies, or in accounts of reflections of characters, and in narration and analyses of dreams; emergent, as in characterization of Criseyde; developmental, as in characterization of Troilus through account of his maturation and ennoblement by love and other influences, and of his "ascent" from experience to experience, from insight to insight, symbolized by a movement upward from celestial sphere to celestial sphere; lyrical, as in songs of Troilus and Antigone; epistolary, as in letters of Troilus and Criseyde; et al.

Context, Setting, Atmosphere: tragic, in setting in besieged and doomed city of Troy; royal/aristocratic; martial, as the tragedy of a soldier's love; chivalric/courtly/medieval, in mirroring and use of customs, institutions, ideals, conventions of later Middle Ages; classical/heroic/pagan, in setting of tale in heroic age of pagan Greece and Troy; domestic, in reflection of routine and manners of royal and aristocratic households; seasonal, with critical events occurring in Maytide, the season of love; astrological-meteorological, as in setting of pivotal action of Book III;[14] planetary; cosmic or cosmological, as in proem to Book III; pre-Christian, pagan;

Christian; mundane and super-mundane; *et al.*

Thematic Modes: amorous; destinal; politic; psychological; astrological-scientific; philosophical; ethical; cosmic; mundane and supermundane; religious and theological, in expression of concepts of religion of love, of pagan faith, and of medieval Christianity; *et al.*

Such a tabulation hardly calls for comment. Most of the evidence for its validity lies open in the text even to the neophyte student of *Troilus;* what may not be immediately clear in that text has been explicated by Chaucerians from Lounsbury and Kittredge to those of our latter day.[15] One must indeed grant variations in emphasis and at times outright contradictions in their explications. Yet these very differences and contradictions attest to the richness, the complexity, the multivalence of Chaucer's achievement. There are, to be sure, contemporary scholars who argue that the complexity of the *Troilus* is only one of structure, mood, style; in theme and purpose, they maintain, Chaucer's poem is monolithic, or if polylithic, only so in the presence within it of the four levels of meaning ascribed to inspired scripture: literal, allegorical, tropological, and anagogical.[16] Yet few would deny that it may be justly described as at once quasi-historical romance, love story, tragedy, philosophical meditation, psychological fiction, problem poem, and throughout as an instance of "Troilus Agonistes."[17]

The internal complexity of Chaucer's *Knight's Tale* has long been sensed if not always specifically noted by its commentators.[18] On its surface simplistic and conventional if not naive, close and repeated examinations have revealed in it an extraordinary richness of texture, almost a kaleidoscopic shifting in tone and color, a subtlety, even a profundity in perception. To be sure, the varying emphases of the commentators have at times concealed rather than revealed the multiple types and sub-types of romance and other genres, the shifting aspects that appear under changing lights and from different vantage points, which are successfully united and brilliantly displayed in the tale of Palamon and Arcite. To the eclectic vision, one not distorted by a monolithic bias, these types and modes and aspects emerge almost in a linear order as one proceeds from the tale's opening to its closing verses. Such an emergence I have sought to suggest in the listing below of its multiple sub-genres and aspects, departing from the linear order only to group together closely related modes and sub-genres.

Emerging Aspects of the *Knight's Tale*

Romance of classical antiquity (matter of Greece and Rome):
classical and pagan myth and legend; legend of ancient Thebes;
Theseus legend; quasi-historical or legendary romance; quasi-
classical epic medievalized by Chaucer

Maytide romance, at once native English and archetypal; a
folk tale in its Maytide rites, proverbial wisdom, theme of
sworn brotherhood

Chivalric romance: tale of courtly love, tale of conflict of love
and sworn friendship; *question d'amour* or love debate; tale
of deeds of prowess on field of battle or of· tourney

Comic romance or romantic comedy; high comedy; tragi-comedy;
tragic romance or romantic tragedy (from point of view of
Arcite); anti-romance or romance exaggerated and parodied

Still-life romance or *static* tapestry of medieval life: martial
array, armor, courts, duels, tourneys, gardens, groves, dungeon
towers

Pageant-romance or proto-dramatic and *dynamic* mimesis of
military campaigns, royal ceremonies, processions, hunts, tourneys, Maytide rites, funeral rites, parliaments, nuptials

Quasi-realistic if anachronistic narration and description of
medieval life: its courts, dungeons, tournaments; ceremonies,
customs, institutions, laws, marriage alliances, treaties, medi-
cal diagnoses and treatments[19]

Political romance: developing themes of foreign wars, dynastic
and city-state conflicts, crusades directed against tyrants,
maintenance of hegemony of super-powers, parliamentary
sessions, treaties, marriage alliances

Philosophical romance: *exemplum* of and meditation upon
influence of planetary powers; *exemplum* of Boethian
philosophy; *exemplum* of principles of plenitude and re-
plenishment; meditative-ironic-humorous commentary on
youth, love, and the human condition

Tale of preordained suffering of mortals — *sunt lachrymae
rerum* — or pathos-romance[20]

Tale of youth's maturing through love, suffering, and sacrificial
atonement; tragi-comedy of conflict resolved through sacrifice, love, forgiveness, reason, and submission to necessity
and providence; tale of divine, natural, and human order
achieved through sacrifice and mediation by the Primum
Mobile's agents, Saturn and Theseus

Romance of archetypal themes and patterns of war and peace, governance of world and of earth's peoples and commonwealths, rites of spring, building of temples (theater-arena with shrines of gods), public ceremonies, sacred games, rivalries in love, rituals of sacrifice, funeral rites, joyous nuptials

These genres, sub-genres, modes, and themes of the *Knight's Tale,* it should be emphasized, are pervasive through the entire romance, although they may be explicitly developed only in certain passages. Familiar instances are the themes of astrological influences and Boethian philosophy. Themes and modes explicit throughout the narrative are without question primary, yet others less prominent may be of almost equal importance in its structure and *sententia.* All coexist as variant facets of one unified composition, whether in full harmony or in balance or in vital and significant tension. A recurrent error in the interpretation of this and other medieval romances has been the emphasis upon one facet or mode to the neglect if not exclusion of others. Such partial or exclusive emphases have often, one must concede, proved fruitful in their directing of attention to aspects previously neglected or perhaps wholly disregarded. The eclectic critic will recognize the partial validity of such monolithic interpretations, will seek to take account of each of them in his holistic vision of the multifaceted romance.

To what degree were Chaucer and the *Gawain* poet aware of the genre-complexity of their achievements? Of Chaucer's awareness there can be little doubt. His attention to matters of style and form, his eager experimentation with modes and genres, are evidenced throughout his work, not excepting the earlier dream visions, and are given explicit utterance in the *Troilus,* the Prologue to the *Legend of Good Women,* and in almost every stage of the Canterbury pilgrimage to the repentant catalog in the poet's leavetaking.[21] Nor can readers who have been instructed by Kittredge concerning the poet's sophistication in matters of art and human nature doubt that Chaucer must have realized the internal complexity of his poems.[22] At least equally clear to sensitive readers of *Sir Gawain and the Green Knight* are the tones of bemused but delighted wonder, the finely poised ambiguity, with which its poet or his *personae* speak of the course and substance of its narrative. They thus variously designate either the romance as a whole or its moods, patterns, and episodes:

ferlyes, 23; auter in erde, 27; selly in sight, 28; outtrage awenture of Arthurez wonderez, 29; laye, 30;[23] stori stif and stronge, with lel letteres loken, 34; sum auenturus thyng, 93; an vncouthe tale, 93; sum mayn meruayle, 94; of alderes, of armes, of other auenturus, 95; fere sellyez, 239; fantoum and fayrye, 240; gomen, 274; Crystemas gomen, 283; melly, 342; game, 365; couenaunt, 393; meruayl, 466; craft vpon Christmasse, 471; laykyng of enterludez, 472; selly, 475; meruayl, 479; auenture, 489; auenturus, 491; gomnez, 495; anious uyaɣe, 535; passage, 544; Crystmasse gomnez, 683; gomen, 692; heghe ernde, 1051; tale . . . Of the grene chapel, 1057-58; chaunce, 1082; chaunce, 1838; to assay the surquidré [of Arthur's court], 2457; wonder, 2459; ferlyly [Gawain] telles, 2494; chaunce of the chapel, 2496; boke of romaunce, 2521; Brutus bokez, 2523; aunterez, 2527

As the poet moves on from his opening verses toward the achievement of his hero's quest, he unfolds in succession various genres and sub-genres, modes and themes, and patterns of time, place, and action. Of these, the first four and the sixth through their restatement at the close of the poem serve as enveloping frames for its entire narrative.[24] The fifth, "lel letteres loken," is its alliterative verse form that "in londe so has ben longe." Thereafter, within and as part of these enveloping genres, other types and modes emerge to play their roles in the circling "carol" of the Green Knight and Gawain.

Genre-Patterns of *Sir Gawain and the Green Knight*

Enveloping Genres:

1. Member of epic cycle of Trojan exiles and their descendants, 1-15—2523-2525
2. Tale of Britain, blessed and wondrous isle, 13 ff.—2523-2528
3. Arthurian romance, 25 ff.—2522-2528
4. "Marvel of Arthur," 28-29, 93-95, 475, 479, 491 ff.—2522
5. Alliterative romance, 33-36—2530
6. Christian romance, 37 ff., 51, and throughout to 2529-2530

Emerging Genres:

7. Christmas story, 37 ff., 65, 471-473, 500-503, 734, 907, and *passim;* therefore also a —
8. Christmas carol or ring-dance, (37 ff.), 43, 473, 1026 and *passim*
9. New Year's story, 60 ff., 105, 284, 298, 383, 404, 453, 491-

492, 1054 ff., 1075, 1669, 1675, 1968, 1992, 1998-2400

10. "Christmas game," (45 ff.), 273, 283 ff., 465, 471 ff., 495, 683, 692, 981-990, 1105-2518

11. Chivalric romance, (38-53), 94 ff., 903 ff., 970 ff., 1512 ff., and *passim* to 2489-2519

12. Tale of faërie and of giants of myth and folk lore, 136-461, 720-725, 2090-2478

13. Tale of the testing of the renown of a great court, 258 ff., 272 ff., 309-315 *et seq.,* to 2456-2519

14. Tale of covenants, for exchange of blows and of winnings, 285-2510 (especially 285-300), 377-414, 445-456, 487-490, 533-565, 674-683, 1050-1082, 1105 ff., 1383 ff., 1402-1409, 1619 ff., 1668-1685, 1932-1951, 2086 ff., 2212-2238

15. Gawain-romance, (109), 343—2521

16. Tale of the testing and ordeals of young knight, specifically, of his courage, chastity, and *trawthe,* 343 ff., 375—490, and on to 2512 (the "heart-genre" of the poem)

17. Quest-narrative, 394-2238, but especially 448 ff., 487-490, 532-535, 666 ff., 1050 ff., 2009 ff., 2061 ff., 2161 ff.

Other Emerging Themes, Patterns, Aspects:

18. Tale of youth and of a youthful court and era: 54 ff., 85-89, 280-284, 354 ff., 492 ff. (see also 16 above)

19. Sacred calendar of the church year, 37 ff., 500-538, 734 ff., 895-997 and *passim,* 2529-2530

20. Archetypal pattern of the seasons, 60 ff., 491-492, and especially 498-533; also 726-749, 1998, 2006, and *passim* between 726 and 2234 for winter season

21. Tale of terror, usually an ominous undercurrent but at times explicit, 240-245, 413-466, 486-490, 493-499, 530-535, 540-549, 556-565, 669, 674-686, 715-725, 1750-1754, 1851-1858, 1965-1968, 1991-1995, 1998-2006, 2074-2314, 2559-2562

22. Potential tragedy with threat of death and disgrace for Gawain and Arthur and Arthur's court—see citations for 10, 12, 13, 14, 16, 17, and 21 above

23. Christmas "interlude," masque, play, magical spectacle, 470-473, 833-900, 970-994, 1105—1125 (cf. "Christmas game" above)

24. Allegory of the pentangle, 619-665, and of the green girdle, 1827-1875, 1926-1951, 2020-2041, 2338-2438, 2485-2519

25. Miracle of the Virgin, 646-650, 754-772, 1768-1769 *et seq.,* 2361-2365
26. Tale and possible allegory of hunting, *passim* 1102-1951
27. Bedchamber comedy, subdued and sophisticated *fabliau,* 935-980, 1010-1015, 1178-1311, 1469-1560, 1637-1647, 1731-1875, *passim* 2350-2514
28. *Exemplum* of penance, 1867-1884, 2369-2394, 2429-2438, 2494-2518

Still other genres and modes are pervasive throughout the entire narrative or through many of its more critical stages. Gawain's quest is certainly an *adventure,* and is so designated by the poet. It is also, as Bercilak is to explain, a *tale of intrigue,* of machinations directed against Arthur and Guenevere and Arthur's knights by Morgan and against Gawain's "trawthe" by Bercilak and his lady. All of the third fit and much of the second are in the *comic mode,* specifically, that of *high comedy* or the *comedy of manners* of sophisticated aristocratic folk. The high comic mode re-emerges at the close of the romance in the laughter with which Arthur's court responds to Gawain's report of his adventures. In the technical sense of a tale with a relatively happy outcome, *Sir Gawain and the Green Knight* is accurately described as a *comedy.* Since its ambiguities and complications are not resolved in joyous nuptials, it cannot be called a *romantic comedy.* The truth is, the ambiguity in the exchanges between Gawain and Bercilak's lady and of Bercilak's own role and character carries it at times beyond the bounds of *romance* and *comedy* into the realm of *irony.* I am not aware that critics have put it beside *Troilus and Criseyde* as an instance of early *psychological fiction.* The subtlety of the poet's analyses of Arthur and Gawain and of Gawain's dealings with Bercilak and his lady would seem to justify such a designation.

Hardly less than the *Knight's Tale, Sir Gawain and the Green Knight* is *proto-realistic* in its representation of the court life, ceremonies, feast, dress, armor, modes of hunting and dressing game, and architecture, characteristic of fourteenth-century England. The "procession of the seasons" (498-533) in the second fit is as real, as true to nature, as it is archetypal. The poet's account of Gawain's journey through North Wales and into the wilderness of Wirral, his description of the rugged landscape of Bercilak's hunts and of the Green Chapel, his evocation of the bitterness, the white splendor, the nocturnal storms of winter, blend trium-

phantly the modes of *romance* and of *realism*. Today we tend
to view as utterly *romantic* the *pageantry,* the moving tapestry,
the splendid *spectacles* in green and gold and white, with music
of instruments, with song and dance and carols, of Arthur's
Camelot and of Bercilak's castle. It is true that the poet here
composes in the *nostalgic mode,* for there was regret in his heart
and in those of his audience for the lost glories of the first
years of Arthur's reign. Yet there is still much in the spectacle,
the pageantry, of the poem that mirrors the richness, the splendor
of the courts of the Plantagenets and of the great nobles of
their time. In its festive scenes, the poem becomes almost a
masque or *revue* or *musical,* much idealized to be sure, of the
life of the aristocracy in late medieval England.

Somber scholiasts of our own time have ruled that the tale
of Gawain's testing is no more than an *exemplum,* a *morality,*
more precisely an *allegory,* of an austere Augustinian ethos.[25] For
such a monolithic judgment, one must ask for grounds more
relative than the text provides. Yet one can freely grant that
the poet's piety, the clarity and fineness of his ethical sense, his
humorous and tender charity which is no stern patristic *caritas,*
are ·as manifest in his verses as his sense of the ambiguities and
ironies of mundane and supermundane nature and conduct. His
irony is more than double-edged, cutting through the code and
conventions of courtly love, of "luf-talkyng," and through the
rash decisions and self-deceptions of the youthful and therefore
almost innocent hero.

For after all the exegetes and scholiasts have departed, *Sir
Gawain and the Green Knight* remains a *tale of mystery* in every
sense, in the mystery of Gawain's challengers, in its continuing
and unresolved enigmas and contradictions.[26] What casuist can
resolve the puzzle presented by Gawain's "full confession" and the
priest's "sure absolution" on the eve of the young knight's own
personal doomsday? To what strange land rode "the knyght in
the enker grene"? The tale has been called and rightly so a
tale of suspense; and most certainly it is one in the suspended,
the ambiguous state in which the reader is left at its close.[27] In
this and in many other ways, it may also be justly called a *tale
of surprise.* From the Green Knight's headlong rush into Arthur's
court, through the sudden rising "abof a launde" of Bercilak's
castle, the stealthy and unexpected entrance of his lady into
Gawain's bedchamber, the Green Knight's unmasking of himself

at the Green Chapel, to Gawain's return to Camelot, the narrative is marked by occasions of heart-shaking, mind-sundering
surprise. Astonishing to the listener or reader expecting a tale
of more conventional kind must be the poet's shifts in genre
and mood. Gaiety, terror, irony alternate as his narrative moves
on from Camelot's Christmas caroling to the rude and primitive
challenge to a beheading game which cuts it short, to the high-
spirited course of Bercilak as host and hunter, through the subtle
comedy of his lady's fencing with an embarrassed but susceptible
Gawain, to the axe-edge balancing between terror and rebirth
at the Green Chapel, and then, as the tale completes its circle,
back to Camelot's caroling, its still unchastened laughter.

In such a circling course, not a few commentators have traced
patterns of myth and folk lore: of solar or green world divinities;
of journeys to death's mound followed by rebirth and a return to
joyous life; of rites of passage, of painful and chastening initiation ordeals.[28] In response, critics of monolithic and positivistic
schools have discounted the presence of such archetypal patterns
or have suggested that they exist only on the subliminal levels
of the poet's mind and of the minds of his medieval audience.[29]
Yet it seems rash to deny some degree of awareness of mythical
and archetypal themes to the poet whose verses name "Morgne
the goddess" (2452), and who described aspects of Gawain's adventure as "ferlyes," "selly in sight," "outtrage awenture of
Arthurez wonderez," "sum mayn meruayle," "fere sellyez," and
"fantoum and fayrye." And clearly marked for audiences of any
era are the quest-pattern of Gawain's "heghe ernde," his "anious
uyage," and its life-renewing if chastening outcome for the hero.

The complexity, the polylithic nature, of the medieval romance
is, as we have seen, something manifest, first, in the range and
the multiple number of varieties and sub-types of the genre
and, second, in the complexity, the multiple modes and facets,
the balanced or contrasting or cross-bred sub-types of the more
notable exemplars of the genre. The theme is one that may
suggest certain reflections, certain directions for inquiry by students of genres and of literary history. The movement of each
of the grander genres, such as the epic, the drama, the novel,
and, I would add, the romance, is toward the full realization of
its potentialities. In so moving, each genre tends also toward
variety and range in modes and sub-types and toward complexity
of the individual work. If the genre is one with a dominant, a

central position in its period and culture, it may seek to absorb allied or competing literary genres and forms of quasi- or non-literary discourse. In such an imperial stage it may become encyclopaedic, even cosmic in mode. In this or in an earlier stage, certain of its exemplars may approach the highest degree of art attainable by the genre and its practitioners, a degree not again to be approached until the genre experiences a rebirth in another age and culture. In its native setting the genre may then enter upon a long period of decline, may experience an Alexandrian *untergang,* one marked by works largely derivative, "artificial," deficient in humaneness and breadth of conception. In such a stage or in a later one, parodic and ironic compositions in scorn or jest of the master-works may appear: mock epics, anti- or counter-romances, burlesque dramas, anti-novels.[30]

Viewed from a higher perspective, the course the major genres run is cyclic: from proto-literary ritual and myth and legend and folk tale to the proto-epic and proto-drama and proto-romance to the high and classical forms of each genre to the increasing complexity of polylithic forms to the emergence of ironic and parodic modes and thereafter perhaps to demonic myth and ultimately and hopefully to a reborn Golden Age of celestial and heroic myth. Such a grand circuit Northrop Frye has brilliantly traced and illuminated in his *Anatomy of Criticism.* Viewed from such a perspective, this would be the course of romance in its great age: from pagan myth and heroic legends and the lore of the folk through proto-romance to high romance to the complex, the polylithic forms we have been here examining and beyond them to those first stirrings of irony and parody in Jean de Meun and Chaucer, which gaining in strength in Dunbar and Rabelais were to culminate in Cervantes.

A single work of polylithic kind may indeed exemplify the grand cycle of its master genre; may traverse the complete course from the paleomythical to the neomythical; may, as we have seen, in such a course shift and poise allied or conflicting tonalities, modes, sub-genres. So Chaucer's *Troilus* moves from pagan myth and ethos through the modes of cosmic and human love expressed in its third book to the ironic and tragic modes of its descending action to the Christian myth of its Epilogue. Its companion romance, the *Knight's Tale,* follows a not dissimilar course from legends of Thebes and Theseus to the modes of chivalric romance through good-humored irony and intense pathos to the resolution achieved through the acceptance of the quasi-philosophical myth of the Primum Mobile and his instruments, the stellar Saturn and the civic Theseus. Gawain's quest has its roots in pagan *mythoi* and in the lore of still quasi-pagan folk and at least a surface resolution in a quasi-Christian penitence. Its dominant tonalities are those of romance and comedy, yet the tragic mode is present in threatening shape. The prevailing comic and romantic modes verge at times upon the tragic, at times upon the ironic, from Gawain's arrival at Bercilak's castle to the teasing if joyful reception of the hero upon his return to Camelot. Not altogether unlike, although on a vaster scale and encompassing almost a millenium, is the meandering course of Arthurian and indeed of all chivalric romance from the quasi-mythical mode of *Culhwch and Olwen* to the high romance of Chrétien through the tragic mode of the Tristan and Lancelot romances to the neomythical mode of the Grail quest. The theme is a grand one, made almost infinitely complex by transcultural and translinguistic influences and by the consequent metamorphoses and rebirths of motifs in continental and British lands. It remains to challenge our attention and to call for our further inquiry.

TEXAS CHRISTIAN UNIVERSITY

A Metrical and Stylistic Study of "The Tale of Gamelyn"

Neil Daniel

The Tale of Gamelyn[1] is a metrical romance preserved in twenty-five manuscripts of Chaucer's *Canterbury Tales.* Little is known of the place and date of authorship except that the poem was not written by Chaucer. The dialect of the poem suggests that it was written in the north or northeast midlands fairly early in the fourteenth century. The poem has held an important position among Middle English romances partly because of its connection with the *Canterbury Tales* and partly because it was the narrative source for Thomas Lodge's *Rosalynde: Euphues Golden Legacie* (1590), which provided the plot for Shakespeare's *As You Like It.* Also, it tells a good story.

No good study of the prosody of *The Tale of Gamelyn* has been done. In the introduction to his edition of the poem Skeat gave the matter some attention.[2] But his treatment of the poem is based on his analysis of the metrics of Chaucer; it proceeds no further than a cursory attempt to set up types of half-lines based on the arrangement of accented and unaccented syllables; and it leads him to the conclusion that many of the lines have the same "lilt" as "Sing a Song of Sixpence." He ends up by saying that

> no one who is not well acquainted with the rules for the scansion of Chaucer has much chance of success in scanning Gamelyn. The best he can do is to pronounce every final *-e* as a distinct syllable (unless it is obviously elided or very much in the way), to treat the terminations *-ed* and *-es* as forming distinct syllables, to lay a heavy stress on every accented syllable, to pronounce the words *very slowly and deliberately,* using the old pronunciation as described in my Introduction to Chaucer's Man of Law's Tale, p. x.; and *then* perhaps he may trust to a well-trained ear. Perhaps the most important of all these hints is that which enjoins slowness and deliberation. If read rapidly after the modern fashion, there may still seem to be a sufficient metre; but it will have no sort of resemblance to that with which the author was himself familiar.[3]

William Ellery Leonard has given the metrics of *Gamelyn* more attention than any other scholar. In his article on "The Scansion of Middle English Alliterative Verse,"[4] he handles *The Tale of Gamelyn* as though it were a part of the alliterative revival, and he goes to some length to demonstrate that there is no metrical difference between the lines of *The Tale of Gamelyn* and the alliterative long lines of *Piers Plowman*. Other commentators on the poem, without attempting any thorough analysis of the verse, have offered only tentative solutions to the meter of the poem. Loomis and Wells, for example, have both suggested that the irregular couplets of *Gamelyn* might be recast as ballad stanzas,[5] and Donald B. Sands says, "The line is a seven-stress affair . . ." and its irregularities "make the verse seem rough and unpolished in the extreme."[6]

A careful analysis of the versification of *The Tale of Gamelyn* should serve several purposes. As a result of offering a judgment on the meter it should shed light on an important editorial problem associated with the poem, the selection of the proper copy text, the best manuscript available for the study of textual problems. In addition it should introduce *Gamelyn* as evidence in the on-going inquiry into the prosodic systems of Middle English poetry. In this connection I hope to show that the poem does not fit easily the prosodic system of Chaucer nor that of *Piers Plowman*, but that it falls somewhere between those poles, partaking of both traditions.

The first question that enters into a metrical analysis of a Middle English poem is the non-metrical question whether the structure of the lines depends upon rhyme or alliteration. For in very general and much over-simplified terms there are two streams that make up the English poetic tradition: the native accentual tradition, stemming from Old English poetry and its Germanic antecedents, in which the two halves of each line are bound together by alliteration; and the imported syllabic tradition, from Old French and medieval Latin verse, in which groups of lines are linked together by end-rhyme. In the accentual tradition the number of syllables in a line is not metrically significant, though of course there are natural lower and upper limits on the number of syllables that can be used to write a line of a given number of stresses. In the syllabic tradition, the number of syllables is metrically significant, though the accentual nature of

English makes it inevitable that arrangement of stresses will enter into the metrical system. There is no natural link between accentual meter and alliteration on one hand, or syllabic meter and end-rhyme on the other, only the historical connection and traditional association.

The Tale of Gamelyn is written in rhymed couplets; there are 902 lines, 451 rhyming pairs. The rhymes have been examined in some detail by Lindner[7] and by Skeat.[8] In general the rhymes are simple—*place/grace, name/game, Þer/broÞer,* etc.—and good *Þee/Þee* (11. 363-64) is a rich rhyme, the only instance in the poem. *Now/now* (11. 93-94), *anoÞer/oÞer* (11. 445-46), and *Þe/Þe* (11. 399-400) are repetition rather than rhyme; and there are three weak rhymes in the poem: *wit/bet* (11. 111-112), *gate/scape* (11. 575-76), *chanoun/nom* (11. 781-82).

But there is also alliteration in *The Tale of Gamelyn* although the commentators have generally dismissed it. Typical is Sands's remark that "alliteration is only incidental and confined chiefly to stock, conventional phrases."[9] While the structure of the lines cannot be said to depend on alliteration, as the couplet structure depends on its end-rhyme, there is alliteration in nearly half of the lines. Sometimes it is indeed incidental or ornamental; for example in 1. 61,

And alle myn oÞer purchas   of *l*ondes and *l*eedes,

the alliteration on *l* is confined to the second half-line. As it does not cross the caesura, it serves no structural function. "Londes and leedes" has the ring of a stock phrase or formula, and in fact the phrase occurs four times in the poem. A list of repeated alliterative phrases of this sort sheds some light on the verse technique of the poem.

Alliterative Pair	*Lines*
lithen/lesteneÞ	1, 169, 289, 341, 551, 769
bote/bale	32, 34, 631
stond/stille	55, 102, 238, 473, 571, 599
stoon/stille	67, 263, 395, 423
stalked/stille	617
londes/leedes	61, 71, 104, 895
ram/ryng	172, 184, 280, 281, 283

Often the alliteration does cross the caesura and joins the two halves of the line in just the manner we would expect in poetry of the alliterative tradition. Lines 589-592 will illustrate the combination of end-rhyme and alliteration that characterizes the poem.

Atte posterne *g*ate *G*amelyn out wente,
And a good cart staf in his *h*ond he *h*ente.
*A*dam hente *s*oone ano*Þ*er gret *s*taf
For to helpe *G*amelyn, and goode strokes he ʒaf.[10]

In a count of 232 of the poem's 902 lines, I find 107 lines (46.1%) in which there is no alliteration on stressed syllables, 48 lines (20.7%) in which there is only ornamental alliteration, and 67 lines (28.9%) in which the two halves of the line are linked by alliteration on stressed syllables. There are ten lines which I have not figured into the percentages because the alliteration is questionable (does *s* alliterate with *sch?*) or it falls on syllables which are not clearly stressed syllables. The percentage of lines linked by alliteration is too high to be accounted for by chance.

That *The Tale of Gamelyn* has both rhyme and alliteration suggests that the poem bridges the gap between the two traditions of English poetry. It is my purpose to show that the metrics of the poem supports the same conclusion.

The second issue which enters into a metrical analysis but is not itself a metrical question is whether to pronounce the final *-e*. In the passage quoted on p. 19, Skeat has suggested that we pronounce every final *-e* as a distinct syllable. His suggestion does not accord well with current opinion on the phonology of Middle English. In general it is felt that in the time and place of the composition of *Gamelyn*, that is in the fourteenth century north or northeast midlands, final *-e* had ceased to be pronounced, certainly in colloquial speech except in some set phrases such as *atte last*. It is also widely held, however, that in the poetry of Chaucer the final *-e* usually counts as a metrical unit whether or not it would have been pronounced in colloquial speech. The only reliable internal evidence that bears on this problem is the rhyme words. But the one instance that could be construed as rhyme on a final *-e* in *Gamelyn* is the rhyme of *leute* with *be* in lines 657-58. The *-e* in *be* clearly must be pronounced. But the word *leute*, from the French *leauté*, meaning loyalty, is a loan word, presumably with a French pronunciation, and it sheds no light on the pronunciation of the final *-e* in the words of native stock.

The importance of the final *-e* in a metrical analysis is that whether or not it is pronounced determines the number of syllables in any line where a final -e occurs. In the absence of evidence in the rhyme words, the only grounds on which a decision can be made are metrical. The unavoidable circularity in this determination invalidates any argument based on the final -e. Only after some decision has been made concerning the meter of the poem can we return to the issue of the final -e and make some useful judgment about whether or not to pronounce it.

We come then to the problem of scanning the lines of *The Tale of Gamelyn*. It has been pointed out that Skeat never really solved the meter of the poem. Indeed, he said at one point in his introduction to the poem, "But this is a slippery matter, which I leave to the reader's discretion."[11] Leonard's rather full treatment of the meter of *Gamelyn* is not directed primarily at *Gamelyn,* but at the rhythm of *Piers Plowman.* He takes for granted that we scan the long line of *Gamelyn* as a seven-stress line, four plus three. To illustrate his reading of the poem he gives us first a passage from *Gamelyn* in the Middle English.

> Litheth, and lesteneth   and holdeth your tonge,
> And ye schul heere talkyng   of Gamelyn the yonge.
> Ther was ther bysiden   cryed a wrastlyng,
> And therfor ther was set vp   a ram and a ryng;
> And Gamelyn was in wille   to wende thereto,
> For to preuen his might   what he cowthe do.
> "Brother," seyde Gamelyn,   "by seynt Richer,
> Thou most lene me to-nyght   a litel courser
> That is freisch to the spores   on for to ryde;
> I most on an erande   a litel her byside".
> "By god!" seyde his brother,   "of steedes in my stalle
> Go and chese the the best   and spare non of alle
> Of steedes or of coursers   that stonden hem bisyde;
> And tel me, goode brother,   whider thou wolt ryde".
> (11. 169-182, Skeat's edition)

Then he translates the poem into Modern English, "to put its scansion out of all doubt."

> Heark ye, and listen ye   and hold ye your tongue,
> And ye shall hear a tale told   of Gamelyn the young.
> In the shire anear was   cri-ed a wrestle-ing,
> And for a prize was set up   a ram and a ring.

And Gamelyn he devis-ed   to wend him thereto
For to prove in true might   what he'd learn'd to do.
"Brother", said this Gamelyn,   "by sainted Rich-er
Thou must lend me tonight,   a little cours-er,
That's a fresh one to boot-spur,   on for to ride;
I must on an errand   a little here beside."
"By God," said his brother,   "of steeds within my stall
Go and choose for thee the best   and spare of none of all
Of stallions or of coursers   that stand there side by side,
And tell me, good my brother   whither thou wilt ride".[12]

It is clear that Leonard is pronouncing the final -e. He substitutes
"he devis-ed" (four syllables) for "was in wille" and "wend him"
(two syllables) for "wende." And it is clear, when he translates
"That is freisch to the spores" as "That's a fresh one to boot-spur,"
that he is following Skeat's injunction to pronounce -es as a distinct syllable and to pronounce each word deliberately. His seven-
stress rhythm is what Marie Borroff calls a "compound" rhythm.[13]
George Stewart, making the same kind of analysis of ME verse
as Leonard has done, calls it dipodic rhythm.[14] Both Leonard
and Stewart illustrate this compound meter, in which heavy
stresses alternate with light stresses, by referring to English
nursery rhymes, especially "Sing a Song of Sixpence." In the
nursery rhyme,

Sing a song of six-pence
A pocket full of rye
Four and twenty blackbirds
Baked in a pie,

the stresses on *song, pence, full, twen-, birds,* and *in* are less strong
than the stresses on *sing, six, pock-, rye, four, black, baked,* and *pie.*

Marie Borroff pays close attention to Leonard's handling of the
meter of *Gamelyn* and *Piers Plowman,* for Leonard's conclusions
about the alliterative long line of *Piers Plowman* would apply with
equal force to the meter of *Sir Gawain and the Green Knight.*
She rejects Leonard's seven-stress theory, at least as it might be
applied to *Gawain,* and she exposes some of the unconscious
ad hoc manipulations in Leonard's analysis. Leonard had composed
a companion line for one of Langland's to yield the seven-stress
couplet,

There was junketing o' midnight,   a jump down and up!

> There was laughing and lowering   and "let go the cup!"[15]

To illustrate that the same device could yield a four-stress couplet, she composed her own companion line:

> There was music and mirth, both downstairs and up,
> There was laughing and lowering and "let go the cup!"[16]

My reaction to Leonard and others who would use "Sing a Song of Sixpence" as a model for the meter of *Gamelyn* is that they are not paying attention to the reading their scansion implies. It is true that "Sing a Song of Sixpence" can be read with a compound rhythm and might be chanted in that manner by children at play. But if one were to stand before an audience and read it as serious poetry, and especially if the poem were longer than sixteen lines, one would likely suppress the sing-song quality of the compound meter and read the poem in four-stress couplets.

But before coming to a conclusion about how *The Tale of Gamelyn* should be read, it is necessary to consider the various possibilities. It is possible to dismiss rather quickly and on objective grounds the possibility of its being in the accentual-syllabic tradition of the poetry of Chaucer. In order for *Gamelyn* to be scanned by the same methods that are used for *Cursor Mundi* or *The Owl and the Nightingale* or *The Book of the Duchess,* there would have to be, within reasonable limits, uniformity in the number of syllables per line. How many syllables there are to a line depends of course on whether or not the final *-e* is pronounced. Holding that judgment in suspension for the moment, the range in line length for *Gamelyn* is either 8-16, with an average of 11.4, if the final *-e's* are not counted; or 10-18, with an average of 13.1, if the *-e's* are counted. In either case, the range in line length is too great to be accommodated by a system that depends on the number of syllables per line.

If the lines are not to be measured by the number of syllables, they must be measured by the number of stresses. But the number of stresses in any given line is not an objective fact; the reader has considerable latitude in how he places the stresses. Borroff provides a model for testing the four- and seven-stress theories in her analysis of *Sir Gawain and the Green Knight.* Following the practice of most theorists in prosody, she places the stresses on the syllables that would naturally receive stress in prose. The stresses are determined initially by syntax rather than by metrical considerations. She then arranges the lines into three categories: (1) metrically clear lines indicating a four-stress scansion; (2) metrically clear lines indicating a seven-stress scansion; and (3) metrically ambiguous lines which can be read without distortion according to either scansion. As she points out,

> if the four-stress scansion is "correct," lines of groups 1 and 3 will be the rule and those of group 2 the exception; if the seven-stress scansion is correct, 2 and 3 will be the rule and 1 the exception.[17]

Using the same approach, I find that for *The Tale of Gamelyn* the number of categories must be increased. (1) There are many lines which sound best with four stresses. Some illustrations:

Líthen and lésteneÞ   and hérkeneÞ a-ríght   (1)
He cóuÞe of nórture   and móchil of gánèe   (4)
And bygán with his hónd   to hándlen his bérde   (80)

These lines can be read with seven stresses, but they sound then labored and over emphatic. (2) There are other lines which sound most natural in seven stresses. Examples are:

The éldest wàs a mòche schréwe,   and sóne hè bigán   (6)
Gód may dòn bóote of bàle   Þát is nòw y-wróught   (32)
Crístes cùrs móte Þou hàue   but Þóu bè Þat óon   (116)

To read these as four-stress lines would be to rush the lines and to remove the emphasis from words whose importance and grammatical function require at least secondary stress. (3) There is a third category, perhaps a sub-class of the seven-stress line, in which a reading according to the natural prose rhythm yields six stresses. Some such lines:

To hélpen délen his lóndes   and dréssen hèm to ríghtes. (18)
Of álle his góode stéedes   nón was hìm biléued   (86)
GóÞ and béteÞ this bódy   and réueÞ hìm his wít   (111)

The first half of each of these lines could be forced into four stresses, but in each case three stresses seems to fit the sense and syntax of the line. (4) There is a large group of lines which reveal a combination of four-stress (simple) and seven-stress (compound) systems. Sometimes the first half-line has four beats and the second half-line only two

>The góode knìght cáred sóre,   sík Þer he láy   (11)
>Séelde ʒe sée óny héir   hélpen his bróÞer   (40)
>Fór to lóken or Þóu were stróng   and árt so ʒíng   (148)

and sometimes the first half-line has two valid stresses and the second half-line has three

>Thei cámen to Þe knìght   Þere he láy fùl stílle   (50)
>Gámelyn was líght,   and Þíder ʒàn he lépe   (123)
>BróÞer, saide Gámelyn,   cóme a lìtel néer   (135)

(5) By far the largest category is made up of lines which are metrically ambiguous. They can be read either as four-stress or as seven-stress lines without doing violence either to the natural prose rhythm or to the method of scansion. Taking a passage at random, we can scan lines with four stresses, although it is necessary in some lines to put in extra secondary stresses.

>Gámelyn stòod on a dáy   in his bróÞeres ʒérde,   (81)
>And bygán with his hónd   to hándlen his bérde.
>He Þóught on his lóndes   Þat láyen vnsáwe,
>And his faíre ókes   Þat dówn were dráwe;
>His párkes were bróken   and his déere réued;   (85)
>Of álle his gòode stéedes   nón was him biléued;
>Hise hóuses were vnhìled   and fùl ýuel díght;
>Thó Þoughte Gámelyn   it wénte nought a-ríght

The same lines can be scanned using seven stresses per line, although occasionally a secondary stress is made to fall on a syllable that could not receive stress in prose.

>Gámelyn stòod òn a dáy   ìn his bróÞeres ʒérde,   (81)
>and bygán wìth his hónd   to hándlèn his bérde.
>He Þóught òn his lóndès   Þat láyen vnsáwe,
>And hìs faíre ókès   Þat dówn wère dráwe,
>His párkes wère brókèn   ànd his déere réued;   (85)
>Of álle his gòode stéedès   nón was hìm biléued;
>Hise hóuses wère vnhílèd   and fùl ýuel díght;
>Thó Þòughte Gámelỳn   it wénte nòught a-ríght

The conclusion that seems to emerge from this examination of the possibilities is that the poetry can be read in any way the reader wants to read it. And although that may seem capricious and unscientific, I think there is some truth in that conclusion. If the reader chooses to read the poem in seven-stress lines, he will find the lines fairly regular, but he will frequently be required to stress syllables for metrical rather than linguistic reasons, and he may have to count rests in lines that do not have enough stressed syllables. And he will be committed to a sing-song rhythm which frequently over-emphasizes words that have no special importance. If the reader chooses the four-stress rhythm, he will find that he must frequently either rush important words to fit them into the meter, or suspend the rhythm as Hopkins does in his outriders.

The key to the reading of *The Tale of Gamelyn* is in its oral nature. Recent studies in oral tradition and transmission, stimulated by the work of Milman Parry and Albert B. Lord, have gone far to suggest that a vital oral tradition, developed in the Old English period, was still active as late as the fourteenth century.[18] Evidence of oral performance in *Gamelyn* is to be found in the frequent references to the audience. The poem is divided into seven narrative sections by recurrences of the stock address to the audience (or some variation of it): "Lithen and lesteneþ and herkeneþ a-right, and 3e schulle heeren . . ." (11. 1-2, 169-70, 289-90, 341-43, 551-52, 615-16, 769-70). Lindner suggested that the metrical irregularity of the poem might be explained as evidence that the poem was sung.[19] It should be pointed out, however, that the poem never mentions singing; twice the poet refers to talking (11. 170, 616). Further evidence of the oral nature of the poem is the preponderance of stock phrases, which may occur four, five, or six times, usually in proximate lines, often in the same metrical position in the line.

Phrases	*Lines*
Lithen (eþ) and lesteneþ	1, 169, 289, 341, 551, 769
Cristes curs mote he (thou) have	106, 114, 116, 818
I swere (and swore) by Cristes oore	139, 159, 231, 323
(and) he bigan to gon	126, 220, 498
and 3e schulle heeren	2, 770
and 3e schul heere talkyng (gamen)	170, 290, 342, 552
yuel mot 3e (I, thou, he) þee	131, 363, 448, 720
as so mote I þee	379, 413
so mote I wel þe	577

(alle) Þat my (Þi) fader me (Þe) biquaÞ 99, 157, 160, 360
whil he was on lyue   20, 58, 157, 225, 228
a (Þe) ram and a (Þe) ryng   172, 184, 280, 283
sky Þer he lay   11, 21, 25, 33, 66
Þer he lay (full stille   23, 50

The style, as will be suggested by the stock phrases, is repetitious and not consciously artistic. The poet consistently prefers an easily-remembered phrase to an original one. The implications of the oral style, it seems to me, are that the poem should not be read slowly and deliberately, as Skeat suggested, and that the meter should not be worried in the presentation. When read fairly rapidly and without undue attention to the number of syllables per line, the lines fall into the easy four-stress pattern that has characterized most popular English poetry from the earliest Anglo-Saxon times.[20] There will be frequent variation of the four-stress line by a compound rhythm; sometimes a single half-line will have light stresses alternating with the major stresses, and sometimes the whole line or several lines in succession will have a dipodic structure. But even when the light stresses intervene, the principal movement of the line is determined by the persistence of four major stresses. And as Sands says, after making no effort to resolve the metrical inconsistencies of the *Gamelyn* meter, "The surprise comes, however, when *Gamelyn* is read aloud; its lines then appear, if not elegant, certainly competent and quite appropriate to the matter of the poem."[21]

It remains then to draw some conclusions from this analysis of the style and meter of *The Tale of Gamelyn*. For example, some statement can be made about the pronunciation of the final *-e*. As it turns out, the meter of the poem does not impose any imperative; since the final *-e* will always be an unstressed syllable and since the number of unstressed syllables is not metrically significant, the issue remains in the realm of dialect study, to be settled on some other grounds than metrical. But the meter lends some reinforcement to those who regard the *-e* as silent. As Marie Borroff says, "We may expect that *-e* will be pronounced as a syllable less frequently by those who read the alliterating line as one of four simple units than by those who read it as compound throughout."[22]

Another problem on which this study sheds some light is a rather specialized editorial problem. In his edition of the poem

Skeat used the Chaucer manuscript Harley 7334 as a copy text, making corrections from the other manuscript versions available to him. In my doctoral dissertation, a new edition of *The Tale of Gamelyn*,[23] I argued that another manuscript, Corpus Christi 198, is a more reliable text of the poem. It is not within the scope or purpose of this paper to recapitulate that whole argument. It is only necessary to point out that an important influence in Skeat's choice of Harley 7334 was that the Harley manuscript more nearly fit Skeat's conception of the metrics of the poem than any other manuscript. For example, in line 2, twenty-four of the twenty-five manuscripts have "And 3e schulle heeren   of a doughty knight." Harley 7334 has "And 3e schulle here a talkyng   of a doughty knight." In line 3 most of the manuscripts have "Sire Iohan of Boundys was his name"; Harley 7334 has the unique reading, "Sire Iohan of Boundys   was his righte name." In each case the unique variant gives a reading which is most easily read as a seven-stress line; most of the manuscripts have a four-stress line. In my estimation, therefore, the metrics of the poem argue against Harley 7334 as the best text. And I agree with Eleanor P. Hammond's Preface to *English Verse Between Chaucer and Surrey* that the most reliable text of any poem is the best single manuscript (in the case of *Gamelyn,* Corpus Christi 198) rather than a composite made up from a variety of manuscripts. Particularly in the matter of metrics, the editor's unconscious prejudices concerning the prosody are more likely to confuse than to clarify the text.[24]

The most important implications of this paper are the ones least easy to state—implications about the development of Middle English prosody and about the whole process of metrical analysis. In the development of separate prosodic systems in the English tradition—the native system of a four-stress line with alliteration, and the romance system of accentual-syllabic meter with rhyme—*The Tale of Gamelyn* occupies an unusual position. It fits in both traditions and may provide a clue concerning the reconciliation and blending of those traditions. The two traditions come together with some jarring effects in the fifteenth-century verse of Lydgate and Skelton. And although it is not my purpose to get into the tangled region of fifteenth-century metrics, it seems to me that *Gamelyn* points in the direction of a solution by demonstrating that the distribution of stresses is a more important consideration than the number of syllables.[25]

Finally, the confusion over the proper reading of *Gamelyn* and other Middle English poems says something important about the methods we use to analyze metrics. That the *Tale* was a popular romance intended for oral delivery is important: the poet was apparently un-self-conscious about the meter. Certainly he paid little attention to counting syllables. Presumably he wrote in a style that felt easy and natural to him. And with the exception of the person who copied out MS Harley 7334, the scribes were able, generally, to copy what the poet had written without being disconcerted by the meter. The controversy over the reading of *Gamelyn* is really a controversy between scholars of the late nineteenth and early twentieth centuries on the one hand, and scholars of the middle of the twentieth century on the other. And it reduces, in the long run, to a conflict of metrical taste. To illustrate briefly with materials other than *Gamelyn*, Frye's analysis of iambic pentameter lines (he uses Shakespeare and Milton as his leading exhibits) would lead us to read many of Chaucer's five-stress, decasyllabic lines with four stresses:

Whán that áprill with his shóures sóote
The dróghte of Márch hath pérced to the róote

(CT, 1-2, Robinson text)

This reading is based on the principle that we should read the lines naturally, "giving the important words the heavy accent that they do have in spoken English."[26] Skeat, accustomed to paying close attention to syllables and hearing a regular alternation of heavy and light, would hardly tolerate such liberties with Chaucer's line.

I do not wish to argue that contemporary opinion on metrics is better founded or closer to the fourteenth-century understanding than the opinion at the turn of the century. My point is that we are likely to find in whatever poetry we analyze the rhythm that we have been conditioned to find most natural. Or to put it in another way, prosodic analysis does not generally discover the meter of the poem; instead it provides a meter for the reader which, if it fits, does not violate the language of the poem. And of course we can never know what the audience of the fourteenth century would have heard or liked to hear. This conclusion casts some suspicion on my suggestion (p. 25) that the sing-song quality of the dipodic rhythm would be tiresome. All I can say with real

assurance is that I would not read the poem that way. But considering the subjectivity of meter—the fact, for example, that we don't
even know what stress is[27]—that may be sufficient. The study of
prosody and metrical analyses of early literature, like all other
kinds of literary criticism, must be a continuing task, and every
study must be re-evaluated and redone in each succeeding
generation.

TEXAS CHRISTIAN UNIVERSITY

John of Angoulême
and His Chaucer Manuscript*

MARTIN MICHAEL CROW

Fonds Anglais 39 *(Ps)*, a Chaucer manuscript in the Bibliothèque Nationale, is an unassuming volume of eighty-four folios, written on paper, bound in red morocco with the royal coat of arms of France stamped on the cover.[1] This Paris manuscript is an exceedingly faulty copy of the *Canterbury Tales,* of which it lacks, besides several links, most of the *Squire's* and *Monk's Tales,* most of the *Rime of Sir Thopas,* over six hundred lines of the *Canon's Yeoman's Tale,* all of the *Cook's Tale, Melibeus,* and the *Parson's Tale.* It is written throughout in one hand by a professional scribe who signs himself at the end 'Duxwurth scriptor.' The handwriting, in double columns and uniformly neat, is pointed charter or 'court hand,' and it dates the manuscript as of the first half of the fifteenth century.[2] Certain other facts enable us to place the date as probably before 1430.[3]

The history of the making of *Ps* may be written under two heads, external history and internal,—the former remarkable for its fullness of detail, the latter for the puzzling problems raised as to medieval methods of manuscript production.

I

The external history of *Ps* is projected upon a background of war and imprisonment, of exile and disappointed love. The clue to this romantic story is found within the large capital letter which begins the first line of the manuscript, where is drawn, rather crudely, a shield with three fleurs-de-lis, differenced by a lambel of three pendants, the first of which is charged with a tiny crescent, —the coat of arms of John, count of Angoulême.[4] That the tiny coat of arms on the first leaf of the manuscript indicates correctly its ownership finds conclusive proof in an inventory of the count's library, made June 1, 1467, just one month after his death. Here the Chaucer manuscript is described as follows: 'Ung romant, en anglois, rimé, en papier, commancant, ou premier feuillet, "want tath aprilh" et finissant, ou penultime "aliberons apetite".' The words 'aliberons apetite' are a misreading of 'a lykerous appetite' (H 189)—the French cataloguer evidently knew no English—and these words occur at the end of next to the last page, just as the fifteenth-century description declares. Furthermore, the manuscript contains a table of contents and numerous corrections made in

John of Angoulême's known handwriting. There can be no doubt that it was his manuscript.[5]

The original owner of the Paris manuscript of Chaucer's *Canterbury Tales,* John of Angoulême, was a royal prisoner in England for thirty-three years, 1412-1445. He was a younger brother of Charles of Orléans, the poet, himself a captive in England for a quarter of a century (1415-1440), and a half brother of the great military commander Dunois, the Bastard of Orléans, champion of Joan of Arc. John was the son of that Louis, duke of Orléans, who was treacherously murdered in 1407 by the duke of Burgundy, and of Valentina Visconti, of the Milanese house of despots. Rated, according to Pierre Champion, 'the fourth person of the crown of France,'[6] John was both grandson and grandfather of a king, grandson of Charles V and grandfather of Francis I. Because he was a person of high rank and for his release was demanded a huge sum, which poverty-stricken France found it difficult to raise, he remained in exile a third of a century.

Angoulême was not taken prisoner on the field of battle, but was given into the hands of the English as a hostage, along with six others, to guarantee payment of the 210,000 crowns agreed upon in the treaty of Buzancais, November 14, 1412.[7] He was a youth of but thirteen years when he became a hostage to the duke of Clarence, commander of the English forces.[8] No one thought the hostages would be held long; but many a chapter in the history of the Hundred Years War was to be unrolled before the count should see his native land again.

Bad luck seemed to beset Angoulême from the beginning of his captivity. In 1415 came Agincourt and the capture of Charles of Orléans, who had had charge of raising the ransom demanded for his brother. In 1416 occurred the death of the duke of Berry, who had agreed to help ransom Angoulême, and after Berry's death his estates no longer made payments.[9] With Charles of Orléans left to shoulder the whole burden of the ransom, with the family estates falling into ruin during his absence, and with the English remaining insatiable in their demands, Angoulême's position seemed well-nigh hopeless. The story of the two brothers' many futile attempts to secure their release is long. They tried many expedients. In 1417 they exhausted their resources to raise the ransom sums, but failed.[10] In 1422 they entered again into negotiations with the English, offering as part payment a jewel known as 'la belle chapelle d'Orléans,' worth 40,000 crowns; unfortunately, the English allowed a Venetian appraiser to escape with it, and the princes were crushed. It was nearly ten years before they tried again to raise the sums demanded, and again they failed. But meanwhile John and Thomas Beaufort had been taken prisoners by the Scotch, who at that time were allies of the French, and the two Orléans brothers flattered themselves that they could be exchanged for the Beauforts. John Beaufort was, however, exchanged for another French prisoner, and upon his return to England, by an ironical turn of fortune, became master of Angoulême instead of being exchanged for him.[11]

In 1429 occurred a fortunate event, the Bastard of Orléans' capture of William de la Pole, duke of Suffolk.[12] William de la Pole, who married Alice Chaucer, Geoffrey Chaucer's granddaughter, was himself a poet and a close friend of John of Angoulême and Charles of Orléans, the latter of whom he had secured permission to guard during his English imprisonment. The Bastard let Suffolk return on parole, and Suffolk never forgot the kindness. He used his influence to aid the two brothers, dedicating to secure their release what he would have paid for ransom.[13] It was hard for the princes to understand why, with the industry of the Bastard in France and of Suffolk in England, they still could not secure their release.

In the decade 1430-1440, a half dozen attempts were made to marry John to some wealthy princess who could pay his ransom. The first match was proposed in 1431, with the daughter of Nicholas III of Ferrara, notorious as the father of twenty-two bastards. This plan failed, perhaps fortunately. In 1432 and again in 1437, negotiations were made for the hand of Jeanne, eldest daughter of Viscount Rohan, but without success. Unsuccessful also were attempts made to win the hand of Marguerite of Savoy, of Jeanne of Béthune, and of a cousin of Frederick IV, emperor of Germany.[14]

Neither by ransom nor by marriage did it seem possible for Angoulême to escape. One other way lay open, a triumphal exit which the prisoner refused to consider. The council of Basle, before choosing Amédée VIII in 1439 as pope in place of the deposed Eugène IV, considered electing John of Angoulême. He refused, perhaps because Charles VII still recognized Eugène IV, or because he thought the council was overstepping its authority.[15]

In 1440, after twenty-five years of captivity, Charles of Orléans managed to free himself.[16] In 1442 the Bastard of Orléans concluded a treaty permitting Angoulême to cross the Channel into territory held by the English. In Cherbourg the final negotiations were undertaken. But as the English captors were still reluctant to part with their prisoner, negotiations dragged on interminably, despite the untiring efforts made in Angoulême's behalf by William de la Pole, duke of Suffolk.[17] The ransom was nearly doubled and Angoulême long refused to sign the agreement. Frightened at the prospect of his captivity beginning all over again, he finally yielded. Toward the end of March, 1445, at Rouen, the count was made to go through a ceremony of hearing all the papers read to him again and of making renewal of his oaths in the church of St Antoine. Then, after thirty-three years of captivity, he was at last set free.

While in England Angoulême belonged until 1421 to the duke of Clarence; from 1421 to 1439 to his widow, Margaret, duchess of Clarence; from 1439 to 1444, to her son by her first marriage,[18] John Beaufort II, duke of Somerset, upon whose death Angoulême passed into the keeping of the duchess dowager, Margaret of Somerset.[19] These different masters, all members of the same family, intrusted the count's keeping to an English squire, Richard Waller, who kept his prisoner first at Clarence's residence in London, then at the castle of the duchess of Clarence at Maxey, near Peterborough, and occasionally at Groombridge, Kent. So far as the facts can be determined from the unedited itinerary of Angoulême, it seems that he spent all of his time in these three places.[20]

Rarely was the count permitted to see his brother Charles or the other hostages who were delivered with him. He had occasionally the company of his chaplain, Denis de Vaucourt, of his preceptor, Colinet Goulon, and of his scribe, John Duxworth, who copied for him at least two manuscripts, the *Canterbury Tales* and part of the Latin *Dialogue of St Anselm.*[21]

Secluded and guarded in England, how did Angoulême while away the time? Forbidding himself to touch dice or cards, he spent his long leisure hours in playing the harp, in exercises of piety, and in reading and copying books.[22] As a youth he had been initiated into the study of letters by his preceptor, who gave him a collection impressively entitled *Flos Florum Compilatus ex Sacris Dictis Doctorum Ecclesiae et Moralium Philosophorum.*[23] That book gave him, no doubt, the idea for a treatise of the same kind, *Cato moralisé,* which he composed in England and brought back with him to Angoulême, where the autograph manuscript remained until 1562 chained in the choir of the cathedral.[24] An excellent Latinist, he read many works of Latin writers and dignified the scribal profession by himself copying nine volumes of Latin works: a psalter, *Meditations of St Bonaventura* ('doctor seraphicus'), *Chronicle of Martin the Pole,* Boethius' *Consolation of Philosophy,* Petrarch's *Treatise on Prayer* and his *Donat Contemplative,* a treatise of Alain de Lille ('the universal doctor'), *Prayers of St Augustine,* and part of the *Dialogue of St Anselm.*[25] This list shows that he turned to religious and philosophical books for consolation. Yet he must have enjoyed the secular *Canterbury Tales,* since he annotated his manuscript and prepared a table of contents in his own hand, and he must have enjoyed the secular *Geste des nobles francois,* a kind of contemporary chronicle addressed to him.

We have seen how the prisoner spent his third of a century in exile. We have seen how he finally was freed and returned home. Of his life from 1445 till his death in 1467 we have a few pleasant glimpses. He was welcomed to the gay court of Charles VII at Chalons, where festivities were redoubled in his honor, and on a guard-leaf of his *Geste des nobles* he wrote the program of a ball where he took part in a Burgundian dance. He noted the steps executed by the beautiful queen of Sicily, by the sprightly Madame de Calabre, and by the pleasure-loving dauphine, Margaret of Scotland.[26] A study of his portrait, reproduced by Thevet in 1584 from a window of the church of the Celestines in Paris, makes it hard to picture, dancing with the gay ladies of the court, this solemn man with his bent figure, his furrowed brow, large sad eyes, sunken cheeks, drooping mouth, and long emaciated hands.[27]

In 1449, Angoulême married Marguerite of Rohan, of the same family in Brittany into which he had twice failed to marry while a captive in England. To them was born a son, Charles, in 1459.[28] The family lived almost all the time in the province of Angoulême, in their residence at Cognac, which a contemporary poet called 'a second paradise.'[29]

It was in his chateau at Cognac that the count had his library. In an apartment hung with red serge, which was called 'la salle de retrait de Monseigneur,' he kept, in a great cupboard with four doors, about a hundred and sixty manuscripts. In accordance with his simple tastes they were modestly bound in wood, cardboard, or shamoyed leather, or even with just a leaf of parchment.

Although the inventory of his library, made after his death in 1467, gives but meager descriptions of his books, Dupont-Ferrier has been able to identify forty-five of them in the Bibliothèque Nationale and to study in these volumes the habits of the count

as a student and a scribe.[30] It is apparent that his library was not
for mere show. Everywhere there is evidence of his care to facilitate
research: rubrics, side-notes, running titles, foliations, tables of
contents, corrections, commentaries, glosses, synonyms. The notes
in the Boethius, observed Dupont-Ferrier, are especially instructive.
The whole work is in his own hand—a hand distinguished by
firmness and regularity, yet lively and rapid and expressive of
personality. Of the *Consolation* the count wrote an analysis,
apparently composed by himself, marked passages for further study,
and added full notes, written evidently a little at a time as he
read and studied. Some of these notes are highly abbreviated and
thus show that the count was an experienced scribe. Other manuscripts show that he collaborated with his hired scribe, e.g., the
Dialogue of St Anselm. In the first part of this book the hand is
that of John Duxworth, the count writing only the running titles,
rubrics, etc.; but from folio 233 r, the text is entirely in the count's
own hand.[31] How he and Duxworth collaborated in the making
of *Ps* we shall see later in detail.[32]

The books in Angoulême's library show his intellectual and moral
tendencies. He preferred to all others books of liturgy and prayer.
His favorite writers, as shown by the manuscripts most annotated,
were St Augustine, St Anselm, St Bernard, St Bonaventura, Pierre
d'Ailly, and Jean Gerson. He liked especially moral philosophy, and
we may assume he wished to enlighten himself as to his duties
both as a man and as a prince. For this purpose he read Friar
Lorens' *Somme des vices et des vertus,*[33] Alain de Lille's
Anticlaudianus, and Alain Chartier's *Curial.*

Though the count read history, he was not much interested in
any epoch but his own. To history he seems to have preferred
romances, of which he had at least half a dozen. Of poets he read
Jean de Meung, Guillaume de Lorris, Petrarch, and Boccaccio. Also
he read the marvelous adventures of Marco Polo and of Mandeville.[34]

Theology and moral philosophy first, then romance, history,
poetry, and travel books—one sees the count's predilections. Also
one sees from a list of his books that most of his authors were
Christian, although he included some pagan, e.g., Aristotle, Terence,
Cicero, Ovid, and Valerius Maximus. Boethius he of course considered Christian. One notes that no copy of Virgil is listed.

The languages Angoulême knew were French, Latin, and English.
Of Greek he must have had no knowledge; he possessed not a single
work in that language.[35]

Angoulême wrote both prose and poetry. His *Cato moralisé* I have already mentioned. His *Oratio ad Crucifixum,* a short religious poem in French, is printed by Charavay.[36] He wrote also *Le poème contre tout péché,* composed when he was but ten, and another poem, *Jeunnesse.* 'But in reality'—I translate from Dupont-Ferrier —'he never composed an original work. To read, make résumés, compile indefatigably, never to discard the tyranny of accurate memory, eternally to live under the yoke of the thought of others, and to make the accumulation of the knowledge thus acquired lead to a harmonious development of his religious and moral nature— such appears to be the double task John of Angoulême imposed upon himself.'[37]

Besides this picture of the count in his study, absorbed in the reading, transcription, and commentation of manuscripts, we have, from the latter part of his life as told by the none too trustworthy Jean du Port, three other pictures, highly contrasted. First we see him in 1452 winning military honors at Fronsac in the conquest of Guyenne and later entering Bordeaux with banners flying and guidons of blue taffeta emblasoned with fleurs-de-lis.[38] Then we see this studious and saintly man in the incongruous setting of a medieval court of love, a solemn figure among a circle of beautiful damsels and poet minstrels whom his wife gathered about herself and her husband in their home at Chateau-neuf-sur-Charente. Among these minstrels was the poet Vaillant, whose works appear in a beautiful manuscript made for Madame de Rohan about 1455. Angoulême himself transcribed one of Vaillant's poems, *La cornerie des anges.*[39] The third picture shows the count clothed in gray, with doublet and sackcloth, 'stealing away,' according to Jean du Port, 'from the chateau and its merry guests without saying a word to anybody, going on foot among the good people of the country, drinking and chatting with them about times past, enquiring after those who were good householders, who cultivated well the earth, . . . and after those who did the opposite. He corrected trespassers, and when people had differences he brought them together and made peace and exhorted them to live righteous lives in the fear of God and to love one another as brothers. He seemed to make reborn the Golden Age.'[40]

The last is the picture which seems best to reveal the true character of this meditative, somewhat melancholy man, the man who was called John the Good,[41] the man who during his solitary exile transcribed treatises on philosophy and morality, the man who was considered for elevation to the papacy, who only fifty years after his death was considered for canonization as a saint,[42] and who has in our times been commemorated, in the gardens of the cathedral at Angoulême, by a statue in the attitude of prayer.[43]

II

Such is the story of the original owner of the Paris manuscript of the *Canterbury Tales*. From Angoulême's library the manuscript passed to the collection of Francis I, thence into the Bibliotheca Regia, now the Bibliothèque Nationale.[44] Seldom do we know so much as the name of the person for whom a medieval manuscript was made. Here we have not only the name of the owner but also a full account of his life, which, I shall show presently, throws some light upon the baffling problem of how *Ps,* with its numerous errors and its remarkably complicated textual relationships, was put together.

From a study of the manuscript itself, we learn how Angoulême and his scribe, John Duxworth, collaborated. The manuscript was copied throughout in the hand of Duxworth, who, as a study of the dialect readily shows, was a Northerner.[45] We find, for instance, examples of Northern *a* for Chaucer's Midland *o,* as in *stane* for *stone, awne* for *owne, hald* for *hold, lang* for *long.* We find many examples of the Northern plosive *g* for Chaucer's *y,* and of Northern plosive *k* for Chaucer's *ch,* as in *gyve* for *yeve, gaf* for *yaf, kirke* for *chirch, whilk* for *which, dyke* for *dich, perke* for *perch, busk* for *bush, benk* for *bench,* etc. We find in the regular plurals and genitives of nouns the Northern inflectional ending *-is* *(-ys)* generally substituted for Chaucer's *-es,* as in *wurdis* and *londys.* (That is, before a consonant in the lightly stressed final syllable of a dissyllabic word, *e* often becomes *i.*) We find the Northern verbal ending *-is* for Chaucer's *-est* and *-eth* in the second and third person singular present indicative, as in *longis* for *longest* and *havys* for *haveth.* Occasionally a Northern present participle in *-and* occurs, the past participles of weak verbs usually end in Northern *-id* in place of Chaucer's *-ed,* and Chaucer's frequent prefix *y-* is often dropped from past participles. Also, Duxworth uses certain Northern words, as *sho* for *she*, *thaire* for *hir*, and *thaym* for *hem*, *ky* for *kyn*, *childer* for *children*, *quert* meaning *health*, and *muck* meaning *dung*.[46]

In the making of corrections, both Angoulême and his scribe had a hand, but with varying purposes. Duxworth, whose motto seems to have been neatness at any cost, made about 120 corrections, most of these of accidental mistakes. One set of corrections he made from his original faulty exemplar or exemplars, another set from a much better exemplar, which we should like to think belonged to Alice Chaucer and was lent through her husband, William de la Pole, to his friend, Angoulême.[47] Angoulême's corrections, about 300 in number, show on the one hand a strong editorial tendency, and on the other the close following of an excellent exemplar, probably the same one used by Duxworth for his second set of corrections. Angoulême's editorial corrections, all unique readings, are obviously meant to improve the meter or clarify the sense of his exceedingly faulty copy of the *Tales*.[48]

In the study of unique variants in our manuscript, we of course do not have, as we do in the study of corrections, handwriting tests to show who made the changes. We cannot be sure even that some of the unique variants were not in the exemplar. From a study of the habits of Duxworth and Angoulême as seen in their corrections, however, we can be reasonably sure that such unique variants as Duxworth introduced were either accidental or for the purpose of hiding mistakes in copying, and thus avoiding erasures and deletions. Therefore I believe Duxworth sometimes composed certain crude spurious lines, in order to perfect the riming couplets which he had accidentally disarranged; perhaps at other times he composed in order to supply gaps in his exemplar. In the copying of rime royal stanzas, the scribe sometimes got into almost inextricable difficulties, necessitating rearrangement of the whole stanza and also the composition of spurious lines, so that he sometimes came out with eight or nine lines instead of the original seven. But in other places from two to eight spurious lines might be introduced for no other obvious reason than to add something to the content; these lines it would seem Angoulême might have composed. Two examples will suffice: In the *Merchant's Tale*, after E 2126, we find

> What lovere is this world withinne
> That castith by sleight his love to wynne?

And after line F 784 in the *Franklin's Tale* we find

> But every wrong mot redressid be
> Sum what by pacience and not al by cruelte.

Could these couplets have expressed some of the prisoner's philosophy?[49]

Without hesitation may be attributed to the owner of the manuscript also the omission of certain parts of the *Tales*. After but twenty lines of the *Squire's Tale,* Duxworth writes, probably at Angoulême's dictation, 'Ista fabula est absurda in terminis et ideo ad presens pretermittatur nec ulterius de ea procedatur'; after but thirty-two lines of the *Monk's Tale* the scribe writes, 'Non plus de ista fabula quia est valde dolorosa.'[50] One wonders if Angoulême thought it dolorous because one of the so-called 'modern instances' tells that Angoulême's grandfather, Gian Galeazzo Visconti,[51] lord of Milan, in 1385 imprisoned and poisoned his uncle Barnabo Visconti.[52] Of the *Canon's Yeoman's Tale* 650 lines are omitted because 'termini sunt valde absurdi.'

Other unique intentional variants improve the meter, which had been very seriously impaired in our manuscript by the silencing of final *e,*—another proof of Northern influence. Still other changes were perhaps thought of as improving the meaning or the style. We find many words of romance origin substituted for Chaucer's words of Anglo-Saxon origin, such as *noble* for *worthy, virginity* for *maidenhead, honored* for *heried, manners* for *thewes, commandment* for *hest,* etc., and no doubt from the point of view of the Frenchman, Angoulême, these changes were all in the direction of clearness.[53]

We are able to account for many of the peculiarities of *Ps* by explaining them as due to the idiosyncrasies of the scribe Duxworth, or even more likely of his master, Angoulême, whom we can imagine whiling away many a tedious hour of imprisonment in editorial work upon his Chaucer manuscript. But one other peculiarity of *Ps* is even more puzzling than any yet discussed, that is, its extremely varied textual relationships. Except for its constant relationship with *Harley 1239,* with which it forms a pair, *Ps* is, of all the *Canterbury Tales* manuscripts, one of the most variable, changing its affiliations from tale to tale, or even within a tale, and being related, sometimes closely, sometimes doubtfully, to various groups and sub-groups. In places it comes so close to single manuscripts as to lead one to think it might have been copied from them, e.g., in the latter part of the *Summoner's Tale,* where it is near to Ellesmere; in other places, e.g., the *Man of Law's Tale,* it is independent of all known manuscripts.[54]

How can such shifting be accounted for? One might say upon first thought that Angoulême, moving about from place to place in England during his honorable imprisonment, gained access to various exemplars for his scribe, Duxworth, to copy. This is not an unreasonable hypothesis and may account for a few of the shifting affiliations. But the main objection to this hypothesis is the fact that *Ps's* sister manuscript, *Harley 1239,* makes, when present,[55] every textual shift which *Ps* makes. As these two manuscripts are very closely related, agreeing even in the Northern dialectal cast, not to mention numerous peculiar readings, spurious lines, omissions, etc., in all probability they were copied from the same exemplar,[56] and in it we must account for the shifting relationships that appear in its two descendants. The most satisfactory explanation, and one that circumstantial evidence seems more and more to substantiate, is that some manuscripts were made in commercial shops, where several exemplars were present and where several scribes were employed. These scribes, working from day to day, probably took no care to avoid shifting exemplars; sometimes they may have purposely shifted in order to supply matter lacking or illegible in the original. Some practice like this must have been followed in the production of conflate manuscripts, such as I believe the exemplar of *Ps* to have been.[57]

CONCLUSION

Of this five hundred year old manuscript the story, a mingling of fact and inference, we may now summarize. *Ps* was made for John, count of Angoulême, while he was a royal prisoner in England, 1412-1445. It was copied from a conflate exemplar, probably under Angoulême's immediate supervision, by an English scribe, John Duxworth, whose dialect shows him to have been a Northerner. Although from Angoulême's unedited English itinerary we are unable to show that he was ever kept in the North, we do know that his brother Charles was confined for some years in Yorkshire.[58] We may be able yet to show some connection between Angoulême's itinerary and the Northern dialect of his scribe. Both the count and Duxworth inserted numerous corrections in the manuscript—over four hundred in all. Many of these are unique and obviously editorial, but others show the close following of a manuscript of high textual quality, one which might have belonged to Alice Chaucer and been lent to Angoulême by her poetry-loving husband, the duke of Suffolk, who was a close friend of the royal French prisoner. When Angoulême returned to France, his Chaucer manuscript became a part of his Cognac library of 160 volumes and was inventoried in 1467, after his death. From his private library it passed to the collection of his grandson, Francis I, thence to the Royal Library, now the National Library, of France.

The readings of this fifteenth-century French edition of the *Canterbury Tales* are hardly worth a modern editor's consideration. But as a laboratory for the study of scribal habits, *Ps* is invaluable. Its numerous corrections in two hands, its unique variants and spurious lines, its Northern dialectal peculiarities, and its shifting textual relationship throw much light upon medieval methods of manuscript making.

THE UNIVERSITY OF TEXAS AT AUSTIN

An Easter Play in Finland

William G. Stryker

In the library of the University of Helsinki, on two sheets of parchment in a collection of loose manuscript leaves, is a Latin liturgical play for Easter. The catalogue describing the collection lists these particular leaves as belonging to a twelfth-thirteenth century breviary.[1] The play is accompanied by musical notation on four lines, which, according to Haapanen, the cataloguer, is of the school of Metz.

Liturgical plays for Easter center around the visit of the Marys to the empty tomb of Christ on Easter morning, as recounted in the Gospels.[2] Young's *The Drama of the Medieval Church,* the standard collection of Latin liturgical plays, contains or describes over four hundred extant texts of the Easter play, mostly from Germany and Austria, but also including texts from churches or monasteries in France, Italy, England, Ireland, Holland, Switzerland, Czechoslovakia, and Poland. Finland and the Scandinavian countries are neither represented nor mentioned by Young, nor indeed by the authors of the two more recent long studies of the subject.[3] Not only the lone Finnish example but also the half-dozen texts from Sweden published in 1952 have gone unnoticed by students of liturgical drama.[4] In this article I shall present the text of the Finnish play and then describe it and the sub-type it belongs to with respect to stage of dramatic development and textual variants.

The text of the Finnish play follows:[5]

Chorus:

> *Maria Magdalena et alia Maria ferebant diluculo aromata, Dominum querentes in monumento.*

Mul(ieres):

> *Quis reuoluet nobis ab hostio lapidem quem tegere sanctum cernimus sepulchrum?*

Angelus:

> *Quem quaeritis, o tremule mulieres, in hoc tumulo plorantes?*

Mulier(e)s:

> *Ihesum Nazarenum crucifixum querimus.*

Angelus:

> *Non est hic quem quaeritis, sed cito euntes nunciate discipulis eius et Patro quia surrexit Ihesus.*

Mulier(e)s:

> *Ad monumentum venimus gementes, angelum Domini sedentem uidimus et dicentem quia surrexit Ihesus.*

Duo ā:
> *Currebant duo simul, et ille alius discipulus precucurrit citius*
> *Petro et venit prior ad monumentum.*

Duo senes:
> *Cernitis, o socii, ecce lintheamina et sudarium, et corpus Ihesu*
> *in sepulchro non est inuentum.*

Chorus:
> *Surrexit Dominus de sepulchro, qui pro nobis pependit in*
> *ligno, alleluia.*
> *Te deum laudes.*

The "kernel" from which all versions of the Easter play have supposedly grown is the famous tenth-century trope from the monastery at St. Gall, Switzerland:[6]

Interrogatio:
> *Quem quaeritis in sepulchro, Christicole?*

Responsio:
> *Iesum Nazarenum crucifixum, o caelicolae.*
> *Non est hic, surrexit sicut predixerat; ite, nuntiate quia*
> *surrexit de sepulchro.*
> *Resurrexi.*

The trope served as an introduction to the introit of the Easter Mass and, according to the usual hypothesis, was composed around 900 A.D., probably by the monk Tutilo, a known writer of tropes. It evolved into drama when the sentences of the dialogue were assigned not simply to sections of the chorus, but to individuals representing the biblical characters, that is the angel (or angels— Matthew and Mark have one, Luke two) and the Marys. Later the play was expanded and transferred to the end of the matins service on Easter Morning, where it was freer to expand than it had been as part of the mass.

Young groups all texts of the play into three "stages," a classification taken over from Carl Lange.[7] Stage I plays are those containing no episodes or characters beyond the encounter between the angel(s) and the Marys, though some versions show as many as four additional speeches (antiphons) besides the simple question-reply-announcement above, and some also incorporate all or part of the *Victimae Paschali* Easter sequence into the dialogue. Stage II plays include all or part of the added antiphons and are specifically marked by the addition of a second "episode," the footrace of John and Peter to the tomb of Christ, as described in John 20:1-10. Stage III plays are distinguished by the further addition of the *Hortulanus* scene, in which the risen Christ appears to Mary Magdalene. The Finnish text, as we see, is a Stage II play.

The idea underlying the grouping of texts into three stages is that the *Quem quaeritis* play developed gradually and incrementally from the simple St. Gall trope into the complex Resurrection plays containing several episodes. This evolutionary hypothesis has been challenged several times, most recently by Hardison, who studied the chronology of all extant texts. The main problem with the evolutionary idea, as he shows, is that a chronological arrangement of the texts does not support it. To begin with, the St. Gall trope is not the oldest; it is some fifteen to twenty-five years later than an expanded version from Limoges. Another early but expanded text, with added antiphons and quite explicit stage directions, is the famous *Regularis concordia* Easter play, prepared at Winchester 965-75 A.D. With Stage II plays, the evolutionary notion works no better. The earliest such play is an eleventh century text from Aquileia, yet Young illustrates the supposed evolution of the type with plays of these dates arranged in this order: 1462 (he mentions a fourteenth-century text of the same form), thirteenth century, twelfth century, 1495, thirteenth century.[8] Fitting nowhere into the supposed pattern of development is a complex Resurrection play from Ripoll which, dating from the twelfth century, is far earlier than any other complex Easter play and earlier than over three-fourths of all the four hundred-plus texts collected by Young. In summary, Hardison describes the history of the *Quem quaeritis* play not as evolution but as a story of "long periods of stagnation alternating with abrupt and unexplained changes."[9] He believes that earlier critics were mistaken in seeing an analogy between the growth of liturgical drama and biological evolution: "There are changes (often for the worse), but there is no pattern of steadily increasing complexity."[10]

However the Stage II plays came into existence, they do appear to be a different kind of performance from the simple dialogue between angel(s) and Marys. De Boor, author of the most recent detailed study of the *Quem quaeritis* plays, believes that the Stage II plays embody not only a new design but a new concept. The old, simple play is timeless and symbolic, while the expanded one (like our Finnish example) seeks to show what happened at a particular time and place in history.[11] The former is ritual, the latter representational drama.

Through all the expanded versions, though—not only Latin but also vernacular, like the Wakefield play—the core of the play, the three speeches beginning with the angel's *Quem quaeritis,* remains in place. This core, the announcement of the Resurrection, is the central event in Christian history, and as such is protected by a rich accumulation of tradition, association, and symbolism. These are the factors, Hardison suggests, which caused the *Quem quaeritis* play, the first of the liturgical plays, to remain static in so many places for two, perhaps three, centuries while complex plays appeared on other themes (the shepherds and the magi).[12]

When additions to the *Quem quaeritis* do appear, they come at the beginning and the end, informing the audience as to what happened before and after the central event. The *Quis reuoluet* at the beginning, based on Mark 16:3, is the Marys' realistic request for assistance upon arriving at the tomb. (De Boor sees in this line, especially *tegere,* an anachronistic, and thus entirely realistic, reference to a medieval flat grave.[13]) Also realistic is the angel's addressing the Marys as frightened and sorrowing women, rather than simply as Christians. The angel's instructions to the women are more explicit, hence more realistic, in the Stage II plays— they are directed to carry the news of the Resurrection to Peter and the other disciples, not to the world in general. The women, realistically, obey these instructions and report what they have seen and heard to the two apostles. *Currebant duo simul,* based on John 20:4, is a "historical" and realistic addition, and preceding it most Stage II plays have a rubric describing the race to the tomb, thus suiting the action to the word. Though the apostle episode itself is "history," the antiphon *Cernitis, o socii* goes beyond history. In the scriptural account the disciples find the graveclothes and "believe," but they do not display them. The antiphon is a piece of "historical improvisation," justified, in Hardison's opinion, "by the Augustinian interpretation of the Visit to the Tomb as ocular proof of the Resurrection."[14]

We turn now to the matter of textual variants. One would like to be able to associate the Finnish text (hereinafter called F) with some published text, but there are none that it matches very closely in both dialogue and rubrics. De Boor has observed that the Stage II play is wholly a German development—texts from places not German today (e.g., Aquileia, Harlem) were under German church and/or political government in the middle ages.[15] Holding to the evolutionary hypothesis, he has sought an *Urtext* and an *Urheimat* for the Stage II play and finally suggests the dioceses of

Salzburg and Passau in the late eleventh century as the probable home of the form, mainly because of the large number of texts surviving from this region.[16] By the twelfth century, he believes, the play existed in at least two forms, those of Salzburg and Augsburg, the latter closely resembling the eleventh-century Aquileia text. Of these two, F is closer to the Augsburg type. In its particular choice of variants, however, it is closest to a group of later texts (fourteenth to sixteenth century) from Halberstadt and Magdeburg.

These variants are as follows:[17]

1. The introductory antiphon *Maria Magdalena*. Of the five eleventh- and twelfth-century Stage II texts in Young only one (Young I, 631-32) has this antiphon, but most of the later texts have it, as does F.

2. The number of women. Most of the texts provide introductory stage directions which specify either two or three persons to represent the Marys. In F, with its very bare rubrics, we may infer two Marys from the *Maria Magdalena* antiphon, but this interpretation brings the play into conflict with the responsory immediately preceding it in the manuscript: *Dum transisset sabbatum Maria Magdalena et Maria Iacobi et Salomee emerunt aromata, ut uenientes ungerent Iesum, alleluia, alleluia. Versus: Et ualde mane una sabbatorum ueniunt ad monumentum, orto iam sole.* This discrepancy is common, however; it exists in all texts employing the *Maria Magdalena* antiphon and this partic- ular form (the most common of four) of the third responsory of Easter Matins. [18]

3. *sanctum* in the *Quis reuoluet* antiphon. This is the usual form. A variant *sacrum* appears in the Aquileia and St. Lambrecht texts.

4. The number of angels. In specifying one angel, F is in accord with most texts from Bavaria, Austria, Prague, and Aquileia, but not with the Halberstadt-Magdeburg group, which specify *Duo angeli* or simply *Angeli*.

5. *plorantes* in the *Quem quaeritis* antiphon, rather than the variant *gementes*.

6. *Surrexit Dominus* as the closing choral antiphon, rather than *Surrexit enim*. Variants 5 and 6 usually go hand in hand; *gementes* and *Surrexit enim* are confined mostly to texts from Austria and the Alemannic area. Most of the other texts, includ- ing the Halberstadt-Magdeburg group, have the forms shown by F.

In variants 5 and 6 above, F agrees with the Augsburg type and not the Salzburg type, in 1 and 4 with Salzburg but not Augsburg, and in 3 with both. In variants 1, 3, 5, and 6, it agrees with a Halberstadt manuscript of 1440 and a printed Magdeburg breviary of 1491.[19] These texts also have brief rubrics, those of the latter being almost as bare as the ones in F—in contrast with some versions containing instructions about apparel, positioning, manner of speaking, and actions. Some eighteen other texts printed in Young, confined to no particular area but mostly fifteenth and sixteenth-century versions and none earlier than the thirteenth century, have one- or two-word rubrics (e.g. Young I, 322, 626-39).

Comparison on the basis of features mentioned thus far will carry us no further in relating F to any version now in print. F has one detail of phrasing in which it is almost alone, and two unique rubrics. In the antiphon *Cernitis, o socii* the name *Iesu* and the word order following it are shared only by a fifteenth-century Polling breviary (Young I, 627) and a fifteenth-century Brixen breviary (Young I, 651-52). However, both differ from F in other ways; thus this feature leads nowhere.

As is already apparent, and as one would expect, there is much more variation in rubrics than in dialogue, and Young finds many of the rubrics interesting because they indicate a gradually increasing (in his opinion) awareness of the dramatic possibilities of the play. Two of the brief rubrics of F are, so far as I know, unique: *Duo ā* and *Duo senes*. While they do not help us relate this text to any other, it would be some satisfaction if we could at least interpret them. *Duo ā* may stand for *Duo apostoli*. I find no instance in the published plays, nor in lists of manuscript abbreviations, where *ā* stands for *apostoli,* but the fact that one published text (Young I, 629) has *Duo Apostoli* as a rubric to *Currebant duo simul* establishes this as a possibility. Normally, and logically, the chorus sings this antiphon, but Young prints four other versions in which the two apostles sing it (Young I, 354, 361B, 627, 652) and one in which the option is given of having either chorus or apostles sing it (I, 356). This detail proves to be a blind alley too, for all six of these texts (five of which are Austrian) differ from F in other ways. A reading of *ā* as *antiphon* (as in one of the Swedish texts referred to at the beginning) would be conceivable if *Duo antiphon* made sense.

Duo senes may stand for *Duo seniores,* though here again I find no other instance of *senes* used as an abbreviation for *seniores.*

The two apostles are usually directed, in one way or another, to sing *Cernitis, o socii* as they display the graveclothes. One text (Young I, 630) does have *Seniores duo* here, and a rubric consisting of or containing *duo presbyteri* occurs several times.

Of the six Swedish texts, five belong to Stage I and the sixth, from a breviary which Dr. Schmid does not date, is a Stage II play which agrees with F in all the six variants listed above except 4, but it differs in other ways. Between the antiphons *Non est hic* and *Ad monumentum* it contains an antiphon *Venite et videte . . .* , which is shared by many texts of both Stage I and Stage II. Hardison describes this antiphon as a conservative feature, a carry-over from the early ceremonial version of the play, which is in logical contradiction to the angels' immediately preceding instructions to the women to go and announce the Resurrection to the disciples.[20]

The rubrics of the Swedish version differ from any I have seen in other texts. The first three refer to the women as *extra stantes* and the angels as *deintus sedentes,* respectively. Four of the last five rubrics are simply *a* (for *antiphon*), a feature found in several other texts. Dr. Schmid finds the dialogue in her text (including the *Venite et videte)* in agreement with a 1515 Halberstadt breviary (Young I, 315). The rubrics are not much alike, but they are about the same length and they do contain two words not usually found, *sedentes* and, before the *Te deum, finita.*

Thus the likenesses of the Finnish and the Swedish texts, respectively, to two texts from Halberstadt provide some slight support for what would seem a reasonable guess anyway: that the Swedish and Finnish versions may have been obtained from Halberstadt or some nearby church or monastery in northern Germany, e.g., Magdeburg or Wolfenbüttel. Lange and Young both mention but do not print several other Halberstadt and Magdeburg texts which differ from the published ones only in "unimportant variants." It is conceivable that some of these might parallel F more closely.

Haapanen's dating of F as twelfth-thirteenth century, though it may be based on good paleographic evidence and is possible as far as the scanty knowledge of the Finnish Church in the middle ages is concerned, seems rather early with respect to the text of the play.[21] Young lists only four twelfth-century texts of Stage II plays and eleven thirteenth-century ones. The earliest from Halberstadt, Magdeburg, or Wolfenbüttel are of the fourteenth century.

Accounting for passage of the play from Germany to Finland is no problem, for clerical travel between Finland and "the continent" must have been commonplace in the middle ages. Though officially under the archbishop of Lund till 1216 and Uppsala after that, the Finnish bishopric was taking its directions straight from Rome in the early 1200's, rather than through the archbishop. Finnish students were studying in numbers at the University of Paris from the beginning of the fourteenth century and át various north German universities from 1404. Though the Finnish Church in these centuries was small—one bishopric with about forty parishes and churches, nearly all in the "old, settled or southwestern part of Finland"— it was relatively strong and active and very much a part of the Roman Catholic Church.[22] Thus it is not in the least surprising that a ceremony as popular as the *Quem quaeritis* play should have found its way to Finland.

SAN FERNANDO VALLEY STATE COLLEGE

"Everyman": The Way to Life

Jim Corder

Contrary to our customary judgment that it is confined solely to the hours of the hero's death, *Everyman* is a dramatization of the universal man's journey *through* life to its end.[1] Once we recognize that the play renders the complete pilgrimage of youth to age and death, we can see anew the artistry of the work, a tightly-compressed representation, not of the time of death alone, but of man's discovery and enlightenment in life and his final triumph in death.

In a recent discussion of *Everyman* in another context, David Kaula directed attention to the fact that even as Everyman approaches the grave, he is not ready to meet death, for he "must undergo the actual process of aging and dying."[2] I should like to expand this suggestion and argue that the play's theme is not the hero's discovery of the way to Christian death, but his discovery of the Christian way to life.

When the summons comes and Everyman learns that he must die, the play very early reaches the moment of its greatest intensity. Everyman's speech following the summons tells the dreadful urgency of time that weighs upon him. But, as Kaula has shown, once past that speech, the sense of urgency is never again so strong. This diminution of urgency is the first clue that indicates a much greater time-lag between summons and death than we have always assumed. This time-lag, which is equal to the complete life of the hero, is then made clear to us in the foreshortening of the hero's full normal life span by the dramatic sequence of appearing and departing characters. The parade of characters patently shows that Everyman does not die almost immediately after the summons but lives out a full life. Summoned in his youth, he grows, ages, and dies.

Following his summons—to which I will return a little later—Everyman first meets Fellowship and begs his company on the journey. Fellowship, of course, refuses to accompany him:

> For no man that is living today
> I will not go that loath journey.

Everyman then meets and is in turn forsaken by Kindred, Cousin, and Goods. Then, after his encounters with Good-Deeds and Knowledge and the insight they bring him, Everyman meets Discretion, Strength, Five-Wits, and Beauty. They accompany him on his journey to the grave, Five-Wits in particular being an important figure in Everyman's growing perceptions. But when Everyman approaches the grave, he is again deserted by friends. At this point, it is important once again to notice the order in which Everyman's friends depart:

Departing in this order early in the play
> Fellowship
> Kindred
> Cousin
> Goods

Departing in this order as Everyman nears the grave
> Beauty
> Strength
> Discretion
> Five-Wits

The sequence of departures provides a sound psychological record of man's progress from early manhood through age to death. The departure of the first four friends early in the play accomplishes the first stage of Everyman's growth, for abandoned by these friends, all of whom represent things outside himself, he is left, as moral men all are left, with only his own character and actions to determine his fate. It is as foolish, I suppose, to contend that one loses his friends thus in the bloom of life as it is to assume, as others have in reading the play, that they all leave a man lonely when he faces death. We must remember that, given the context, their departure is the only means the dramatist has for showing Everyman's awakening and maturing. What is important about their departure is Everyman's consequent realization that the friends do not offer a medium for salvation. That the friends are gone is not so important as Everyman's finding the insignificance of such externals—a discovery common, not to every man, but to most long before the moment of death. It is a discovery, indeed, which more often signals the *arrival* of manhood and attendant knowledge of our solitariness than it does the *departure* of life.

The departure of the second group of friends dramatizes realistically the process of aging; in this way is Everyman made concrete. I think we can safely assume that, as in the play, beauty does go first, to be followed by strength, which departure signifies illness and the failure of the body. The body failing, the mind soon fails, and discretion departs, followed shortly by conscious sense, here represented by Five-Wits. All this change is the process of years, not of hours. *Everyman,* then, dramatizes a complete adult life-span. Knowing this, we know that the messenger, when he warns Everyman of death, summons him to life.

Viewing the summoning of Everyman as the dramatic metaphor for human mortality—life lived from birth under sentence of death—rather than as the literal action of the play, suggests possibilities for new theatrical interpretation. The actor playing the title role now has an opportunity to present Everyman's lifespan. What seems called for is a non-realistic acceleration of aging to match the concentration of the play's action. Since Everyman leaves the stage only once before his death, the actor presumably must eschew the aid of makeup and simulate the progress from youth to maturity to old age in bearing, voice, and gesture.

But before concluding with this assertion of the play's meaning, I must turn back to the first of the play and reconcile God's instructions to the messenger with this assumption that the play depicts an entire life rather than a day of death. It has been argued that the words of God and of the messenger clearly indicate that Everyman must die immediately. If this were so, it would controvert what I have said earlier; but nowhere in the speeches of God or of the messenger is there any specific, unambiguous statement that Everyman is to die presently. The speeches indicate only that he will die. God bids the messenger, Death, to go to Everyman and

> show him in my name
> A pilgrimage he must on him take,
> Which he in no wise may escape;
> And that he bring with him a sure reckoning
> Without delay or tarrying.

Death goes then to Everyman and tells him,

> A reckoning he needs will have
> Without any longer respite.

This summons sounds immediate and ominous until we remember
the sequence I have discussed earlier, which shows a life lived out
past the urgency of the play's beginning, and until we remember
what is announced in the prologue as the heart of the play. The
messenger announces a "moral play,"

> That of our lives and ending shows
> How transitory we be all day.

He announces, we should notice, that the play treats of both our
lives and *ending*. He goes on then to say,

> Man, in the beginning,
> Look well, and take good heed to the ending.

These words of the prologue tell the theme of the play,
man's discovery of the regeneration and peace in the Church
brought about by his earlier discovery of his own mortality, an
experience as demanding and fearful and perhaps as painful as
death. Finding that he is mortal, Everyman is abandoned—at first.
But Knowledge guides him. Told in the beginning to take heed
to his ending, which is always inescapable, he follows this knowledge. As the remainder of his journey clearly shows, he turns to
the Church, observes its necessities, and lives out his life in the
sanctity of the Church and the Christian manner. Summoned by
the knowledge of death, he turns to life, to die a Christian death
only after a fully recorded life.

TEXAS CHRISTIAN UNIVERSITY

'Haf owre to Aberdour':
A Note on "Sir Patrick Spens"

ALLAN H. MACLAINE

The famous closing stanza of the finest version of *Sir Patrick Spens* reads as follows:

> Haf owre, haf owre to Aberdour,
>   It's fiftie fadom deip,
> And thair lies guid Sir Patrick Spence,
>   Wi the Scots lords at his feit.

Professor Francis J. Child, in his monumental edition of *The English and Scottish Popular Ballads,* identifies Aberdour as the small town near Fraserburgh in the district of Buchan in the northeast corner of Aberdeenshire; and all subsequent students of the ballad have accepted this judgment.[1] There are, in fact, two Aberdours on the east coast of Scotland: the one in Buchan just referred to, and the Aberdour much farther south in Fife on the Firth of Forth. Child believes that the northern Aberdour in Buchan is the place intended and that the ship went down near there somewhere off the coast of Aberdeenshire. With uncharacteristic lack of caution he flatly dismisses Aberdour in Fife as a possibility, asserting that "the southern Aberdour, in the Firth of Forth, cannot be meant."[2]

This conclusion by Child is apparently based on two assumptions: (1) that the ballad deals with an expedition to Norway with a shipwreck on the return trip; and (2) that "haf owre" means half way between Norway and Scotland. For the moment let us accept the first assumption—a large and shaky assumption in view of the fact that only four of the eighteen versions of the ballad recorded by Child mention Norway at all; even Child himself is uncertain about the Norway connection and says, "I do not feel compelled to regard the ballad as historical."[3] The second assumption, that "haf owre" means that the ship was half way home from Norway and approaching the Aberdeenshire coast at the time of the wreck, is open to even more serious question. The plain fact is that almost all versions of the ballad contain clear associations with Fife and with the waters surrounding Fife—the Firth of Tay and, above all, the Firth of Forth. For this reason, among others, I suggest that Aberdour in *Sir Patrick Spens* means the seaport in Fife and not the town in the northeast corner of Aberdeenshire.

By its very nature the ballad is careless about geography, and such carelessness is especially evident in ballads that are as old and widespread as *Sir Patrick Spens*. Undoubtedly this piece in its earliest form recorded an actual event with real people and places; but in the process of oral transmission over long stretches of time and space the original story became blurred by changes in place-names and character-names, by the grafting on of new details and the dropping out of old ones, resulting in all kinds of confusions. Sometimes, as the distance from the germinal event increased, factual impossibilities were introduced for the sake of catchy phrases or rimes. In Version D, for example, the shipwreck is located "nore-east, nore-west frae Aberdeen"; "nore-east" makes sense, but "nore-west" is impossible (dry land). In the face of all the contradictions and imponderables it is obviously impossible to reconstruct the prototype story of this, or any other, ancient ballad with certainty. The best that the student of *Sir Patrick Spens* can hope to do is to work out a geographical interpretation that makes good sense in itself and is more probable than other possible interpretations in the light of the total evidence available. Professor Child's identification of Aberdour simply seems to me *less* probable than the other alternative which he rejects out of hand.

The most consistent geographical feature of all in this ballad is that the king "sits in Dumferling toune" (eleven out of eighteen versions recorded by Child). Let us take this, then, as established fact: the king is at Dunfermline in Fife, to which Aberdour on the Firth of Forth is the nearest seaport. The next most frequently used place-name in the poem is Aberdour; in six versions the wreck occurs "haf owre to Aberdour," though in four other versions the place is given as Aberdeen. It is significant that in all of the Aberdour versions the ship is heading *to* Aberdour, never *from* Aberdour. At any rate, the king in Dunfermline plans to send Sir Patrick Spens out on a dangerous sea voyage. Sir Patrick, while "walking on the sands" somewhere in Scotland, receives the king's order to "come at his command." The ship is loaded with "Scots nobles," and there is a voyage that ends in disaster "haf owre to Aberdour."

Given this set of generally consistent circumstances, what possible interpretations may be given to the phrase "haf owre to Aberdour"? As I see it, there are only three solutions that have any degree of plausibility. (1) The wreck may have occurred while Sir Patrick was coming at the king's command to receive his commission for a major voyage; that is, while sailing from another Scottish port (such as Leith) to Aberdour in Fife to meet the king at nearby Dunfermline. This interpretation would rule out Aberdour in Buchan altogether. (2) Another possibility is that the phrase may mean the ship sank while *returning* to Aberdour after a major voyage (perhaps to Norway). In this case, Aberdour in Fife would surely be the destination; since the king was in Dunfermline it would make no sense at all for the expedition with important nobles aboard to return to Aberdour in Buchan, a remote fishing port located 150 miles north of Dunfermline. (3) On the other hand, it is possible that neither of the two Aberdours was Sir Patrick's actual destination, that Aberdour is mentioned merely as a landmark or temporary refuge on the way to some other port on the return voyage (perhaps from Norway). This third possibility is the only one that rules out Fife and fits in with Child's theory that Aberdour is the place in Buchan; and, moreover, this interpretation depends very heavily upon the validity of the Norway assumption. Altogether, then, two out of the three possible interpretations, all about equally plausible, strongly favor the southern Aberdour as the place intended.

In themselves, the two Aberdours are about equally qualified to be immortalized in *Sir Patrick Spens*. Both are east coastal parishes with small harbors; both are ancient. Aberdour in Fife has an old church (St. Fillan's) originally founded in the twelfth century and a castle dating from the fourteenth, while Aberdour in Buchan has a castle of comparable antiquity and other evidence of a long history. Though both are insignificant as ports nowadays, there is clear evidence of maritime activity in the past. In this respect, the southern Aberdour has a slight edge in that there are signs that it once served as a harbor for sizable craft, whereas Aberdour in Buchan seems to have sheltered nothing more substantial than a fleet of small fishing boats. In the context of the ballad, the northern town has the dubious advantage of being closer to Norway; but Aberdour, Fife, has what to my mind is the far greater and more certain advantage of nearness to Dunfermline —it is, in fact, one of the nine parishes of the Dunfermline district of West Fife.

Let us consider further the evidence of the other place-names in this ballad. In eleven out of the eighteen versions, including all of the best ones, "The king sits in Dumferling toune," only seven or eight miles from Aberdour on the Firth of Forth. If the king had his headquarters in Dunfermline, it would be most natural for him to send out a ship from the port close by, such as Aberdour or Kirkcaldy or Leith. All of the other place-names in the eighteen recorded versions (except Aberdeen and Dumbarton) lie within a radius of thirty miles from Dunfermline—Aberdour (eight miles), Kinghorn (thirteen miles), Leith (thirteen miles), Perth ("St. Johnston," twenty-four miles), and Dundee (thirty miles). The only other place-name mentioned is "Inch" in version D: "As I came in by the Inch, Inch, Inch." This is somewhat obscure since an "inch" may mean either an island or a hill, but in this context an island seems much more likely. It is perhaps significant, however, that most of the notable inches off the east coast of Scotland lie more or less on the approaches to Aberdour in Fife. There is Inchcape, for example, off the mouth of the Firth of Tay; and even more probable are the famous inches in the Firth of Forth—Inchkeith, Inchmickery, and Inchcolm. A ship approaching Aberdour would pass within close range of all three inches in the Firth of Forth; indeed, Inchcolm lies at the very entrance to the harbor of Aberdour and is part of Aberdour parish. Thus, "the Inch, Inch, Inch" in the line cited above may well mean Inchkeith, Inchmickery, Inchcolm.

If we accept the Norway expedition, a ship going there might be expected to sail from and return to any of the ports on the east coast, especially from one of those on the Firth of Forth or the Firth of Tay or Aberdeen. West coast ports, such as Dumbarton, would be out of the question. If the king was at Dunfermline, a nearby port would be more probable than Aberdeen, and Aberdour (Fife) would in fact be closest of all. One possibility is that the king in Dunfermline ordered Spens, who was at Leith, to pick up some nobles in Edinburgh and cross the firth to Aberdour where he would meet them for final instructions for the trip to Norway. "Haf owre to Aberdour" they were wrecked in a storm in the Firth of Forth. In this case "Haf owre to Aberdour" may simply mean *in the middle of the Firth of Forth,* in mid-channel. The water there is not "fiftie fadom deip," but it is deep enough (20 to 30 fathoms) to justify this impression in the folk mind. Two of the versions (J and R[4]) say that mattresses from the ship floated ashore at Kinghorn on the Fife coast only five miles from Aberdour; it is obviously inconceivable that mattresses lost off the Aberdeenshire coast would float ashore at Kinghorn. It may well be that the ballad in its earliest versions celebrated a local disaster that had no relation to the expeditions to Norway in

1281 or 1290. Possibly the later "Norway" versions (G and H) substituted Aberdeen for Aberdour simply because Aberdeen was the nearest major port to Norway.

Child's argument is somewhat inconsistent: he says the ballad is not necessarily historical and may not refer to any of the known expeditions to Norway; yet his dismissal of Aberdour, Fife, is based wholly on the Norway theory. If one discounts the Norway theory (and therefore versions G, H, and I), the geographical evidence in favor of Aberdour in Fife is overwhelming. Even if we accept the historical basis for *Sir Patrick Spens* and assume a trip to Norway, the probabilities still point to Aberdour in Fife rather than to Aberdour in Buchan as the place referred to in "haf owre to Aberdour."

UNIVERSITY OF RHODE ISLAND

STUDIES IN

Renaissance

LITERATURE

The Ingenious Compliment:
A Consideration of Some Devices and Episodes in
"The Merry Wives of Windsor"

MARJORIE DUNLAVY LEWIS

When an Elizabethan playwright had the task of providing a script to be presented before an audience of noblemen who were being celebrated for their chivalric virtues, tradition and occasion dictated the conventional themes of love and honor. *The Merry Wives of Windsor* was William Shakespeare's unconventional solution—a play satirizing not love and honor but ridiculous pretenders to love and honor.

Attempting to assign a definite date to the play, scholars have tried to attach the first production to a particular celebration of the Order of the Garter.[1] The date itself is not important for the argument of this essay, but the fact that *The Merry Wives* had a connection with a Garter ceremony is significant. Almost any meeting of members of the order would provide an audience for which many of the events of the play would be particularly amusing and, through an ingenious turn of the playwright's invention, particularly appropriate. Most of the occasional poetry written for Garter ceremonies in the sixteenth century consisted of encomia describing the career and virtues of some of the knights. Shakespeare, instead of praising the life and character of an individual, chose to celebrate the virtues of chivalry and honor presumably possessed by all of the members of the order. *The Merry Wives* celebrates the virtues of gentility and chivalry by presenting a collection of pretenders to honor assuming the terms and conventional attitudes natural to the knights of the audience. In some of Shakespeare's plays, *Henry V* and *Romeo and Juliet*, for example, the comic pretenders were contrasted to the truly gentle figures within the play, but in *The Merry Wives* the real contrast was between the pretenders of the play and the real gentlemen of the audience, who were complimented as the ideal which makes ridiculous the attempts of the pretentious.

No specific source can be found for *The Merry Wives of Windsor*. Most scholars assume that there was a play from which some plot devices were borrowed, but they disagree about whether or not that work was *The Jealous Comedy* or some other lost script.[2] In any event, Falstaff in love is an essential part of the plot regardless of whether the queen herself suggested the idea or an unknown source provided this basic element.[3] The very thought of the fat knight wooing was enough to insure that the play's base would be in the comic possibilities of ridiculous pretensions. Yet Falstaff in love was not enough, and Shakespeare turned to the theme of pretense to honor and social position which he had used to good effect before.

Allan Gilbert has called *The Merry Wives* a "comedy of manners."[4] Such a designation may stretch the definition of comedy of manners too much; however, it is certainly clear that some scenes are sketches of "character and manners" which have definite reference to the contemporary scene. Around the plot concerned with the marriage of Anne Page, Shakespeare weaves a pattern of motifs which treat satirically pretensions to gentility. He employs the motif of the litigious gentleman appealing to the law and not to his sword; the motif of the upstart family excessively concerned about a coat of arms which is too new to be respectable; the motif of the marriage for money as the gentry and the middle class barter position for wealth; the motif of the country bumpkin who mistakes affectation for true courtesy; the motif of knighthoods made cheap and plentiful; the motif of the diminishing retinue; the motif of the avaricious lecher as Petrarchan lover; and the motif of the pseudo-gentleman who exposes his supposed honor to the test of the quarrel. Many of the members of the audience for which the play was intended were or had been notable jousters and fighting men. Indeed, Garter celebrations often included combat at the barriers as, for example, Leicester's celebration of the Feast of St. George in Utrecht in 1586 had done.[5] Knights experienced in weaponry and combat would take special delight in the scenes dealing with the dueling code and the quarrel.

William Green has already pointed out the relevance of much of the material in the play to a particular audience of Garter knights and members of the court. The purpose of this essay is to point out Shakespeare's ingenious use of a particular episode to dramatize the nature of the Order of St. George. The scene which contains the action and those scenes which lead up to it will be examined with the intention of relating them to the dominant comic pattern of the play as well as considering the serious artistic use to which the playwright puts the scene.

The motif of quarreling pretenders to gentility appears in the early scenes of the play in a contention between Falstaff and

Shallow, and the theme is also alluded to in Slender's boasts to Anne Page concerning his fencing lessons. Slender's inept attempts at mimicking the behavior of a gentleman introduces, if only for a moment, a theme which receives greater development in the quarrel between Caius and Evans.

The quarrel of the physician and the priest, which is planned but never completed, consumes a large part of the middle of the play, but the initiating action begins in the first act. In the first scene of Act I, Sir Hugh, the priest, is performing an appropriate clerical duty as he acts as mediator and composer of a quarrel between Justice Shallow and Falstaff. By the last scene of the first act, the peacemaker himself has become a party to a quarrel which seems destined to be tried by the sword. He has received a cartel from Dr. Caius, the French physician, another pretender to honor. Dr. Caius is severely handicapped in his social climbing, however, because he is a physician. That profession enjoyed none of its modern respectability, and the characters in the play reflect all too clearly the contemporary attitudes toward doctors.[6] Caius ministers to courtiers and great gentlemen or so he would have others think, and he boasts of the gentility of his patients in order to bolster his own social claims.

The action which leads up to the challenge which Caius sends Evans is filled with little details which reveal the absurd pretensions of Caius and point up contrasts with the members of the truly chivalrous company watching the performance of the actor in the role of the doctor. Caius bursts in upon his household with his attention centered on an imminent trip to the Court. His sudden advent has forced Simple to hide from him in a closet. Caius is anxious to collect his retinue for his progress to the Court. Since his retinue consists of no more than the awkward Jack Rugby, his concern is delightful in its absurdity especially when this lone bumpkin is contrasted to the uniformed retainers attending the Knights of the Garter and making up a conspicuous part of the audience laughing at Caius.[7]

As Caius bustles about, Rugby collects his weapons, since he will accompany his master armed. Rugby's weapons are not kept close at hand or even suitably placed on wall brackets or racks; instead they have been left on the porch, the usual place for muddy footgear and the homely objects of domestic cleaning. Rugby's weapons form one part of a contrast in the pattern of comparisons between pseudo-gentility and true chivalry which make up the ingenious compliment to the audience. The honorable achievements and arms of the Garter knights were displayed on the walls of St. George's Chapel. If the Garter occasion were one in which new members were installed, the ritual of displaying their weapons would make a significant part of the ceremonies. Rugby's humble weapons with their lowly housing make an extreme contrast to the arms of St. George's Chapel.

Meanwhile, the bustling physician opens the closet door and discovers Simple. Now the steps of the quarrel develop rapidly. Caius calls loudly for his own rapier, but Simple is spared when the jealous Caius learns what Simple's errand has been. Sir Hugh Evans is matchmaking, and his proposed match for Anne Page is not Dr. Caius but Slender. The doctor construes Evans' action as an insult and sends a challenge to Sir Hugh. His choice of a messenger—the terrified and servile Slender, instead of a chivalrous equal—only adds to the sum of his gauche errors made in attempting to follow a code he does not properly understand. Caius's choice of expressions as he gives his cartel to Slender is most inappropriate for a gentleman concerned with his honor:

> You jack-nape, give-a dis letter to Sir Hugh; by gar, it is a challenge: I vill cut his troat in de Park; and I vill teach a scurvy Jack-a-nape priest to meddle or make . . .[8]
> (I.iv.112-114)

The action is now set in motion for the combat between Evans and Caius. While the physician elaborates his plan for the encounter, Dame Quickly points out that Evans is only acting for a friend. Caius is not deflected from his intention by this temporizing observation. The challenge is dispatched, but since the text is not given, the audience has no way of knowing how the physician managed the difficult problem of arranging suitable grounds for the quarrel. Like that pretender of *Twelfth Night*, Sir Andrew Aguecheek, Caius may have constructed a piece of nonsense for his cartel. In any case, Shakespeare evades the problem and leaves the audience aware that whatever the cartel may say, it serves. Instead of concentrating on the challenge, the playwright describes the elaborate formal arrangements for the meeting, including the appointment of an umpire. The Host deliberately satirizes his own assumption of such an office even as he undertakes it, and examples of his satiric comments on pretension will be taken up as they occur in the discussion of the combat scene itself.

In scene three of Act II, Caius and Jack Rugby await Sir Hugh at the appointed meeting place. Caius boasts that the Welsh priest has "saved his soul" by his failure to appear. Raging in frustrated inactivity, Caius decides to demonstrate what he will do to his opponent and urges Rugby to be a party to the demonstration. The wretched servant protests that he "cannot fence" and is saved only by the appearance of the crew following the umpire. When Caius questions why this audience has come, the Host replies gaily:

> To see thee fight, to see thee foin, to see thee traverse; to see thee here, to see thee there; to see thee pass thy punto, thy stock, thy reverse, thy distance, thy montant. Is he dead, my Ethiopian? is he dead, my Francisco? ha, bully! What says my Aesculapius? my Galen? my heart of elder? ha! is he dead, bully stale? is he dead?
>
> (II.iii.24-31)

The Host ridicules the knowledge of medicine and fencing which Caius presumably has mastered. This display of fencing terms satirizes the over-particular Frenchman, and the supposed fencing style of the doctor whose display of form the Host mockingly hints will be formidable. In the allusion to "heart of elder," he suggests by contrast with the expected phrase "heart of oak" that Caius is a coward.[9] The references to Aesculapius and Galen are obvious enough since Caius is a physician, and the more obscure denomination "Ethiopian" may simply be intended to contrast the darker Frenchman to the presumably fairer Englishmen surrounding him.

The aggrieved physician reports that his opponent has not appeared at the appointed field of combat and calls upon the new arrivals to bear witness that he, Caius, has appeared and waited. Shallow suggests that to fight would go against the professions of both. Sir William Segar, Elizabethan soldier and author, had definitely excluded both professions from the "sorts of men" who could be challenged or who could issue challenges to combat when he described appropriate challenges in his treatise on arms, *The Booke of Honor and Armes*.[10] Shallow's objection, then, coincides with martial authority on such matters. This speech by Shallow is the real introduction of an image that builds up throughout the quarrel scene until it reaches a final perfection and distillation in the Host's speech of reconciliation that resolves the conflict. The image is based upon the professions of the two antagonists. Caius, the physician, ministers to the body, and Sir Hugh, the parson, ministers to the soul. This combat will not be a debate but a duello between the representative of the body and the representative of the soul. The concept of the physical and spiritual in opposition was one that had been used frequently in the literature of the medieval period and repeatedly by the sonneteers of the 1590's. Shakespeare himself had employed the conflict of the body and soul in the famous Sonnet 146. The images of that sonnet, of course, are multiple, and there is no dueling image. However, the situation in *The Merry Wives of Windsor* provided an all-too-tempting chance to use the professions of the two combatants in more than one way. This additional use in no way detracts from the primary satirical purpose of the dramatist's use of the two professions. That men so employed should engage in the duello is, indeed, ridiculous. Shallow has pointed this out, and Page, who has been the recipient of Shallow's discourse on the valor of his youth, points out that the "man of peace" has himself been a great fighter. Shallow swallows the bait and begins:

> Bodykins, Master Page, though I now be old and of the peace, if I see a sword out, my finger itches to make one. Though we are justices and doctors and churchmen, Master Page, we have some salt of our youth in us; we are the sons of women, Master Page.
>
> (II.iii.46-51)

Shallow summarizes the profession to which the men who are so bellicose belong, and his re-emphasis upon this only serves to underline the absurdity of the whole situation. The Host takes Caius aside and enjoys himself at the French doctor's expense by making fun of him through his ignorance of English. He calls Caius "Mockwater" and then explains slyly that this is an English expression for "valour." As Caius boasts of his courage and the deeds which he will perform as he fights with Sir Hugh, the Host promises that the priest will "clapper-claw" Dr. Caius. He defines "clapper-claw" as "make amends." The doctor, delighted with the Host, assures him of guests from among his patients. These guests will be no less than "earls," "knights," "lords," "Gentlemen."

Meanwhile, Sir Hugh, accompanied by his second, Simple,

Slender's man, waits for the appearance of his opponent. The choice of Simple as second adds to the satiric effect. The second was supposed to be a man of honor and position whose knowledge of the proper behavior and customs of the duello was a foregone conclusion.[11] Simple is already known to the audience for his naive remarks to Dame Quickly about his master's gallant behavior. He proudly remarks that Slender has "fought with a warrener." This battle with a gamekeeper figures as a great military venture.

As the parson and Simple wait, Sir Hugh makes a speech which describes his violent feelings. Like Pistol and Nym, Sir Hugh is very conscious of the humours. He believes that he is simultaneously choleric and melancholy, and he mutters threats with one breath and emits frightened sighs in the next. As Simple glimpses the approaching Caius, Sir Hugh inquires hastily about the weapons Caius carries. Simple reassures him with the news that Caius has no weapons. Evans, whose gown has been removed for the combat, is unable to decide whether to reassume the garment or leave it off. He paces up and down simulating unconcern as he tries to read. His gown, the book, and the sword are all important props for the teasing of Shallow and Page as they point out the ridiculous situation in which the parson has placed himself:

> Shal. What, the sword and the word! do you study them both,
> Master Parson?
> Page. And youthful still in your double and hose! this saw
> rheumatic day?
>
> (III.i.44-46)

The attention which the gown receives is largely lost upon the modern audience, but as a symbol of his clerical office (Sir Hugh's gown is naturally an academic one), it further emphasizes the folly of this priestly combatant's participation in a secular duel.

Evans tells the new arrival that there are reasons for his behavior, and he speaks disparagingly of the physician. Then as Caius, Rugby, and the Host enter, Sir Hugh apparently offers to draw his weapon. The Host intervenes and suggests that both be disarmed and allowed to question each other. Such final attempts at reconciliation were part of the umpire's duty.

The opponents converse on two levels. In low tones they move toward reconciliation, but in tones meant to be overheard they utter bellicose threats. As they argue about the appointed meeting

place, Evans turns to the Host for confirmation, and the umpire
seizes his opportunity to act as peacemaker:

> Host. Peace, I say! hear mine host of the Garter. Am I
> politic? am I subtle? am I a Machiavel? Shall I lose
> my doctor? no; he gives me the potions and the motions.
> Shall I lose my parson, my priest, my Sir Hugh? no;
> he gives me the proverbs and the no-verbs. Give me
> thy hand, terrestrial; so;—give my thy hand, celestial;
> so. Boys of art, I have deceived you both; I have
> directed you to wrong places: Your hearts are mighty,
> your skins are whole, and let burnt sack be the issue.
> Come, lay their swords in pawn. Follow me, lads of
> peace; follow, follow, follow.
>
> (III.i.102-114)

The Host's speech, which pokes gentle fun at both Caius and
Evans, brings to a successful conclusion the image of the conflict
of body and soul. Neither has been vanquished, and the two are
reconciled. The Host symbolizes the union as he takes their hands
and joins them together. His use of the terms "terrestrial" and
"celestial" serves as a reminder of what the opponents stand for.[12]
The convention of "making up the quarrel" in a dispute between
gentlemen is used here to resolve the quarrel of the body and
soul. The Host's practical attitude as he remarks that he needs
both is most appropriate for the comic treatment of the theme.

But the image of the reconciled body and soul is important to
the Garter theme of the play also. The Order itself combined
concerns that were both spiritual and physical. Knights, who
practiced the active military arts, were disciplined by the Christian institution which represented the spirit. Institutionalized chivalry had affirmed the spiritual dedication of the knight and reinforced this dedication with the vigil in the chapel, an essential
part of the initiation into knighthood. The famous military orders
of the Middle Ages, the Templars and the Knights of St. John,
continued and elaborated this disciplined relationship of physical
and spiritual, active and contemplative. The chivalric orders of
Renaissance courts such as the Order of the Golden Fleece and
the Order of the Garter simply reaffirmed this relationship, although the members were not part of a brotherhood dedicated
to a more rigorous rule enforcing celibacy as the rule of the
Templars did. The members of the Order which first watched

The Merry Wives of Windsor had participated in special divine services which were part of the ritual of the Garter, and the whole celebration honored St. George on his feast day.[13] The saint himself represented the desirable union of physical action in defense of right, governed and directed by the spirit. The reconciliation of spiritual and physical as Caius and Evans clasp hands is a dramatic image of the nature of the institution celebrated by the occasion and Shakespeare's ingenious compliment.

TEXAS CHRISTIAN UNIVERSITY

'By Shallow Riuers':
A Study of Marlowe's
"Dido Queen of Carthage"

John P. Cutts

The opening lines of Marlowe's *Dido Queen of Carthage* effectively set the tone, atmosphere, and themes of gods behaving like less than gods, of the heroic reduced to the sportive dilettante, and of corruption which prevail throughout.[1] Jupiter dangling Ganymede upon his knee while Mercury sleeps, promising him imperial powers and offering him "linked gems,/[His] *Iuno* ware vpon her marriage day" (42-43),[2] almost exactly parallels Dido dangling Aeneas at the end of her chain of command, promising him imperial powers in the powerful present of Carthage to counteract shadowy thoughts of a future second Troy beyond the seas, and offering him for jewels the "golden bracelets, and . . . wedding ring,/Wherewith [her] husband woo'd [her]" (1057-1058). In her delusion that she has thwarted Aeneas' attempt to sail away to Italy, she is temporarily caught out by proclaiming him as a Jove minus a Ganymede and Mercury:

> Now lookes *Aeneas* like immortall *Ioue*,
> O where is *Ganimed* to hold his cup,
> And *Mercury* to flye for what he calles?
>
> (1251-1253)

whereas it is Aeneas who Ganymede-like fills her cup of imperial success, and it is her sister Anna who acts as Mercury her messenger. The main distinctions, and these all redound to Dido's credit, are that Dido is free to seek another mate since her husband Sicheus is dead and that her attachment to Aeneas is wholly the result of the direct intervention of Aeneas' mother Venus in which Dido is more a victim of love's violence than herself a victimizer.

These distinctions are important in other ways, too. It is doubtful that except for Venus' direct intervention Dido of her own accord would fall in love with Aeneas. At their first encounter Dido is at no pains to spare her contempt for the mean, base, common-groom look about Aeneas. Even though she makes immediate preparations for remedying the "outward" deficiency in Aeneas by sending for her husband Sicheus' royal

robe to clothe him in, she knows that this addition cannot sufficiently compensate for the "inner" deficiency, the real source of
her criticism — "*Aeneas* is *Aeneas,* were he clad/In weedes as
bad as euer *Irus* ware" (379-380), if he but bore a noble mind.
Aeneas' claim that his present mean fortunes make him an unfit
companion for a queen despite the greatness of his birth becomes
a hollow justification also when Dido has to remind him to
remember who he is, and to "speak like [him]selfe" (395).
When Aeneas' companions first pointed out Dido to him, his
reply — "Well may I view her, but she sees not me" (368) —
indicates his lack of confidence in himself. He has buried his identity in the coffin with Priam and Anchises, and is forever pausing,
doubting whether it will come back to him. At one of the crucial
points in the play, Aeneas, returning to the wood where he shot
the deer that saved his famished soldiers' lives when first he
set foot upon Carthage's shore, and where he first encountered
Venus disguised as Diana "Hauing a quiuer guirded to her side,/An
cloathed in a spotted Leopards skin" (185-186), comments self-
disparagingly on the *manly* look of his son Ascanius:

> And mought I liue to see him sacke rich *Thebes,*
> And loade his speare with Grecian Princes heads,
> Then would I wish me with *Anchises* Tombe,
> And dead to honour that hath brought me vp.
>
> (952-955)

If only Ascanius were born to put things right instead of Aeneas,
then Aeneas could "wish [him] in faire *Didos* armes,/And dead
to scorne that hath pursued [him] so" (958-959). The irony is
made doubly poignant, however, by the audience's awareness
that Aeneas is not really looking at his son Ascanius but at Cupid
impersonating Ascanius. It is bad enough that Aeneas should be
seeking a way out of responsibility by concentrating on the
manliness of his son, but it is far worse that he should be trying
to pass off his amorous potential as more than his warlike
equivalent, as if such action would indeed give him some real
stature. It is he after all who introduces Dido to the cave and
likens it to the place where "*Mars* and *Venus* met" (999), but
strangely reverses the roles, wishing to be the seduced one rather
than the seducer, pretending not to understand Dido's burning
love for him, asking only if she has fallen "sicke of late" (1019)
and what she means by her "doubtfull speech" (1026).

Whichever way Aeneas is presented he loses stature. He is neither a warrior on the battlefield nor in bed. He bears none of the attributes which Dido lists for all those kings who have been most urgent suitors for her love. He is no Orator who thought by words to compass Dido, and "yet he was deceiu'd" (790); no Spartan Courtier; no Halcyon Musician;[3] no wealthy King of Thessaly; no warlike Prince, Meleager's son, but a Ganymede who will willingly "spend [his] time in [Dido's] bright armes" (22) as long as he can be protected from fortune's "shrewish blowes" (4) and deck himself in the jewels and bracelets that Dido will give him "if [he] will be [her] loue" (49, and echoed at 804). "Come liue with me and be my loue,/And we will all the pleasures proue" is obviously Jove's theme song to Ganymede. His whole speech is rounded with this passionate plea to his love — "Come gentle *Ganimed* and play with me (1). . . . Sit on my knee and call for thy content (28) . . . if thou wilt be my loue "(49). It becomes the theme song of Dido, *after* she has been wounded by Cupid's arrows at Venus' request, as Dido's remarkable lines show:

wilt stay with me . . .
Ile giue thee tackling made of riueld gold,
Wound on the barkes of odoriferous trees,
Oares of massie Iuorie full of holes,
Through which the water shall delight to play:
Thy Anchors shall be hewed from Christall Rockes,
Which if thou lose shall shine aboue the waues:
The Masts whereon thy swelling sailes shall hang,
Hollow Pyramides of siluer plate:
The sailes of foulded Lawne, where shall be wrought
The warres of *Troy,* but not *Troyes* ouerthrow:
For ballace, emptie *Didos* treasurie,
Take what ye will, but leaue *Aeneas* here.
Achates, thou shalt be so meanly clad,
As Seaborne Nymphes shall swarme about thy ships,
And wanton Mermaides court thee with sweete songs,
Flinging in fauours of more soueraigne worth,
Then *Thetis* hangs about *Apolloes* necke,
So that *Aeneas* may but stay with me.
(748, 750-767)

These lines are cruelly parodied by the old nurse's attempted seduction of Ascanius, offering him

an Orchard that hath store of plums,
Browne Almonds, Seruises, ripe Figs and Dates,
Dewberries, Apples, yellow Orenges,
A garden where are Bee hiues full of honey,
Musk-roses, and a thousand sort of flowers,
And in the midst doth run a siluer streame,
Where thou shalt see the red gild fishes leape,
White Swannes, and many louely water fowles.
(1375-1382)

Here again, however, the fact that it is really Cupid disguised as
Ascanius whom the Nurse is attempting to seduce points up the
incredibility of such a courtship were it not motivated entirely
from without. That the old Nurse should be made to suffer
sexual pangs for a boy who has not yet come to age as a man
is a bitter parallel for Dido being made to suffer sexual pangs
for a boy of an Aeneas who can give but lip service to Mars and
Venus and refer to Dido's silver arms "coll[ing him] round about"
(1201) as "female drudgerie" (1205) and refer to kisses as
penalties. Herein lies, perhaps, one of the most potent reasons
for Aeneas' willingness to leave his son Ascanius behind with
Dido, while he puts to sea with his sailors to find out Italy.
In his desperate search of his manhood he is willing to abandon
his "boy" image to Dido. Aeneas has obviously completely forgotten about Ascanius in his preoccupation with his need to
show manly strength in answer to Achates' charge that the kind
of life they are leading in Carthage is "no life for men at armes
to liue,/Where daliance doth consume a Souldiers strength/And
wanton motions of alluring eyes/Effeminate [their] mindes"
(1183-1186). When Dido taunts Aeneas with being false to
her, his first excuse, that he had only left in order to take his
farewell of Achates, carries ironic overtones of bidding farewell
to manliness. His second excuse, that the sea is too rough and
the winds are blowing to the shore, would seem to indicate that
his problems are to be faced on land and not run away from at
sea. Both criticisms are further reinforced by his weakest excuse—
"Hath not the Carthage Queene [his] onely sonne?/Thinkes
Dido [he] will goe and leaue him here?" (1235-1236). He is
desperately trying to make the boy image stand for his strength.
Critics have been unduly puzzled by these lines and have
indicated that there must be an oversight here, because Marlowe

is implying that up to this point Aeneas has forgotten or has been prepared to abandon his son in his attempt to steal away. In order to account for the so-called oversight, it has been suggested that Aeneas had intended to come back for Ascanius "but is catching at straws in his weak attempts to avoid Dido's justifiable anger and distress."[4] To my way of thinking there is no oversight, no need to try to cover up for Aeneas. He is torn with mental struggles, with dreadful feelings of inadequacy, which put him at the beck and call of each new situation which seems to offer a temporary way out of his dilemma. He does not think nor act like a Trojan prince with a divine mission to found an empire, but like a shattered being who cannot restore his self-respect, against whom all occasions contrive to show him in worse lights.

It is very revealing to place Aeneas' account of himself to the unknown goddess who greets him on his first arrival on the Carthaginian shores side by side with his account of himself to Dido. The latter, as we have already observed, leaves Dido the task of trying to make Aeneas think, speak, and behave like a leader of men. The former account begins with the epic stature of a heroic mission

> Of *Troy* am I, *Aeneas* is my name,
> Who driuen by warre from forth my natiue world,
> Put sailes to sea to seeke out *Italy:*
> And my diuine descent from sceptred *Ioue*
> (216-219)

and gradually declines into passive obedience to his mother Venus' direction — "And made that way [his] mother *Venus* led" (221) leading to the stature of an exile, "poore and vnknowne" (227) who has nowhere to hide his head. That he should be rendering this account of himself to a goddess whom he takes to be either Diana herself or one of her chaste train, but whom we the audience know to be Venus herself, is powerfully ironic. Venus cannot direct Aeneas to find out Dido simply by appearing to her son in her proper shape but has to usurp the "chaste" look of Diana to make the whole business look clean and proper, a gift of fortune that is favoring Aeneas. More important, however, than our appreciation of the dramatic irony at this particular point is the total irony of the next in which Aeneas is able, after

Venus has left, to make the discovery for himself that the goddess
was his mother, and lament her going and leaving him there
alone "t]o dull the ayre with [his] discousriue moane" (248),
more like an abandoned putative lover than a dutiful son obeying
his mother's godly behest.

It is with immense relief at the end of the play that Aeneas
can break away from Carthage and Dido under the explanation,
made possible by Hermes, that he now realizes that it was his
mother "that beguild the Queene,/And made [him] take [his]
brother for his sonne" (1450-1451), and that it was no marvel
Dido was in love since she was daily dangling Cupid in her
arms. This explanation is a carte blanche for Dido, not for Aeneas!
And it is made possible not by any careful diagnosis of the
situation and balancing of the evidence, nor by any sudden
clairvoyance on Aeneas' part, but by the *deus ex machina* procedure
of having Hermes directly intervene, bring Ascanius back to
Aeneas, and remind him of Italy which is "cleane out of [his]
minde" (1437). Even with this *direct* prodding Aeneas is temporarily caught out by the restoration of his son Ascanius whom
he had quite literally abandoned earlier. *Now* he expresses anxiety
over where the boy has been so long and instructs Sergestus to
smuggle him aboard their ships "Lest Dido spying him keepe
him for a pledge" — the very excuse he had tried to save his face
with before! No wonder Hermes is provoked to criticize Aeneas
for spending his "time about this little boy" (1459) rather than
giving his ear unto the divine mission. For all his mother's
guidance and Hermes' prodding, Aeneas remains his bungling
self, too much wrapped up in his own unsolvable complex problems
to try to put Troy's right.

His basic dissatisfaction with himself is exhibited in every
way in his dealings with his son Ascanius. Even in the beginning
situation on the shore when Ascanius interjects a real note of
human affairs, calling for succor, his father can only reassure him
by stressing the necessary *mechanical* procedure of building a
fire to dress the meat, though it is fair to notice that Aeneas of
his own accord does take some kind of thought, albeit in a
disciplinary manner, for Ascanius' welfare by bidding him go dry
his drenched limbs at the fire. When Aeneas faces Carthage's
walls and creates in his imagination a living Priam figure out of
stone, his mental lapse is deprecated strongly enough by Achates,
who claims that Aeneas' mind that would have Priam alive again

deludes his eyesight into seeing the statue of Priam come alive. But more strongly Aeneas' lapse is deprecated by his son. For Ascanius to ask him to stop weeping and to point out that the stone is not Priam (330) because if it were Priam would surely smile on Ascanius, is much more damaging to him than Achates' rebuke. The Virgilian source *(Aeneid,* Book I) refers only to "paintings" of the tale of Troy on the walls of Carthage which Aeneas and his followers note. Marlowe's introduction of a stone statue complex considerably enriches the episode, makes it more potentially dramatic, and basically much less flattering to Aeneas.

Aeneas confounds himself in Priam and is lost in the past. His mind is forever harping on the *destruction* of Troy and is dead to hopes and thoughts of making Troy *relive.* It is remarkable that the only zest (1409-1423) he can muster for rebuilding Troy is indeed in Carthage, and this zest is not so much at Dido's request as at the dictates of his own basic desires. Resorting to building a statelier Troy of Carthage is as easy a way out of the mental rigors of the journey he should be undertaking as is his allowing the manly look in his son the task of taking that journey for him, thus affording himself the freedom to wish himself in fair Dido's arms. His zest for building Troy in Carthage is undermined, however, by his choice of a name for the new city. The names his supporters suggest — *"AEnea* by [his] name" (1428), *"Ascania* by [his] little sonne" (1429)—are rejected in favor of "Anchisaeon," his old father's name. The new is confounded once again in the old, and it may be perfectly planned by Marlowe to have Hermes intervene at this exact moment to remind Aeneas of a promising *future,* of the prophecy associated with his son Ascanius, whose descendants will build a *lasting* empire.

Aeneas' discomfort with his son, his willingness to abandon him, to ignore him, not to be a *living* father to him — all stem from his feeling of inadequacy when he compares himself with others' strength and hopes largely symbolized by his son. His need to make a living Priam out of a stone statue points to a much more devastating inadequacy, however — his inability to shake out of a guilt complex with regard to his own lack of manliness and manly action. The stone statue episode, even before Aeneas' *slanted* description of the fall of Troy, indicates a preoccupation with narcissistic negativism. Achates might well wonder why his partner is so rapt withal at the sight of Carthage walls

(297). Aeneas' mind first dwells on the thought of Niobe, "w]ho for her sonnes death wept out life and breath,/And drie with grief was turnd into a stone" (298-300), because he wants to claim that her passions were not as great as his own. Niobe lost *all* her children and all possibility of glory through them: Aeneas has not lost his son Ascanius, is by no means in danger of doing so, and has the promise of the fulfilment of the prophecy of future greatness through him. There is no real parallel except in the sense that Aeneas is determined to make a weeping statue of himself and concentrate on himself to the complete exclusion of Ascanius. What is Niobe to him or he to Niobe that he should weep for her?

That Niobe is a kind of mirror image of himself is made abundantly clear when he turns his weeping attention to the statue of Priam and wishes his prayers "(as *Pigmalions*[5] did)/Could giue it life" (311-312) so that Priam himself could be charged with the rebuilding of Troy. That his mind should be so powerfully deluding itself as to imagine that the statue actually does come alive is to place Aeneas in a situation in which the citizens of Carthage who are seen approaching might well laugh (333) at him and not treat him princely as befits his station. Achates' first reference in the play to Aeneas as his God — "thou onely art our God" (152) — has suffered a remarkable declension into the class of less than dignified mortals when he is afraid Aeneas' conduct will make the approaching citizens laugh. When those so-called citizens turn out to be no strangers but Aeneas' own followers, the underrating of Aeneas is inevitable. It reaches almost a nadir when Illioneus remarks that he hears Aeneas' voice but does not see him, for none of the figures approaching him can possibly be his General, Aeneas (340-341). In the Virgilian source, Aeneas and Achates are enveloped in a cloud which makes the lack of identification feasible. Marlowe has neglected to afford Aeneas such a cover, and it seems to me that this omission is a deliberate dramatic stroke. Aeneas is denied his stature by a series of failures to correspond with what might reasonably be expected of him. His son's remarks to nim are by no means flattering, as we have seen, and neither are Achates'. Their disparaging remarks are reinforced by Illioneus' non-recognition of Aeneas, by Sergestus' ready recognition of Achates (344), and by Aeneas' turning "from his trustie friends" (352) and fading totally into the background, first at the thought of the mention of

Dido and then in Dido's actual presence.

The play has carefully prepared many pointers for criticism of Aeneas as less than epic, heroic, manly, vigorous, before Marlowe allows him his *longest* chance in the whole play to impress himself on Dido and his audience. Aeneas' tale of Troy could well have been nothing more than Marlowe's verse translation of the account in Virgil, and here those critics who hold to the belief that in *The Tragedie of Dido Queene of Carthage* Marlowe is merely versifying Virgil might reasonably expect verification of their thesis. Close investigation reveals, however, that the account is being deliberately slanted and *not* in Aeneas' favor.

The account is prefaced by Dido's request that Aeneas "discourse at large" (401) and "truly" (402), too, how Troy was overcome, because the many tales "scarcely doe agree vpon one poynt" (404). Her placing *"Sinons* periurie" (406), which is the most common explanation for how Troy was betrayed,[6] side by side with and secondary to the possibility that *"Antenor* did betray the towne" (405), a little known explanation which springs from Caxton's and Lydgate's versions of the fall of Troy, invites careful scrutiny. Antenor is closely linked with Aeneas as a traitor to Troy, and, as Oliver has pointed out, the Troy Book "not only relates how 'false Enee' and Antenor conspired against Troy and how Antenor even betrayed the secret of the Palladion (Troy could not fall while the Palladion was safe) but also tells that Aeneas later turned against Antenor and planned to kill him."[7] To ignore Dido's deliberate pointing to Antenor by saying that although Marlowe knew his medieval authorities "he was dramatizing Virgil" is to ignore Marlowe's very careful manipulation of several sources and to miss the direction which he has been painstakingly sign-posting.

It is surely no coincidence that when Marlowe conspicuously diverges from his Virgilian source, it is to present more *personal* details of Aeneas' involvement, which is after all a perfectly natural move since Aeneas tells the tale from his own point of view. Dido has sufficiently provoked the crumbling "stony mace" (410) statue of Aeneas at her feet to arise by suggesting that Aeneas can hardly faint "to remember *Troy?*/In whose defence he fought so valiantly" (413-414). It may be highly significant, too, that Aeneas in order to speak *assumes* the role of Achilles[8] because Marlowe reduces Aeneas' actual involvement in the fight to a minimal and reckless rushing into the enemy's control. T. S. Eliot suggests[9]

that Aeneas' telling of the tale of Troy secures its emphasis by
always hesitating on the edge of caricature and at the right moment
brilliantly exposes the trick of the rhetoric. When the motivation
is diagnosed, the tight-rope balance which Marlowe seems to
make Aeneas take could be categorized as that between outright
distortion and scarcely veiled need to protect himself. Dido will
not let him get away with an attempt at objective accounting, will
not let him leave off at the woeful bringing in of the fatal engine
to baleful Troy, but goads him on the "rest" (455), and sure
enough forces him into a not-so-delicate balance. He has to admit
that his hands were employed in this unhappy work and "did
helpe to hale [the wooden horse] to the gates" (465), and in
preparation for a much more detailed account of his own behavior, prepares his viewers by insinuating that although the
Trojans "banquetted till ouercome with wine" (473) and "some
surfetted" (474), "others soundly slept" (474), among which
latter group he would have us place himself, since he "rose"
(486) when frighted by the noise consequent on the Greeks
breaking the walls of Troy and marching into the streets. His
"involvement" at this stage is purely vicarious as he looks from
a turret and beholds:

> Young infants swimming in their parents bloud,
> Headles carkasses piled vp in heapes,
> Virgins halfe dead dragged by their golden haire,
> And with maine force flung on a ring of pikes,
> Old men with swords thrust through their aged sides,
> Kneeling for mercie to a Greekish lad,
> Who with steele Pol-axes dasht out their braines.
>   (488-494)

Aeneas *looked* and *saw* a great deal of action apparently before
he buckled on his armor and drew his sword *"thinking* to goe
downe" (496; italics mine). This digression was not essential to
prepare the listener for the appearance of *"Hectors* ghost" to
Aeneas bidding him to escape by timely flight. In the Virgilian
source, Hector's ghost appears to Aeneas while he is still asleep,
and Aeneas still in a trance talks to the visionary man. Marlowe
could easily have taken this approach had he wished, but by
making Aeneas enter the witness box as it were and give a
more detailed *time* account of his involvement before a critical
jury, instead of allowing him the godlike stature of arising from

his lofty couch to address an admiringly captivated and attentive audience,[10] he has much reduced Aeneas. Now Aeneas sees the ghost *after* he has looked from a turret on a sea of fiendish activity — almost cowardice on a monument vicariously sharing in slaughter!

Marlowe omits all the details of the Virgilian Hector's ghost passing on to Aeneas the mantle of Troy's dignity, making him the heir to Troy's future greatness, bringing him the venerable statues of the gods, the wreaths and relics of the immortal fire from the sacred choir of Vesta (Book II). He simply has Hector's ghost cry "Aeneas flye,/Troy is afire, the Grecians haue the towne" (502-503). It is as if Marlowe deliberately robs Aeneas of any dignity that might accrue from such materials and instead strips him down to the bare facts of utter confusion and cowardice. Virgil has Aeneas immediately arise to · meet the alarms, resolved on death, resolved to die in arms, rallying and organizing friends and companions to repel the foes, and fired with a sense of honor and inspired by revenge. At one point Aeneas' Trojan troop resorts to the ruse of dressing itself in the armor of slain Greeks so that it might the more successfully wage war upon the Greeks, thus reverting to the wooden horse technique. Marlowe has Aeneas fling forth "desperate of [his] life" (505) and almost immediately run headlong into the mouth of the Pyrrhus bear and the "band of Mirmidons,/With balles of wilde fire in their murdering pawes" (511-512), from which predicament Dido understandably feels it necessary to interject — "Ah, how could poore *Aeneas* scape their hands?" (515). The too ready face-saving answer — "[His] mother *Venus* jealous of [his] health,/Conuaid [him] from their crooked nets and bands" (516-517) — is again a very slanted alternation from Virgil's account in which Venus shining heavenly bright stood revealed before him, purged the dross from his eyes so that he could see that this destruction was brought about by the *gods,* and bade him haste to save his wife, father, and son, and bear in mind the need to remember Troy's future glory. Venus intervenes in the nick of time, because Aeneas wild in rage is about to slay Helen, the cause of the wars, whom he finds sheltering in Vesta's temple. Such rage in Virgil is what Aeneas has been reduced to after he has witnessed the slaughter of the Trojans on a large scale and has seen Priam himself fall. Even in Virgil Venus accuses Aeneas of "unmanly rage" in his vengeance con-

templated against Helen, because there could obviously be no
boast of conquest from a woman slain. But in Marlowe the
slaughter of Priam comes *after* Venus has intervened to save
her son Aeneas, and it is very noticeable that Aeneas is as concerned with the frantic gestures of Hecuba[11] as he is with Priam.
The substitution of the Hecuba episode, not in Virgil, for that of
Helen has the effect of reinforcing the mother fixation.

That the sequence of events is different in Marlowe from
Virgil's account is partly attributable to Dido's intervention and
asking how Aeneas could escape such odds before she has given
Aeneas chance to talk of the destruction of Priam, but it is
surely much more largely attributable to Aeneas' overriding need
to provide some excuse ahead of time for his not taking a much
more active and vigorous role in the whole proceedings. It is
convenient for him to be immediately surrounded by the main
force of the enemy so that he is immediately rendered powerless,
and to be whisked away by his mother Venus *before* he had a
chance to exert himself in a positive way in the most crucial
struggle for the life of Priam.

When Marlowe has Aeneas give the gory details of Priam's
dying, "from the nauell to the throat at once" (550) ripped by
Pyrrhus, it is quite a different Aeneas from the one Virgil describes. Virgil's Aeneas had tried his uttermost to rescue Cassandra,
had had his band of warriors chipped away one by one, had
bravely tackled awful odds, had striven to deserve the death
he sought, and only when he could fight no longer and would
have died, was he somehow borne off, against his will, to a distance
by a growing tide, and hurried hence with only old Iphitus and
wounded Pelias. Marlowe's Aeneas is already in the safe "turret"
of his mother's protection looking down on the carnage of Priam
and once more imagining a statue come to life — *"Ioues* marble
statue gan to bend the brow,/As lothing *Pirrhus* for this wicked
act" (551-552). Marlowe's association of Aeneas with statues is
surely not accidental: it would seem to me to be emphasizing
the "static" in him.

Virgil's Aeneas is hurried by Venus to his own home where
his father refuses to entertain the idea of leaving ruined Troy
and persuades Aeneas to make efforts to save the last remnants
of Troy. Virgil makes much of the family piety of Aeneas:
Marlowe reduces it to nothing. In Virgil, Aeneas is saved from
the dilemma posed by his father only by the miraculous signs

suggesting Aeneas' son's future glory, signs which convince old Anchises that they should all follow where heaven shows the way. With Anchises on his back, his son holding his hand, his wife Crëusa tagging along, Aeneas makes his way and is perplexed enough, when Crëusa does not survive the ordeal, to go back to Troy through all the danger spots searching for her. How cruel is Marlowe's reduction of all this to:

> By this I got my father on my backe,
> This yong boy in mine armes, and by the hand
> Led faire *Crëusa* my beloued wife.
>
> (560-562)

It is as if Marlowe is making Aeneas "guiltily". try to cover up for losing Crëusa. In Virgil the loss of Crëusa is puzzling and circumstantial — Aeneas is not quite sure whether she stopped to rest, lost the way, or became too terrified at the ordeal. In Marlowe Aeneas claims to be leading Crëusa by the hand, a neat change from Virgil, and to lose her in a last skirmish with the Greeks for which there is no parallel in Virgil's account:

> When thou *Achates* with thy sword mad'st way,
> And we were round environ'd with the Greekes:
> O there I lost my wife.
>
> (564-566)

It is the same pattern as Marlowe put Aeneas through before, when the Myrmidons hemmed him round about so he could not go to Priam's aid. Marlowe's Aeneas begs out of responsibility on each occasion by saying the Greeks overwhelmed him to such an extent that he was rendered powerless to help his loved ones. His mother Venus was his excuse for not helping Priam; his exaggerated estimate of his manliness covers up his inadequacy in not securing Crëusa along with his father and son, especially in view of the fact that Crëusa was not just tagging along but was being led by him:

> and had not we
> Fought manfully, I had not told this tale:
> Yet manhood would not serve.
>
> (565-567)

The exaggerated tone is not too far removed from the Falstaffian:

> I am a rogue if I were not half-sword with a dozen of
> them two hours together. I have scaped by miracle I
> never dealt better since I was a man: all would not do.
> *(1 Henry IV,* II.iv.162-164; 167-168)

without the saving grace of good-natured bantering comedy!

It is possible to suggest that somehow Aeneas was more pre-occupied with Achates' coming to his succor than with his own need to defend Crëusa. There is no warranty for the introduction of Achates into this last skirmish in Virgil. Marlowe seems to have been in a hurry to dismiss Crëusa from an episode on which Virgil lavished much attention, and to insert information which is kept from being purely gratuitous by its dramatic overtones. Achates is more than usually wrapped up in Aeneas. The rhetoric of his first speech to Aeneas in the play goes somewhat beyond normal[12] propriety:

> Braue Prince of *Troy,* thou onely art our God,
> That by thy vertues freest vs from annoy,
> And makes our hopes suruiue to coming ioyes:
> Doe thou but smile, and clowdie heauen will cleare,
> Whose night and day descendeth from thy browes
> (152-156)

with something of the tone of Jupiter's address to Ganymede — "1 loue thee well, .../Whose face reflects such pleasure to mine eyes" (2; 24). These speeches are so placed that they provide an effective dramatic juxtaposition. They are the first in each case to introduce both Ganymede and Aeneas. It may be suggested, too, that when Aeneas is confronted with the stone statue complex, his proper confidant is Achates — Aeneas is in fact talking to his own mirror image, and is quite unable or unwilling to listen to its message. Achates thus largely represents a side of Aeneas that is narcissistic, and it may well be that Marlowe is stressing Aeneas' inability to cope with the presence of a Crëusa as later he is unable to deal with Dido. Virgil describes Aeneas going back through the terrors of a burning Troy in frenzied search of his wife, almost in terms of an Orpheus braving the torments of Hades to bring back his wife Eurydice. Marlowe has Aeneas dismiss Crëusa with a half line — "O there I lost my wife" (565) and in the very next breath concentrate on a manhood which would not serve — "Fought manfully . . ./Yet manhood would not serue" (566-567). Oliver's suggestion[13] that "perhaps Marlowe thought the whole story of Crëusa was better played down in a tragedy about Dido" is unflattering to Dido. Cleopatra's accusation of Antony:

> O most false love!
> Where be the sacred vials thou should'st fill
> With sorrowful water? Now I see, I see,
> In Fulvia's death, how mine receiv'd shall be
>
> *(Antony and Cleopatra,* I.iii.
> 62-65)

is more in line with what one would expect of a Dido.

This lack of manliness in Aeneas would seem to be emphasized further by Marlowe's choice of the last accounts, namely regarding Cassandra and Polyxena, given by Aeneas before sorrow tires him so much that he has to ask Achates to speak for him. Virgil does mention the fruitless attempt to rescue Cassandra from the temple of Minerva (not Diana, as in Marlowe) but does not say that Ajax ravished her. The alteration from Minerva to Diana:

> We saw *Cassandra* sprauling in the streetes,
> Whom *Aiax* rauisht in *Dianas* Fane
>
> (569-570)

is surely deliberate. Marlowe's own translation of Ovid's *Elegia VII* has the correct information:

> So chast *Minerua* did *Cassandra* fall
> Deflowr'd except, within thy Temple wall.
>
> (17-18)[14]

He would seem to me to be deliberately calling attention to the passage by altering conspicuous facts. Virgil mentions the ravishing of Cassandra as one of the *earlier* incidents in Aeneas' account of his observations in Troy, when he and his band of warriors disguised as Greeks strewed the streets with Grecian carcasses until Coroebus, one of the band, saw his wife Cassandra being dragged by her disheveled hair and went to her defense, supported by Aeneas and the rest only to find their Grecian disguise made them the target of Trojans trying to defend

Cassandra, and their action and different speech the target
of Greeks trying to ravish her. It seems to me that Aeneas
deliberately transposes the help he gave to Cassandra at an early
stage to this very late and needy moment — juxtaposes it in
fact with the loss of Crëusa. He is trying to give the *impression*
that even if his attempt was unsuccessful, at least it shows an
unwillingness to leave a woman in distress,[15] even when the
weight of the evidence points in quite another direction — his
need to justify himself to himself and to a captive audience.
When we hear the lines about Aeneas' "rescue" of Cassandra:

> Her cheekes swolne with sighes, her haire all rent,
> Whom I tooke vp to beare vnto our ships:
> But suddenly the Grecians followed vs,
> And I alas, was forst to let her lye
>
> (571-574)

the same pattern is observable as with the loss of Priam and
Crëusa — the Greeks overwhelmed him to such an extent that
he was rendered powerless to save his loved ones.

The occurrence of the same pattern yet once more with the
last episode, concerning *Polixena:*

> I lept into the sea,
> *Thinking* to beare her on my backe abourd:
> For all our ships were launcht into the deepe,
> And as I swamme, she standing on the shoare,
> Was by the cruel Mirmidons surprizd,
> And after by that *Pirrhus* sacrifizde
>
> (578-583)

surely clinches the criticism that Aeneas in attempting to cover
up for his own feelings of inadequacy is resorting to the same
excuse, that of being overwhelmed by a sudden band of Myrmidons.
The interpretation is especially fitting for this last incident in
view of the fact that the Ovidian source offers a full account
of the killing of Polyxena by Pyrrhus, but *not* with the aid of
the Myrmidons or at the altar.[16] Marlowe has inverted the episode
of Aeneas' sea labor to try to save Polyxena for the express purpose
of trying to have Aeneas justify to himself his abandonment of
his wife Crëusa. The episode is akin to his abandonment of his
son later in the play, in the sense that it stems from a guilt complex. The use of the theme of ravishing in Diana's temple instead

of in Minerva's, and the added detail of having Polyxena sacrificed, would seem to me to indicate Aeneas' attempt to draw attention to *others' lustful* desecration and profanation and away from his own almost apathetic concern for woman.

Dido's interjection at this point in the tale of Troy to the effect that she dies with "melting ruth" (584) is indeed an ironic comment on Aeneas' thwarted attempts to save Cassandra and Polyxena from being ravished. Before long Dido will openly accuse him of falseness in his excuse for abandoning her, for the "Gods wey not what Louers doe,/It is Aeneas calles Aeneas hence" (1539-1540). Her query about the escape of Helen, "she that caused this warre?" (587), is full of ironic overtones, too, especially in view of the fact that Marlowe makes Aeneas omit the Virgilian episode in which Aeneas himself found Helen sheltering in a temple and would have wreaked a cheap vengeance by slaughtering her if he had not been prevented from doing so by the dazzling appearance of his mother Venus accusing him of being "unmanly" in such thoughts and intentions. Marlowe makes Aeneas *suppress* this episode, and Dido on the other hand bring it to the forefront of attention. It is Dido who issues the final comment on Aeneas' tale of Troy by wishing Helen, the "ticing strumpet" (595), had never been born, and it is she who likens herself to a second Helen (1552; 1556) at the very end of the play when Aeneas is suddenly surprised by a *metaphorical* band of Myrmidons depriving him of his free will (1548). But the sting of her remarks lies in the extension of the Carthage-Troy parallel in her taunting Aeneas with not being "as true as *Paris*" (1554), and in her poignant regret that she does not have a son by Aeneas to lessen her grief by seeing Aeneas in his face (1557-1558). In this last "accusation" lies a remarkable dimension for critical examination of the Ascanius-Cupid affair in the play. Venus gives Dido a child — Cupid: the only child Aeneas can give her is Ascanius!

While Dido brings uncomfortable thoughts of Helen to Aeneas' mind after he has given his version of the tale of Troy, Anna and Iarbus touch other tender nerves by asking respectively what became of aged Hecuba (585), and how Aeneas managed to get back to the fleet again after his vain attempts to swim to shore to help Polyxena (586). Anna's question arising out of sheer curiosity may carry with it the ironic overtones of the implication that Aeneas abandoned Hecuba as he did Cassandra and Polyxena,

and that while he has been busily trying to justify his conduct
with regard to the last two, he has forgotten to come up with
an explanation for deserting Hecuba. It is a very good question
to ask, for Marlowe's Aeneas had recounted that the frantic Queen
had leaped on the face of Pyrrhus:

> And in his eyelids hanging by the nayles,
> A little while prolong'd her husbands life
>
> (540-541)

until the soldiers pulled her by the heels and "swong her howling
in the emptie ayre" (543). There is no correspondence in Virgil
for this action. Virgil's Hecuba chides her husband for being
tardy in resorting to his son's aid, shames him by the references
to his son Hector who would behave like a real Priam were he
alive, and with a last salute embraces him. Marlowe would seem
to have derived his information about the frantic queen from
Ovid's *Metamorphoses,* Book XIII, and to have transposed
Hecuba's outrage on the eyes of the tyrant Polymnestor, who
had murdered her young son Polydorus and to whose charge he
had been committed, to Hecuba's attempted outrage on Pyrrhus.
For her outrage on Polymnestor the Greeks stoned her: she became
a bitch and bit the stones they threw at her. Ovid has all the
celestials deplore the disaster of Hecuba. For her attempted outrage
on the eyes of Pyrrhus, Marlowe's Aeneas abandons her to the
empty air which sent an echo to the wounded King.[17] Hecuba's
part may be deliberately left in mid air, so to speak, because it is
too uncomfortable personally for Aeneas to cast more than a
fleeting glance at it. He does not allow her the *success* she had
with the murderer of her young Polydorus, but only allows her
a frantic "gesture," as vain an attempt to do anything about the
horrible slaughter as his own.

Iarbus' question calls Aeneas' bluff almost as effectively as does
Dido's "how could poore *Aeneas* scape" (515). How did Aeneas
get back to the fleet? If he swam as close to the shore as he
said he did, and this entailed swimming from the deep waters —
"For all [their] ships were launcht into the deepe" (580) — close
enough to see Polyxena standing on the shore and surprised by
the cruel Myrmidons, then he was indeed way out. On the other
hand if it is true, as he says, that Polyxena's cry *"AEneas* stay,/The
Greekes pursue me, stay and take me in" (576-577) moved him
into action so that he leaped into the sea *"Thinking* to beare her

on [his] backe abourd" (579; italics mine), then he cannot have been out of earshot, too far from the shore at all. It would seem to me that Aeneas is using the information he gives about the ships being launched into the deep as his excuse for not getting to the rescue of Polyxena soon enough, and that we have once again an example of his going through the mere motions of heroic deeds, sufficient to lend color to his pretensions but not enough to carry them through successfully.

"As for *Aeneas* he swomme quickly backe" (591) explains Achates as he *rapidly* tries to dismiss the terrible facts of Hecuba's fate by saying nothing was known of her after she was led captive into Greece, and *rapidly* refers to Helen's treacherous betrayal of Deiphobus, another of Priam's sons, and to final reconciliation to Menelaus. It is significant that in Virgil the information about Helen's theft of Deiphobus' weapons while he was asleep and her letting the Greeks into the house is given to Aeneas in Book VI when he meets the mangled shade of Deiphobus in the underworld *after* he has been spurned in his attempted meeting with Dido.[18] Marlowe's transposition of material about Helen's treachery from a much later episode to the present need to answer Dido's question about what happened to Helen would seem to be deliberately employed in order to point to others' patent destruction of Priam's children and away from Aeneas' own lack of real aid to save them.

Iarbus' question takes on greater significance in retrospect when, shortly after and in Dido's next appearance on stage, he is declaring his love to her and is being told that of all the wooers she has had, many of them mightier kings, Iarbus has had the greatest favors she could give. Dido even goes so far as to imply that her favorable and familiar conduct toward Iarbus has resulted in her being "counted light" (648), though she thanks the gods that "no wanton thought/Had euer residence in [her] breast" (651). Iarbus' genuine wooing of Dido has a considerable look of success about it as Dido's own words indicate — "Feare not *Iarbus*, Dido may be thine" (653) — *before* Cupid disguised as Aeneas' little son begins to play with Dido's garments, embrace her, and sing her the song which his "cosin *Helen*" taught him in Troy (662). Even when Cupid's golden arrow touches Dido's breast and the "wanton thought" of love surprises her, thoughts of Iarbus are only with difficulty replaced by thoughts of Aeneas. This episode is surely partial explanation of the "off and on"

effect of Dido's remarks to Iarbus — "O stay *Iarbus,* and Ile
goe with thee" (671); "Why staiest thou here? thou art no loue of
mine" (673). Cupid has to force his presence by demanding
attention each time Dido's love for Iarbus seems about to triumph
over the newly injected love for Aeneas. *Without* Cupid's inter-
ference at the instigation of Venus, whether Dido would fall in
love with Aeneas at all is doubtful. It is for the child's sake that
Dido agrees to love the father well whom until that point she did
"neuer thinke . . . beautiful" (717).

That the role of Iarbus is entirely Marlowe's own addition
to the sources further supports the interpretation that Iarbus'
genuine love for Dido should stand as a foil for Aeneas'. At
the end of the play, it is Iarbus who makes possible Aeneas'
departure from Carthage by furnishing the necessary rigging for
Aeneas' fleet and oars for his sailors. Iarbus triumphs over
Aeneas in this respect. Iarbus' genuine love for Dido motivates
his willingness to provide the means by which Aeneas can under-
take the *heroic* task of attending to the gods' bidding. Aeneas'
heroism is thus made ultimately to depend on an Iarbus! Iarbus'
rushing into death to follow and be with Dido, and Anna's killing
herself to be with her "sweet *Iarbus, Annas* sole delight" (1729)
are the last things in the play and provide a tragic dignity which
is almost entirely lacking in the Dido-Aeneas relationship. Iarbus'
love for Dido and Anna's love for Iarbus are absolutely genuine
and worth dying for. They provide the play with a dimension
that recalls the interplay of more normal human relations caught
in the machinations of ungodly gods and ungodlike heroes.
Aeneas' "love" for Dido, and Dido's love for Aeneas are contrived
and manipulated, in Dido's case entirely by Venus' intervention
for her own political purposes, and in Aeneas' case by his use
of Dido as an escape from his guilt complex over his wife
Crëusa and over Troy, and basically over his own inadequacies
as a man.

In the beginning of the play Marlowe has Iarbus welcome the
Trojan strangers — Illioneus, Cloanthus, and Sergestus washed up
on a different part of the shore from their leader Aeneas —
["a]s *Iupiter* to sillie *Baucis* house" (289). The strangers prove
far less godly than Jupiter and Mercury visiting Philemon and
Baucis. In return for the hospitality they receive, they do not
turn a poor cottage into a rich temple, a poor Carthage into a
rich new Troy, though by their half-hearted attempt they make

things look worse than if they had never tried. Nor are they instrumental in a positive way in rewarding the concept of a love that endures all life's hazards and faces it out to the edge of doom. Only in a negative way do they force into the open Iarbus' intense love for Dido, and Anna's intense love for Iarbus, and show by their almost simultaneous deaths something of the power of love exemplified by Philemon and Baucis. Golding's comment on the Philemon and Baucis episode as evidencing "mutuall love betweene the man and wife,"[19] whom death could not divide, provides us with a safe enough indication of how Elizabethans were likely to have "pointed" the tale.

There is an obvious sense in which Dido herself triumphs over Aeneas, by ridding herself from those "thoughts of Lunacie" (1681) over a runagate which have deprived her of her dignity. In their last meeting, both she and Aeneas are made by Marlowe to resort to the Latin of Virgil's *Aeneid,* deliberately, I would suggest, because each is striving to overcome the difficulty of too present involvement, and trying to bring to bear the strength of the detachment of history, Aeneas hiding behind it, Dido forcing attention on its inhuman coldness and apathy. When this last show-down is over and Aeneas becomes once again the "stranger," it is with immense dignity that Dido again is made to resort to Virgil's Latin and rejoice to go to the shades after invoking land against land, sea against sea, arms against arms in a never-ending series of wars against Rome's peace. Out of her ashes a conqueror shall arise to revenge her — a Hannibal,[20] to threaten the very existence of that new empire which Aeneas will found. In her death she is the phoenix symbol forever generating war against Rome in revenge for Aeneas' treason.

A more powerful triumph over Aeneas is not so obvious. The destruction of Aeneas' sword in that fire, the sword "that in the darksome Caue/He drew" (1703-1704), is a fitting revenge on Aeneas' unavailing manhood. It has to be burnt "first" (1705) because its crime against her is worse than his "technical" treason. Infected by Cupid's arrow, Dido was deluded into thinking Aeneas' sword would satisfactorily do its master's turn, but all it has done is tantalize and frustrate by non-performance, just as its master tantalizes and frustrates by the empty look and non-practice of heroic proportions. The adored "God" (152) that visited Carthage shores becomes a "Serpent that came creeping from the shoare" (1573) and slinks away flaccid and incapable of engendering. The serpent that Dido "for pitie harbord in [her] bosome" (1574) compares unfavorably, too, with little Ascanius whom she sheltered there not knowing it was Cupid. This comparison is further strengthened by Dido's treatment of the old Nurse as a "[t]raytoresse too keend and cursed Sorceresse" (1629) for letting her "boy" go for some petty gift. The old Nurse considered Ascanius would be a "twigger" — a prolific breeder, when he became a man.

Even the garment in which Dido clothed Aeneas when first he came on shore, the garment "which *Sicheus* ware" (375), has to perish in the final conflagration. This garment had given Aeneas the *royal* look, yet his own demeanor was base. It was in the name of Sicheus that she saluted him after the cave incident — "*Sicheus,* not Aeneas be thou calde" (1054), affiancing him with Sicheus' wedding ring. It was in the magic of the name of Sicheus that she whistled him back from his first attempt to sail away — "siluer whistles to controule the windes,/ Which *Circes* sent *Sicheus* when he liued" (1216-1217). It was in the splendor of Sicheus accompanied by Moors and Mauritanians that she wished to exalt his ride through the "Punicke streetes" (1273) albeit on *her* "Gennet" (1272) — not a Barbary horse, or stallion, or symbol of male strength.[21] It was a reconstituted Sicheus who was to make her "immortall with a kisse" (1329), in whose looks she was seeing eternity. Like Faustus she has in some sense been ravished by splendid magical visions, but unlike Faustus she is the *victim* of the joint machinations of Venus-Valdes and Juno-Cornelius, who have led her into this execrable art without her knowledge, let alone her will, and Aeneas in this context is nothing more than a magician's "spirit" conjured up to "liuely resemble" (*Faustus,* 1059) an epic hero, rather than the true substantial body. Her contribution is to clothe the vision in her late husband's garments and commit it all to the fire of revenge.

OAKLAND UNIVERSITY

Peele's "Old Wives' Tale" and Tale-Type 425A

JAMES T. BRATCHER

In Peele's *Old Wive's Tale,* the soothsayer, Erestus, calls himself "the white bear of England's wood."[1] Outwardly one who lives by alms, he represents in truth a young man who labors under a spell. The crabbed magician Sacrapant, in envy of his former fine fortune and marital happiness, has cruelly enchanted him: Erestus must appear as a wizened beggar by day and a bear by night. He complains,

> And when the sun doth settle in the west,
> Then I begin to don my ugly hide.[2]

Two other victims of Sacrapant's magic liven the play—Erestus's lady Venelia, who runs "madding" in the woods, and the distressed damsel Delia, who languishes as Sacrapant's cherished but forced mistress. These two unfortunates will briefly reappear later in this study. Primary interest focuses on the "bear of England's wood" motif, which offers, it will be argued, a significant key to one of Peele's major folklore sources for the drama.

Although not itself of central importance to the play-within-the-play (Erestus makes no entrance as a beast,[3] nor does his animal form materially affect the plot), the motif nevertheless effectively imparts the atmosphere Peele seeks. Signaling a chain of like marvels in his "curious *mélange* of nursery tales,"[4] it unmistakably introduces a "wife's tale." Like other ingredients of the farrago, moreover, it appears genuinely to reflect some element of a granny's tale familiar to a late sixteenth-century English audience; accordingly, scholars have kept an eye out for Peele's traditional source for the man-bear theme among other rustic influences. To date at least two folklore pedigrees have been suggested for Erestus's *alter ego.*[5]

Writing in a commentary published almost seventy years ago, F. B. Gummere would assign the motif to Peele's broad (and here unquestioned) indebtedness to the folktale "Childe Roland."[6] Sarah L. C. Clapp, in a 1926 study, "Peele's Use of Folk-Lore in *The Old Wives' Tale,*"[7] evidently countenances Gummere's accounting for the theme; at least she does not question it in relying heavily on his commentary. This one derivation, however, appears

to rest very dubiously on the following points: (1) The wizard
Merlin as he figures in the folktale functions much as does Erestus
in the play—he advises wayfarers. (2) Traditionally, as is known,
Merlin is a shape-shifter. While these points can be easily granted,
they do not yield convincing results. As the tale has come down,[8]
Merlin does not function in "Childe Roland" as a shape-shifter,
much less as a white bear specifically.

A more recent suggestion would link the "bear of England's
wood" with the bear-prince of "Snow White and Rose Red." In
the introduction to her *Folktales of England*,[9] Dr. Katharine M.
Briggs comments on Peele's play as "a treasury of references to
tales which have now been lost." By way of illustration she writes:
"[Tale-]Type 426, 'Snow-White and Rose-Red' (Grimm, No. 161)
is unknown in oral tradition in England, but it may have been
known there two hundred years before the Grimm brothers found
it in Germany, for the enchanted bear plays an important part
in *The Old Wives Tale*." (As noted, Erestus *as a bear* plays no part
whatever.) The trouble with this somewhat circuitous identification of Erestus with the bear in the Grimm tale is that Tale-Type
426, in which two girls befriend a bear who turns into a prince,
forms a literary concoction that the Grimms incorporated not
from oral tradition but from a questionable collection of tales
published in 1818. Thompson thus impugns the story.[10] While undoubtedly Peele's white bear came from a folktale somewhere in
his ken, it did not originate in this particular narrative.

As a result of widespread tale-collecting in this century and
the last, it becomes possible to fix the origin of the "bear of
England's wood" in a tale-type as yet unassociated with *The Old
Wives' Tale*. This is Type 425A, "The Monster (Animal) as
Bridegroom." The story of course has wider repute under its
classical title, "Cupid and Psyche." In broadest outlines it resembles "Childe Roland," the source of Peele's basic plot, in being
the story of a quest for lost kin. As a convenience one may provide
the following synopsis based on postclassical versions.

Through one or another set of circumstances a beautiful
girl becomes the bride of a "monster" or a supernatural animal.
The bridegroom may possess a partly human form, like winged
(and in this context, matured) Cupid, or he may be a bear, bull,
wolf, dog, bird, etc., that becomes a man only at night. Whatever
the variables in these respects, he treats the girl lovingly and

keeps her in luxury, providing fine lodging and succulent foods. In time she comes to regard him as her proper husband: in many of the variants she has children by him. He has admonished her, however, in the keeping of some observance, such as not looking on him at night or not revealing his name; and when she breaks the taboo, he has to abandon her. Distraught, she searches the ends of the earth for her lost husband. When at length she finds him, he ordinarily resides in the keeping of an enchantress who has given him a drug that causes forgetfulness. By bribing the enchantress with magical objects she has acquired in the course of her search, the wife gains permission to pass three nights by her husband as he sleeps. Each night she calls his name and beseeches his remembrance of her, reciting, typically,[11] an unspelling charm. This instance of the charm comes from an Irish text collected in the last century:

> Three babes I bore for thee,
> Three basin full of tears
> I shed for thee.
> Seven long years I spent
> Climbing up the glass mountains [*sic*],
> And my bonny bull of oranges
> Will you not turn to me?[12]

On the third night, which brings the third recitation of the charm, the husband's memory returns and the pair reunite in conjugal bliss.

That Peele knew a variant of this tale, involving a bear as the bridegroom, and drew on it for his "bear of England's wood" seems virtually certain in view of evidence to be presented. That he appropriated other story elements—such as the wife's charm—provided for by the tale is less conclusive; but the likelihood gains cogent support in the white-bear borrowing as substantiated below. This firm point of indebtedness recommends our noticing, in due course, features of the play which remain otherwise unaccounted for in commentary on Peele's sources. These concern the deranged condition of Venelia; the considerate manner in which Sacrapant maintains captive Delia; the drug that Sacrapant forces on Delia; and the mock charm and accompanying petition by which Eumenides, the knight who has quested long and far for Delia's hand, revives her and makes her his own. (Eumenides' romantic overture has been accounted for in part, as a borrowing from Robert Greene, but the folktale still has its claim to make.)

First, to establish the paternity of Peele's "white bear of England's wood" as Tale-Type 425A, one may offer sample excerpts from variants of the tale published either in this century or the last. No text from Peele's day has come to light, although, to note an obvious consideration to be taken up directly, the best-known recension of the tale dates from the second century A.D. when Apuleius polished the story for inclusion in his *Metamorphoses* (Englished, as *The Golden Asse of Lucius Apuleius,* by William Adlington in 1566). Excerpts from modern variants follow.

> The youngest girl's husband was very good-looking, but he always wore a long white coat made of bearskin, so the folks called him White Bear Whittington.[13]

> That was the white bear, who threw off his beast shape at night; but she never saw him, for he always came after she had put out the light . . . . [14]

> She got off [his back] and went on in the house. The white bear came in behind her, says . . . "From now on I can be a man of a night and stay with you here and be a bear of a day, or I can be a bear of a night and sleep under your bed and be a man of a day."[15]

> Der was a bull name King Henry and, in de day, Bull-of-all-de-Land [cp. "England"]. Well, in de day him put on bull clo'es an' de night him turn man."[16]

> Every day he [identified in this variant as "wolf of the greenwood," cp. "England's wood"] was to roam the greenwood; but when night came, he could return to his own home in human form.[17]

Other instances of the tale may be cited as corroboration, most notably the "Black Bull of Norroway" mentioned in the *Complaynt of Scotland* (1549) and a nineteenth-century Irish text that converts the Norwegian bull into the "Brown *Bear* of Norway."[18] At this point the evidence appears to be more than sufficient to link *The Old Wives' Tale* with "The Monster Bridegroom."

One repeatedly finds, among other animal bridegrooms figuring in the tale, (1) a white bear who (2) alternates between animal and human form. Except for the fact that Erestus is, of dramatic necessity, a man by day instead of by night, these details correspond to the nature of his enchantment. (This statement obviously grants that in other respects Erestus hardly duplicates the folktale bridegroom.) Moreover, (3) the names assigned to the bridegroom offer semantic and phonetic approximations of "the white bear of England's wood." On the one hand, the "brown bear of Norway" (cp. "bull of oranges," i.e., of the district Orange? or pertaining in some way to King William III?[19]), only slightly removed from the black bull of the title given in the *Complaynt,* would appear to stand on the far side of Peele's patriotic English bear in the process of folklore fading and transmutation. On this side, one detects echoes of "England" or "England's wood" in "Bull-of-all-de-Land" and "wolf of the greenwood." The most distant American cousin of the Norwegian bull, one may note, seems to be the pet bear of Nance Bowers, a backwoods beauty of the Crockett almanacs. Nance rides the bear, as does the bride in variants of the folktale. His cognomen is "king bear of Mud Forest,"[20] a suitably homely removal from the romance-evoking "white bear of England's wood."

Interestingly, Peele could have met with Tale-Type 425A in Apuleius's *Metamorphoses,* from which, as Thomas Warton first observed,[21] he appropriated the name of Sacrapant's sorceress-mother, Meroe. The monster bridegroom of Apuleius's chapter "Cupid and Psyche" is not, however, a bear but the winged son of Venus. Thus it seems reasonable to assume that in addition to his formal training Peele drew on early boyhood recollection for his knowledge of a folktale about a white bear, Cupid in "degenerate" form, who took a mortal bride. There exists slight evidence textually to support the conclusion that he first encountered the tale between, say, the years 1556-71 (within which span, coincidentally, Adlington's translation of the tale in its widest-known literary form appeared). Near the start of *The Old Wives' Tale,* the page Frolic says in response to Madge's, the old wife's, storytelling preamble: "I have seen the day, when I was a little one, you might have drawn me a mile after you with such a discourse."[22] It is tempting to read the sentence as autobiography, although as solid evidence it counts for little more than does Fantastic's reference to Madge's "discourse" as "No better hay [attraction] in Devonshire,"[23] in view of the possibility that Peele's father—an obvious source for his presumed early knowledge of the tale—hailed from Devonshire.[24] It may be observed that the "hay" allusion has a proverbial ring; Devonshire, at any rate, was noted both for agriculture and for rustics who relished fireside marvels.

It remains to consider other likely elements Peele extracted from "The Monster Bridegroom" in compounding his "curious *mélange.*" While more tenuous than the small but firm point of indebtedness thus far examined, and while also, to some extent, the common stock of folktales and romance literature, four additional similarities between tale and play deserve attention. Together with the white-bear borrowing, they produce, one may maintain, a telling *ensemble* which urges our reckoning Tale-Type 425A among major influences on *The Old Wives' Tale.*

1. Venelia's madness recalls the distraught condition of the abandoned wife of the folktale. For example, Apuleius as rendered by Adlington describes Psyche as one "who is a vagabond, and runneth about the Countries," having "hurled her selfe hither and thither, to seeke her husband."[25]

2. Sacrapant supports captive Delia with utmost regard for her comfort. In particular, he magically causes a table to spread in answer to her request for "the best meat from the King of England's table, and the best wine in all France, brought in by the veriest knave in all Spain."[26] Assuredly the folktale offers no basis for the political satire, but otherwise: "and there too was a table ready laid, and it was as grand as grand could be. Then the white bear gave her a silver bell; and when she wanted anything, she was only to ring it, and she would get it at once [from unseen sources]."[27] Apuleius *via* Adlington prescribes "royall meats [foods] . . . all sorts of divine meates and wines . . . brought in, not by any body, but as it were with a wind, for she saw no person before her, but only heard voyces on every side."[28] The voices are of course those of attendant spirits, counterparts of Sacrapant's "Furies."[29]

3. When Delia's brothers discover her at the magician's abode, she fails to recognize them owing to the "potion of forgetfulness"[30] that Sacrapant has administered. The potion, variously designated as "sleepy drops," "a sleepy dram," or "laudanum," is

a recurring element of the folktale.[31]

4. Notice has been taken of the charm the folktale wife recites over her husband. The charm offers a striking parallel with *The Old Wives' Tale*. As an example of it added to the one already quoted, the following instance occurs in an Ozark Mountain text collected as recently as 1950. Here "fire cliff" bears its name because of the imagined effect of sunlight on a glass mountain: Irish and English variants of the tale carry the title "The Glass Mountain," which refers, of course, to the site of the enchantress's castle. In the Ozark text the wife says,

> Three children born to you,
> The red sea crossed for you,
> The fire cliff climbed for you,
> Old White-Bear, look at me![32]

In its recounting of past sacrifices, including far travels, and charging the loved one with an obligation on that score, the recitation finds a counterpart in Eumenides' speech near the conclusion of Peele's play. The wandering knight says to Delia in waking her from drugged forgetfulness, here mouthing a romantic cliché (italics mine) that nevertheless reflects, it is possible to argue, the fire-cliff, glass-mountain imagery of the wife's incantation:

> God speed, fair maid, sitting alone,—there is once. God speed, fair maid,—there is twice. God speed, fair maid,—that is thrice . . . . [Delia wakes and Eumenides continues in verse:]
> Thou fairest flower of these western parts,
> *Whose beauty so reflecteth in my sight*
> *As doth a crystal mirror in the sun;*
> For thy sweet sake I have cross'd the frozen Rhine;
> Leaving fair Po, I sail'd up Danuby
> As far as Saba, whose enhancing streams
> Cuts twixt the Tartars and the Russians;
> These have I cross'd for thee, fair Delia:
> Then grant me that which I have su'd for long.[33]

Structurally both the folktale charm and Eumenides' verse overture form periodic sentences, and in their specific import they could hardly be closer.

To be sure, difficulties obtain in suggesting Peele's indebtedness at this juncture, despite remarkable similarities and the supporting evidence of other borrowings. It has long been recognized that four lines of Eumenides' speech parody lines in Robert Greene's *Orlando Furioso:*

> . . . I furrowed Neptunes Seas,
> Northeast as far as is the frozen Rhene;
> Leaving faire Voya, crost up Danuby,
> As hie as Saba, whose inhauncing streames
> Cuts twixt the Tartares and the Russians . . . .[34]

But if a part of the speech had literary inspiration, it is also clear that the scene in its entirety mirrors folklore. Whereas the context of the lines in *Orlando Furioso* resembles nothing in Peele's play, the folktale in question presents an exact analogy: removal of a spell. No less evident is the satirical intent of Eumenides' introductory lines ("there is once," etc.) as a travesty of folklore charms. In view of what this study has revealed, one cannot easily ignore the folktale wife's incantation in relation to the travesty. (The charm constitutes, incidentally, a memorable feature of the tale; MacEdward Leach has reported that in Jamaica it is all that remains.[35]) On this accounting, the incantation happily afforded Peele the opportunity to parody Greene—whose lines supplant the wife's recital of hardships—while answering to the broader object of his spoof: romantic resuscitations.

On the whole, then, there are compelling grounds for adding Tale-Type 425A to the list of folklore sources of Peele's most unusual, and like its sources, perennially pleasing play. Apart from this tale-typé and theme of the enchanted carolers of Kölbigk,[36] the sources are treated in the Clapp article cited above.[37] In addition to linking Tale-Type 425A to *The Old Wives' Tale,* the present study has indicated the currency of a "white bear" variant of the tale in sixteenth-century England.

UNIVERSITY OF TEXAS AT EL PASO

"These Are But Toyes"

KARL E. SNYDER

From the accession of Henry VIII to the outbreak of the Civil War, masques were a consistently popular stage spectacle, equally so with all classes of people. No one took them seriously as art. Sir Francis Bacon's reference to them as "but toyes" [Essay XXXVII, "Of Masques and Triumphs"] gives a fairly accurate idea of the attitude toward these shows. The wide appeal of this type of entertainment is likely due to the nature of the English people themselves, for after the Restoration, the masque did not disappear but became more closely identified with the drama itself, that is, the spectacular elements of the masque entered the play. And even at the present time, the Christmas pantomime is a form of the masque.

The masque of the seventeenth century is bracketed by the names of two makers, Jonson and Milton. Many other names appear in connection with the composition of the masque, especially Inigo Jones as he designer and Ferrabosco and Lawes as musicians. But few of the many masques composed in the period were given more than once. Only those which, for one reason or another, caught the fancy of the king or queen or some other influential court personage could hope for a second production. One of the few great successes in the masque presented before Charles I and his queen, Henrietta Maria, was Thomas Heywood's *Love's Mistress*, or *The Queen's Masque*. This work was presented three times during one week before the king and queen and then later acted at the Phoenix. Thus it had at least four productions, a record few other such works can match. Yet critics and historians of drama of the period tend consistently to ignore it as a part of the genre. Welsford makes no mention of Heywood or the work and, although Nicoll has two references to it in the body of his text on the Stuart Masque, he does not include it in his "List of Masques Presented." The question remains then why other masques are always considered in discussions by critics and historians.

One of the answers may very well lie in the source of the quarrel between Jonson and Inigo Jones. As so many of the writers upon the period have pointed out, Jonson, a man of large ego, felt that the inventor, the poet, was supreme in the masque. But whatever the invention was, it had to be turned into a stage

spectacle before it became a masque. The ability to create the
stage spectacle was Inigo Jones' province, and the musical settings
were always assigned to those skilled in that art. And when Jones
got a better by-line than Jonson for a given presentation, Jonson
was not happy. Furthermore, Jonson's feeling that the poem
outranked all other elements in the production has been shared
to a large extent by literary critics and historians. Therefore,
regardless of the fact that *Comus* is an occasional piece, given
only one production by amateurs, at least until after the Restoration, literary historians rank it as the epitome of the masque, on
the basis of its poetry only, not on any basis of production. Even
though Lawes wrote the music for *Comus,* one wonders if the
members of the Bridgewater family were all trained singers; and,
in spite of the many references to *Comus* in volumes of history
of the drama, Milton's work is essentially non-dramatic. It might
appear, then, that a work like Thomas Heywood's *Love's Mistress,*
with its three spectacular productions including stage machinery
designed by Jones, and with its own musical score, might just
possibly be a better exemplification of the masque-in-action than
some more famous poem such as *Comus.*

It is true, of course, that the subtitle, *The Queen's Masque,* was not
given to Heywood's work until after the command performance
for the King's birthday, and perhaps his intent at the outset was
not to write a masque. But Heywood was never an original writer;
he followed the patterns and the trends of his time. And as the
Stuart period drew toward its close, the masque, even in the
hands of Jonson, was showing the inevitable blending of the
stage play and the spectacular entertainment which was to be so
characteristic of the Restoration stage. Furthermore, Heywood's
classical materials were obviously parallel to much of the material
used as a basis for the masque in general.

A major distinction between most of the court masques of the
1630's and Heywood's work is the length of the latter. Much
more plot and dialogue appear in his work than in the ordinary
masque. Jonsonian masques of the early part of the decade have
a kind of argument explaining the allegory to be represented by
the songs and dances, but one finds in these works a meager
amount of dialogue and practically no plot at all, and, consequently,
little of dramatic interest. But Jonson had used extensive dialogue
in earlier works. For example, in *News from the New World*
(1621), the rather long introductory dialogue, satiric in tone,

is a type of anti-masque and is also a playlet in itself, and *The Gypsies Metamorphosed* has a good deal of dialogue. So Heywood had ample precedent for expanding the plot and dialogue elements of his masque-play, and by the mid-seventeenth century a typical form of the masque had evolved. A spoken chorus, an instrumental overture, or a grand vocal chorus opened the entertainment. Then speech—monologue or dialogue—, songs, dances, and scene shifts were alternated so that the audience witnessed varied stage activities to avoid boredom. In particular, musical numbers were so arranged that no two similar dances followed one another; nor did a solo voice follow one of a similar quality. The scene variations often were limited only by the size of the treasury, some of the more glorious productions costing at least $50,000 in present money.

Heywood had a double training for his stage work. He was a writer of plays for the public theater, a most popular and prolific playwright. He learned from this work to fashion plot and to write dialogue and certainly at times more than competent verse. But he also was engaged from time to time by the City Companies to construct the entertainments which accompanied the progress of the Lord Mayor at his installation. These entertainments were largely composed of staged scenes allegorical in nature, with speeches by one or more persons. Music, except as it pertained to the procession, did not hold a prominent position. But the relationship of music to the stage was a standard element of the theater. So when the time came for Heywood to write a play that was destined to be seen by the regal eye, he was trained to satisfy both the spectacular and the dramatic. Furthermore, he had the subject matter, classical-allegorical, which was a favored type of matter to use for the plot basis of a masque, for he had earlier labored diligently to turn the whole of classical mythology into drama in his plays of the Four Ages, Gold, Silver, Brazen, and Iron. Out of this classical background he took the Cupid and Psyche story and created a play-masque.

The dramatized version of the Psyche myth is framed, in Heywood's version, by a Chorus of two characters, Apuleius and Midas, representing the opposed views of Art and Ignorance. Though the dialogues follow a Jonsonian pattern of satire, the characters, with their asses' ears, relate to the anti-masque, that is, the grotesque to set off the beautiful. Apuleius speaks, in the Induction, of "this sphere spangled with all these stars" and at

the end of the play of "the planets in their places." This faint
hint suggests that the gods and goddesses of the play may have
been part of the stage frame, probably sitting in some of the
cloud machines for which the Stuart masque stage, especially in
Inigo Jones' designs, is famous.

The play proper opens with recorder music and is set in the
Temple of Apollo at Delphi, thus allowing Inigo Jones a splendid
opportunity to design a transformation which would convert the
setting of the Induction into the Delphic temple. Apollo speaks
during the scene. The stage directions are a simple *Enter* and *Exit*.
But stage machinery could make the speech of the god much more
effective than the directions suggest by having the actor descend
and ascend, or by having the statue metamorphosed into the actor
and back again. Such a majestic appearance would also be accompanied by music, either instrumental or vocal chorus.

The temple scene is followed by one which suggests the bower
of Venus. Again the stage machinery was probably used to alter
the scene, with the entrances and exits of Venus, Pan, Apollo, and
Cupid managed by the use of the planetary spheres spoken of
earlier. Recorders are also introduced to open this scene. Music
to bridge from one scene to the next was a commonplace of the
theater, but in the masque in which much scenery and many
machines are used, music also helped to cover the noise of the
scene change itself.

Since Cupid in this scene makes reference to the rock on which
Psyche is to be abandoned, the rock itself must have been part of
the scenic effect. The following scene, with no music bridge
indicated, brings Psyche and her family to the rock, and the stage
direction says she climbs upon it; thus a practical rock is necessary.
Zephirus is commanded by Cupid to take Psyche from the rock
to Cupid's bower, whereupon Zephirus carries Psyche out in his
arms, a banquet is brought in, and he returns still carrying Psyche.
While Zephirus is off stage, the scene with the rock must change
to Cupid's bower, and Psyche says in her speech after her return
that she was brought on "unseen wings," suggesting perhaps only
a figure of speech, but allowing also for the possible use of the
cloud machine. The banquet table is transformed in the course
of the scene from a plain table to one spread with "all delicates."
As Psyche muses concerning the table, Echo answers the last words
of Psyche's speeches, a device that seems to indicate the use of the
dying fall in music.

At the end of this scene, as Cupid and Psyche exeunt into the bower, the scene closes upon them, preparing the stage for the return of Apuleius and Midas and the introduction of the anti-masque in its full form, a series of seven solo dances by seven types of asses, followed by explanation of the allegorical meaning of the Cupid and Psyche story.

Act II opens in Cupid's bower. Again the echo device is used, and the text refers to loud and still music. The sisters arrive and depart apparently by way of the cloud machine. Recorder music accompanies the entrance of Zephirus with the bags of gold to be given to the sisters.

Following a scene of straight dialogue at Admetus' palace, the scene shifts to an unspecified country area where we are entertained by comic word-play between a clown and a group of country swains. This scene is the first part of an anti-masque which is completed at the end of Act II by a dance between the country swains and country wenches. Cupid enters the country scene, perhaps from above since he shoots a love arrow at the Clown. When Midas remarks, at the end of the act, that the echo at the beginning of the act was pleasing, his comment indicates the probable addition of musical accompaniment to the speech of the echo.

Act III has many masque-like attributes. The scene opens upon Cupid's bower, where Psyche is discovered with the lamp. Following Cupid's curse upon Psyche for her transgression, the bower is transformed and laid waste by Boreas and the storm. A country scene follows with Apollo and Pan engaged in a music match made of two songs, a lyric in praise of Apollo and a song consisting largely of puns on the word *pan*. Midas is the judge, and his taste leans toward the pun. Then Boreas reenters with Psyche transformed and ugly, recorder music accompanies Cupid as he descends and ascends, other gods enter—probably by the machinery of the planetary spheres again—and Venus' revenge on Psyche begins with the assigning of the impossible tasks. Finally Midas and Apuleius close the scene with choric comments, followed by another anti-masque dance, this time one of grotesque contrarieties.

Act IV is short, containing a first scene in which Cupid's shackles are struck off by Vulcan in his smithy, a second in which Psyche is sent off to Hades for the box of beauty, and a final one in which the country characters sing a comic song.

Act V begins with the scene in Hades during which a banquet

is set forth, the scene closing to "hideous music." After an in-
determinate scene with the clown and the false box of beauty,
the scene turns to Admetus' palace where Psyche enters, once more
transformed into the beautiful immortal goddess so as to be fit
to be Cupid's bride. There follows, as is so typical of the masque,
a general dance of the gods and goddesses, after which Midas
and Apuleius close the play with an epilogue.

The number of dances, songs, scenic transformations, and musical
interludes in the play are a good indication of why the play was
given the secondary title of *The Queen's Masque.* The work is
also, however, a play; and as such it shows the skill with which
Heywood could interrelate the arts of poetry, music, dance, costume,
and spectacle into an entertainment which was, for its time, the
wonder of the Stuart Stage.

TEXAS CHRISTIAN UNIVERSITY

Maia's Son:
Milton and the Renaissance Virgil

ANN GOSSMAN

Virgilian echoes abound in the poetry of Milton. From the days when he vowed that he would "strictly meditate the thankless Muse" through his last major poems, Milton demonstrates a Virgilian sophistication in the use of allusion, a stylistic debt to Virgilian words and phrases, and a Virgilian sense of form. No one would deny that Milton read Virgil studiously as a boy and retained and renewed his knowledge of Virgil in later years.

Yet, like most other learned writers of the sixteenth and seventeenth centuries, Milton often demonstrates a familiarity not only with the primary sources, such as Plato or the Bible, but also with the available glosses, commentaries, and translations. Davis P. Harding has established, for example, that Milton knew both Ovid and the Renaissance allegorizations of his mythology.[1] The question that this paper attempts to answer is: Could Milton have been influenced by allegorical commentary on the *Aeneid*, and, if so, in what way?

Such commentary began in the post-classical centuries and continued through the Middle Ages and Renaissance. Of the transitional or post-classical commentaries, that of Fulgentius is the most significant. The major commentary of the Middle Ages on Virgil is that of Bernard of Sylvester. In the Renaissance the most extensive and accessible such commentary is that of Christoforo Landino. Because Bernard's commentary has been almost entirely unavailable for centuries and was not accessible to Landino or to Milton,[2] this paper will touch upon it only in passing. The commentaries of Fulgentius and Landino will be compared, examined in the light of Platonism and Neo-platonism, and explored for their possible bearing upon *Paradise Lost*.

Fabius Planciades Fulgentius, who belongs to the late fifth or early sixth century, addresses his work on Virgil to Chalcidius, who may have been the translator of Plato's *Timaeus*.[3] The work takes the curious form of a dialogue between Fulgentius and the spirit of Virgil. Usually, as in the medieval dialogues between pupil and master, the Socratic roles are reversed: the former asks questions and the latter supplies the answers. Fulgentius' purpose was to extract any wisdom in the *Aeneid* consonant with a rather Platonic Christianity. His allegorical technique is to exploit the hidden significance in proper names by the extraordinarily in-

genious use of etymology and to interpret the poem as an allegory
of the human experience. The etymologies, like those of Isidore
of Seville, are absurd by modern standards; but the allegorical
reading, even when most farfetched, does at least endeavor to
establish the universality of the poem.

"Arma virumque cano" ("Arms and the man I sing") furnishes
Fulgentius with a wealth of meaning (p. 743). *Arma* he explicates
as *virtus,* courage in battle; for *vir* (the man, the hero) he reads
sapientia, wisdom of thought. These qualities combined comprise
perfection. There is no need to suppose a debt, but it is worth
noting that Milton describes his universal man, Adam, in similar
terms: "For contemplation hee and valour formd."[4] Fulgentius
proceeds to another parallel. Christ combines *virtutem* (power)
and *sapientiam* (wisdom). Thus Aeneas and Adam can be taken
as Christ-like in terms of these two qualities.

Fulgentius is troubled by the force of the gods in the *Aeneid.*
Virgil seems to be blaming fortune, rather than human weakness,
for adversity, whereas Plato, he observes, attributes fortune and
misfortune to one's own wisdom (p. 745). But Fulgentius returns
the mastery to man when he translates *primum* (first) as "prince"
and explicates the word as inner kingship or the improvement
of natural gifts. Thus he can wrest from *arma virumque . . . primum*
a three-fold subject matter: physical substance, sensitive substance,
and education, a scheme which sounds like the Platonic tripartite
soul (p. 747).

The labored ingenuity of the next section may be summarized
briefly. The shipwreck is the danger of birth. Aeneas does not
recognize his mother because he is still allegorically in his infancy,
but when he buries Anchises he is an adolescent resisting parental
authority (pp. 751-752). None of this part influences later writers.
Its only significance is that it reflects, however crudely, a belief
that the *Aeneid* is a general mirror of the human experience.

In the fourth book, according to Fulgentius, Aeneas is a young
man, interested in hunting and in sex. He commits "adultery"
until Mercury warns him away. Here, Dido is the temptation of
the flesh, and Mercury stands for thought. "So maturity casts off
the bonds of love, but scorned love dies, burned out into ashes"—
such is the heartless appraisal of Dido's suicide (p. 752). Most
critics have seen in Virgil's Dido a brilliant transformation of
Homer's Circe and Calypso, possibly in the light of Euripidean
tragedy. Structurally, the episode is much more important to Virgil

than to Homer because it is the most poignant test of Aeneas' renunciation of his own will in favor of his divinely appointed imperial destiny. But Fulgentius reduces the episode to the same level as other temptations, allegorically read, and does injustice to the complexity of Dido. Both he and Bernard reveal the typical medieval mistrust of woman in equating her with lust, just as Augustine confesses that he wept for Dido in his pagan days, but scorned such tears when he became Christian.

Book VI of the *Aeneid* is the most interesting for medieval, Renaissance, and modern critics. Servius was probably the first to see it as an allegory of the descent of the soul from its star to the body; Bernard devotes half of his commentary to the role of Book VI as "a mystic account of the soul in the human body."[5] Fulgentius allots it more space than any other book. He treats Aeneas' appeal to the Sibyl as the beginning of his initiation into the mysteries (p. 753). Part of the preparation for the descent he sees as intellectual. When Aeneas plucks the golden bough, for instance, Fulgentius comments that the study of letters, especially of Plato, is indeed golden (p. 754). Aeneas descends and crosses the river—abandons youth and is ferried by Charon or Time (p. 755). Afterwards, Tricerberus is placated, for the honey of wisdom soothes calumny. Aeneas sees the punishments of pride and avarice (p. 756). (Fulgentius erroneously assumed that Aeneas saw Tartarus rather than simply hearing about it.)

When Aeneas surrenders the bough to Proserpina, Fulgentius says that his eloquence shines before the queen of knowledge. Then he finds Musaeus, gifts of the Muses, and Anchises, the way of seriousness (pp. 758-760). Anchises is further explained as life in one's own native land, where God is the Father, the source of wisdom (p. 760). Here Aeneas learns the secrets of nature. At this point, Fulgentius reproves Virgil for mentioning reincarnation: "You have so much insight, even prophetic wisdom. How could you put *that* in, among such sweet fruit?" But Virgil sweetly replies, "If I didn't put something foolish and Epicurean in among the great Stoic truths, I wouldn't be a pagan. Only you whom the sun of truth illumines can know the truth!" (pp. 761-762). Naive as the conversation is, it asserts a medieval and Renaissance commonplace more effectively formulated by Milton, who asserts that his poetry can surpass the classical literature if the Muse, Holy Light, will enable him to speak of "things invisible to mortal sight."

Thus the Sixth Book of the *Aeneid* with its Platonic and ancient
Neo-platonic core of meaning, the section on the World Soul
and reincarnation, has to be modified in favor of Christian theology.
But such portions of Platonism as can be reconciled with Christianity, especially the moral wisdom, the cultivation of the soul, and
the expectation of eternal life in union with the supreme source
of value—these Fulgentius can keep and affirm. And he can
therefore assert that the spiritual quest for truth and goodness,
a theme which unites Platonic and Christian thought, is the
essential theme of the *Aeneid*. Thus Milton's *Paradise Lost* too can
show man's attempt, which divine grace makes possible, to find
by reason and love the way back from disobedience to God.

The Sixth Book of the *Aeneid* is especially important to Landino,
who wrote two commentaries on the poem. The shorter of the
two is an actual commentary widely reprinted marginally in
school texts of the poem; the other, from which it is condensed,
takes the form of the third and fourth books of his *Camaldulensian
Disputations*.[6] This longer work is the one that will be cited in
this paper. Landino, a fifteenth-century writer influenced by Ficino,
begins with a reference to Plato's dictum that poetry is not
given by human art but seizes our minds by a divine frenzy,
and that poets are divine bards. Wisdom, for Landino, is knowing
one's duty in the light of good and evil. The greatest good is
to be united with God, who is truth. Poetry is justified as
conducive to this end, especially because it employs allegory, as
did Christ (pp. 56-57).

When he begins to unveil the allegory of the *Aeneid,* Landino
reveals his continuity with post-classical and medieval traditions
evident in Fulgentius and Bernard. For example, he speaks of
Aeneas' departure from Troy as a transition from the first age
of man. The shipwreck is not birth here, but Troy is the stage
in which the youth has no wisdom except what nature has given,
no aim except pleasure, and little interest in the soul. Pleasure
must die with Troy when the hero departs, guided by his mother,
Venus (p. 63 v).

Landino makes much of this goddess, who is no longer simply
desire, as medieval man would identify her. In the light of the
Florentine respect for the celestial Venus, she is nothing less
than divine love, and she impels one to follow knowledge. Of
course there is a terrestrial Venus, Landino knows—she is concerned in the union of man and woman, and her companions are

Ceres and Bacchus, and "her rewards are country pleasures" (p. 64 r). The two Venuses are natural love and the love of heavenly ideals. Landino does not mention the love between two mortals that leads to love of the divine. Terrestrial Venus is identified as the one whom Paris followed. Landino duly cites *Phaedrus* and *The Symposium.* "Intelligence in the angelic mind is captivated by love to know the beauty of God." He adds: "She emanates from the World Soul and creates the force that brings lower things into being and gives rise to matter in the world" (p. 65 v). Both Ficino and Pico had felt the need of reconciling Plato and Plotinus on the subject of the two Venuses. Ficino had distinguished *amor divinus, humanus, ferinus* (heavenly, human, and bestial love) in *De Amore,* VI, vii, 1345 ff.[7] Pico's commentary had pointed out that Plato distinguishes the celestial Venus from Aphrodite Pandemos (or from *Venere Vulgare*); but he had divided terrestrial Venus into *bestiale* (sensual) and human, the image of the higher Venus, capable of leading to her.[8] Logically it would seem that there ought to be three Venuses, but the authority of Plato is strong. For Landino two Venuses and two Cupids suffice, and these simply have to do with begetting and with contemplating. The Venus who directs Aeneas to Italy leads him to that good land which is true wisdom.

Landino realized that Virgil did not write the whole poem as a Neo-platonic myth of the soul, but that he intended in part an allegory of the physical process of creation and in part an allegory of the soul. Although his central concern was with human felicity, he had to state it in a cryptic way in order to be safe from detractors, and he had to put in a few legendary trappings for the sake of Augustus (p. 65 r). After this digression, Landino explains that the heavenly Venus shows that Troy (the body) must perish, because Pallas (wisdom) despises it. As Landino elevates Venus, he reduces the mortal parent, Anchises, to "what Christians call sensuality." Anchises (the lower soul) lingers in Troy until the higher soul bears him away (p. 69).

As Aeneas is carried over the sea (appetite), Landino digresses on intellect and will and Plato's chariot. For him, Right Reason must be the charioteer. If Aeneas weeps over his departure from pleasure to virtue, one should remember that fortitude and temperance are hard won. Landino proceeds to a little homily in which Dido is the backslider, but this passage comes before the account of Carthage (pp. 69-70). The short Odyssey of Book

III is treated in terms of temptations, chiefly to avarice and pleasure (pp. 71-79). In Book IV, Juno is seen as the desire for imperial honor, the merely practical or prudential, rather than celestial reason (pp. 81-82).

At this point Landino digresses to explain the "golden chain" of being. Christian and Plotinian ideas are combined in this chain, which begins with the "essence" of God and proceeds through power, wisdom, fate, the world soul, celestial demons, aethers, airs, waters, lands, and finally to matter, the formless source of all material bodies (p. 94 r). He stresses the extremes, God and matter. The latter is suggested to him even by the forest in which Aeneas meets Venus (p. 92 r), probably because the same word, *sylva,* means both "forest" and "matter" (Greek, *hyle).* Aeneas sees Venus in mortal form because our knowledge in this life is immersed in the material.

Few modern readers would find Venus' arranging a love affair with Dido for her son a Neo-platonic or angelic action, but Landino does see it in this light. Juno is imperial power, and Dido is the civic life. Since "divine wisdom can manifest itself in social life," Venus evidently expected her son to manifest goodness in civic affairs (p. 94 r). But Landino eventually blames Dido only slightly less than Fulgentius and Bernard had done. This time she represents, not lust, but the active life at the expense of the contemplative. Aeneas enters the cave with her— "some people misguidedly seek wealth, honor, and empire in the body" (p. 94 v). Thus Aeneas is ensnared in toils as dangerous as Circe's and forgets contemplation. But Mercury, who represents this way, rekindles his mind with the desire to seek Italy, and Mercury bids him to remember Ascanius—the future or eternal life (p. 95 r). An echo of the medieval reading is heard when Landino calls Dido's suicide typical of the rage of lovers and madmen (p. 100 r).

In Book VI the Sibyl's cave is identified as mind or world soul or perhaps the soul of the Sibyl, inspired by Apollo (truth), so that in the dark Aeneas may see this light. Carvings in the temple depict the Cretan story, which is evil. Landino explains, "First we must contemplate evil so that we may be strong enough to abstain" (p. 103 v). This is good Miltonic doctrine: by Adam's sin we fell into the "doom" of "knowing good by evil." Milton explicates Spenser in these terms: "describing true temperance under the person of Guion," Spenser "brings him in with his palmer through the cave of Mammon, and the bower of earthly bliss, that he may see and know, and yet abstain."9

Aeneas descends, undergoes various trials, and finally meets Proserpina, who has here declined into merely the lower or sensual soul; she must be given the golden bough—wisdom (pp. 110-112). Citing Ficino's commentary on the *Timaeus,* Landino sets up three orders: wisdom, providence, and fate. Then he discards fate and substitutes reason or order as more consonant with Christianity. In an attempt to reconcile the mythology and the philosophy of the poem, he considers the Orphic equation of Jupiter with the World Soul, but again he discards a reading too difficult to reconcile with Christianity. There is no fate apart from divine providence, he asserts, which exists in the mind of God and may be called fate when applied to mortal concerns. Milton formulates this orthodox Christian opinion in similar terms by having God assert:

. . . Necessitie and Chance

Approach not mee, and what I will is Fate. (*PL* VII, 172-173)

Landino continues his Christian emphasis on free will and Providence rather than fate. He suggests that Charon and his boat may represent the soul and free will, or Charon may represent Grace (p. 118 r). Cerberus is mere nature, the body, or evil (p. 123 r). Since Aeneas needs only theoretical knowledge of evil, not experience of it, he does not actually see Tartarus but only hears about it from the Sibyl. Such knowledge is valuable, because whoever knows what the vices are like will abstain from them. By resisting various temptations and terrors, Aeneas comes to accept God's plan and to be united with Providence (p. 127 v). Presumably, having had the vision of truth, he can subordinate his will to the will of God and voyage forth to seek true wisdom—Italy. Landino ignores the implications of the philosophical theory of reincarnation and the political significance of the Roman Empire.

It would seem that for Landino's purpose the *Aeneid* might as well end with Book VI. The Commentary in the *Camaldulensian Disputations* does so. For the modern reader, it does not seem that Aeneas rises above civic virtue to contemplation, but just the reverse. After his vision or philosophical contemplation, he feels justified in proceeding to the active life, in which he exhibits, in fact, the very Roman virtues of military and civic ability. Only the allegorical technique can save Landino's reading, but that reading must be a very selective examination of the poem.

The first two books of the *Disputations* are devoted to the problem of the active *versus* the contemplative life and the nature of the Summum Bonum. To Landino it was evident that the contemplative life excels the active. Spenser and Milton, on the other hand, have their heroes follow Virgil's practice rather than the allegorized version suggested by Landino's reading. Like Plato's philosopher who returns to the cave after he has seen the light, Spenser's Redcross Knight is required to descend from the Holy Hill of Contemplation to fight the dragon. Even when he has seen the heavenly Una unveiled, he must use this vision, too, to inspire him in his continued service to Gloriana in the active good life. In much the same way, Milton's Adam is allowed to see the future course of mankind in a vision and to receive a prophecy. Then he must go forth in greater peace of thought, having "his fill of knowledge, what this vessel can contain." Michael enjoins him to add faith, virtue, patience, and love to knowledge and to perform "Deeds to [his] knowledge answerable" (*PL* XII, 582).

Even in writing a new sort of epic, Milton deals more with the active life than with the contemplative, and he is closer in that respect to his classical originals than to commentaries and allegorized versions. Yet the active life did require redefinition in a poem whose hero was Adam. And in redefining it, Milton is closer to the commentaries than to the classics in one respect: the vision of man's activity as a moral struggle and his valor as that dedication that will lead him to eternal life with God. What Fulgentius and Landino sought in the *Aeneid* was a universal moral myth for humanity. Their allegorical visions help to account for some of the non-Virgilian elements in episodes whose model was clearly the *Aeneid.*

The clearest instance of such an influence is Milton's treatment of Raphael. As editors have noted, Milton draws upon Isaiah's account of the Seraphim (6:2): "Each one had six wings: with twain he covered his face, and with twain he covered his feet, and with twain he did fly." Milton adds a rich description of the colors of the wings, a comparison with the Phoenix in flight, and other details. By comparing Raphael to Hermes, who descends like a cormorant in the *Odyssey* (V, 50 ff.), or to Mercury in the *Aeneid* (IV, 252 ff.), Milton suggests a parallel function for Raphael and Hermes:

  . . . Like Maia's son he stood,
And shook his plumes . . . *(PL* V, 285-286)

The synthesis of Isaiah's seraphim and the classical god is further developed by the detail that the third pair of wings

               his feet
Shaddowd from either heele with feathered maile.

                         (PL V, 283-284).

Raphael comes from the apocryphal *Book of Tobit,* which inspired Christian artists to depict him in the guise of a traveler. Usually he has only one pair of wings, however, and his hand is raised "in the attitude of a warning gesture, as though to say, 'Take heed.' "[10] Although ranking high in the hierarchy of Heaven, Raphael is not always identified in *Paradise Lost* as a seraph, for Milton does not strictly observe the nine orders of *The Celestial Hierarchy.* And like the other angels, Raphael is clearly free to vary his apparent age, sex, shape, and accoutrements. It is worthwhile to consider why Milton should stress the likeness to Hermes.

First, it is appropriate for Raphael to exhibit both human and celestial attributes. He must appear discernibly higher than Adam in the scale of being, and yet sufficiently like him to be his friend and guest in Paradise. Thus Raphael, who brings authentic tidings of invisible things, comes trailing clouds of celestial glory. His appearance suggests the visions that have inspired the prophets. His likeness to the Phoenix, symbol of Christ's resurrection, and his rainbow-colored wings reinforce the suggestion of heavenly mercy and God's promise that man shall be restored after the Fall. By contrast, Michael, who appears afterwards, is the image of the true warfaring Christian who has put on the armor of the Lord. His garments also have the rainbow hue, but his appearance is more suitable than Raphael's for an encounter with fallen man. Both angels offer Adam extensive education. In this role, Raphael goes considerably beyond the function of Hermes or Mercury.

In the *Aeneid,* Mercury's duty is to warn Aeneas to leave Dido and to go forth and fulfill his destiny. All that Hermes had done for Odysseus was to effect his release from Calypso and provide him with the magic Moly as a protection from the enchantments of Circe, though Homer cites instances (in Book I of the *Odyssey*) in which human beings are partly responsible for their own sufferings—Aegisthus, for example, who disregarded the warning of Hermes. The parallel in *Paradise Lost* is that God sends Raphael to warn Adam against disobedience,

> Lest willfully transgressing he pretend
> Surprisal, unadmonished, unforewarned. *(PL* V, 244-245)

Part of the warning takes the form of the narration of the War in Heaven, in which Raphael presents Satan as a historical example of evil and as a present threat to Adam's happiness. But Raphael does not neglect to warn Adam against another potentially dangerous influence—that of Eve. "In loving thou dost well," Raphael admonishes, "in passion not," *(PL* V, 588). The denunciation of carnal pleasure seems harsher than Adam and Eve can at this point have deserved; but in light of the allegorization of Hermes as temperance[11] and of Dido as the desires of the flesh, the admonition is clearly appropriate. Thus Adam, like Aeneas, is being advised to put his loyal obedience to God ahead of any other love or loyalty that might separate him, not from a future earthly kingdom, but from his future heavenly one.

The warning about Eve's beauty is much more than the admonition concerning temperance or the release of the hero from female charm. It is part of an entire sequence in which Milton has Adam educated in the right use of all good things. Raphael frequently equates fruit with knowledge, for both require temperate, gradual assimilation. He presents no literal Moly, but he does speak of a figurative tree, emblem of all creation, which proceeds to work up from its roots to the "bright consummate flower" and its perfume. Through this emblem (*PL* V, 469-505) he reveals the way in which all things proceed from God and, if not corrupted, return to Him. There is no precedent for this passage in Homer or in Virgil, but if Hermes or Mercury is the guide of thought or contemplation, as Fulgentius and Landino took him to be, and if Raphael and Hermes are already associated and both are synonymous with wisdom, there is every reason why Milton should have Raphael so instruct Adam.

It is impossible to prove the direct influence on Milton of such commentaries as those of Fulgentius and Landino. Milton's synthesis is the logical continuation of the Christian humanism, especially the Christian Neo-platonism, of the age preceding his. Pico della Mirandola, for example, had written:

> Let us bathe in moral philosphy as if in a living river. Yet this will not be enough if we wish to be companions of the angels going up and down on Jacob's ladder, unless we have first been well fitted and instructed to be promoted duly

from step to step . . . by the art of discourse or reasoning
. . . inspired by the Cherubic spirit, using philosophy through
the steps of the ladder, that is, of nature, and penetrating
all things from center to circumference . . . Theology will
show us the way and as a comrade lead us. . . . When we
have been so soothingly called, so kindly urged, we shall
fly up with winged feet, like earthly Mercuries . . . and enjoy
that wished-for peace . . . of one accord in the friendship
through which all rational souls not only shall come into
harmony in the one mind which is above all minds but shall
. . . become altogether one.

Urging man to work up from the contemplation of nature to
theological piety and the worship of God so as to behold at last
His brilliant splendor, Pico exhorts that man call upon three
angels, Raphael, Gabriel, and Michael. Of the first of these
he says, "Let us summon Raphael, celestial physician, that he
may set us free by moral philosophy and by dialectic."[12]

Milton's Raphael expounds just such a metaphysical view. By
discourse he strengthens Adam's reason, he leads him to contemplate the universe from center to circumference, and finally
he urges him to measure all things according to God. If Adam
and Eve prove obedient, Raphael tells them, they may look
forward to going to heaven and participating with the angels
in the blessed vision of God. Their progress must be by gradual
steps; the image of Jacob's Ladder and that of the Golden Chain
are one. Raphael is not merely Adam's Mentor on earth, but
also "calls the mind back to heavenly things through the power
of reason"[13] and reveals divine matters through the power of the
poetic veil that Milton has created. Thus the Hermes of Homer's
poetry and the Mercury of Virgil's *Aeneid,* who acquired new
allegorical life in the post-classical centuries, combine with Biblical
angels whose powers the Neo-platonists had extended, into that
magnificent synthesis, Milton's Raphael. Fittingly Adam thanks
the angel:

Well hast thou taught the way that might direct
Our knowledge, and the Scale of Nature set
From center to circumference, whereon
In contemplation of created things
By steps we may ascend to God . . . . (*PL* V, 508-512)

Matthew Prior as the Last Renaissance Man[1]

FRANCES MAYHEW RIPPY

The Renaissance as the Golden Age of Modern Man was a nineteenth-century invention which has lost some of its gilding in the twentieth century. The first instance of the use of the term "Renaissance" listed in the O.E.D. was in 1840. To writers of the preceding period (the Restoration and eighteenth century), the Renaissance was simply "The Last Age," or lumped with that next period as "Modern" as the Latin and Greek classical period was called "Ancient" and the thousand years of the Middle Ages between deprecatingly dismissed as "Gothick." During the rest of the nineteenth century, under the impetus of Symonds, Pater, and particularly of Jacob Burckhardt and his *Die Kultur der Renaissance in Italien* (1860), the Renaissance came to be thought of as indeed a golden age, in which science was reborn, in which humanism sprang up full blown, with man as the measure of all things, in which naturalism flourished, along with nationalism and religious ferment, in which a critical and skeptical interest was taken in all matters intellectual, in which Greek and Latin literature was rediscovered and restored. The Renaissance was, above all, the age which produced the Renaissance man, a whole man with an immense range of secular talents and interests, performing in all these fields with sprezzatura, the easy and effortless grace of the talented amateur. A magnificent age, in short, whose crowning accomplishment was to produce us.

For two chief reasons, it is difficult for twentieth-century historians to define the Renaissance so broadly and so enthusiastically. For one, careful study of the Middle Ages has revealed there earlier forms of the naturalism, humanism, skepticism, and interest in the classics which were supposedly reborn in the Renaissance. Even the Renaissance exploratory voyages now seem closely linked to medieval motives. Likewise, writers in the new field of history of science point out that the science which moved forward so impressively in the thirteenth and early fourteenth centuries was then strangely quiet until the late sixteenth century. If a close reading of the Middle Ages discovers little that was dead there, then we are less sure that all these qualities and approaches and movements can properly be said to have been reborn in the Renaissance.

Moreover, it is hard for us in the twentieth century to be quite sure that having produced us was an unmixed blessing. Our command of technology has enabled us to destroy one another with unprecedented efficiency. From making man the measure of all things we have moved somehow to measuring man with all things, to computerizing him rather than making human values our measurement. Thus, if the Renaissance indeed produced us, our twentieth-century gratitude is tempered with misgivings.

For these two reasons, for many modern historians the Renaissance has shrunk to a movement from the mid-fourteenth century to the early years of the sixteenth century, centered in Italy and marked by a sharp revival of interest in Greek belles lettres. The other characteristics which Symonds, Pater, and Burckhardt saw as distinctively Renaissance are shown to be found in the preceding periods as well or are not seen ·as notably present in the Renaissance.

But literary critics learn slowly and grudgingly from historians. Just as we still insist that Richard III was hunchbacked and diabolical (what are modern historians when put up against Shakespeare?), so we know in our hearts that the Renaissance is a Very Good Thing. Thus, teachers of Chaucer and Dante are apt to point out that their men are really "early Renaissance," and many of us who work in the Restoration-eighteenth century will announce that our man, whoever he is, is the "last Renaissance man."

Nor is this position indefensible. The favorable concepts which have clustered about the term Renaissance for the last 130 years—naturalism, humanism, skepticism, classicism, nationalism, religious· ferment, in short, the interests of the talented, versatile Renaissance man—are found, even emphasized, in English literature of the fourteenth through eighteenth centuries. These are the qualities which we are most likely to mark in the literature of those centuries, the qualities in it which we find most attractive and most distinctive.

Therefore, I should like to suggest (with no abject apologies to the cultural historian, though with some uneasiness) that Matthew Prior (1664-1721), the Channel Row tavern boy who rose to be Minister Plenipotentiary in France, to succeed John Locke as Commissioner of Customs, to draw up in the Treaty of Utrecht Matt's Peace, to be Linacre Lecturer at St. John's College, Cam-

bridge University, and to be the most important poet practicing
in England between the death of Dryden in 1700 and the poetical
ascendancy of Pope in 1714, has some claim to be considered
the last Renaissance man.

Even by the narrow definition of modern historians, Prior
has some right to that title (except by being born too late), for
he showed throughout his lifetime an unusual interest in Greek
belles lettres. One of the four full-length published studies of
Prior is Engelbert Frey's 1915 Strassburg study, *Der Einfluss der
englischen, französischen, italienischen und lateinischen Literatur
auf die Dichtungen Matthew Priors*[2], and to these four national
influences we could surely add that of Greek literature. Although
the connotations of the term belles lettres are such that we hesitate
to call the *Iliad* belles lettres (is it too long and too serious to be
belles lettres? is it more than merely beautiful?), it is nevertheless
significant that Prior's most extended piece of literary criticism is
his "Observations on Homer. A Letter," an account of Prior's
study of the *Iliad*. Moreover, many of Prior's lyrics are modelled
upon the Greeks; some even indicate in their titles the Greek
source which Prior is imitating: "The Third Ode of Anacreon,
Translated" (1703), "In Imitation of Anacreon" (1708), "The
First Hymn of Callimachus. To Jupiter" (1708), "From the Greek"
(1718—an imitation of Meleager's epigram), "The Second Hymn
of Callimachus. To Apollo" (1718), "Written in Imitation of a
Greek Epigram," and "Cupid a Plowman from Moschus." Still
others of his poems deal with Greek subjects—"Democritus and
Heraclitus" (1718)—or use Greek models (especially Pindar and
the *Greek Anthology*) without specifically acknowledging them.

These Greek sources afford Prior an opportunity to do one
of the things which he did best—to domesticate the myth, to take
a mythological subject which might be treated seriously and instead clothe it lightly and mockingly in modern garb. When Prior,
for example, finds Anacreon's Cupid at his gate, "All Wet and
Cold, and wanting Light" (1. 12),[3] he lets him in: "I gave the
Child an easie Chair/Against the Fire, and dry'd his Hair;/
Brought friendly Cups of chearful Wine,/And warm'd his little
Hands with mine" (11. 19-22). It is too late when he discovers
Cupid's true nature, as Cupid, in a spurious test of his wet bow,
wounds him: "This done, the Rogue no longer staid,/But leap'd

away, and laughing said,/Kind Host adieu, we now must part,/ Safe is my Bow, but sick thy Heart" (11. 31-34). The poet plainly disbelieves in this folksy, furtive Cupid, though the wound which he gives may be real enough.

If the definition of the Renaissance may be extended to include Latin literature as well as Greek, then Prior is indeed a Renaissance man, having produced many poems based on Latin models (predominantly Horace and Ovid), as well as almost fifty pages of poetry and prose in Latin. One of Prior's first poems, written in 1685, when he was twenty-one, was "A Satyr on the modern Translators," and he never lost his interest in the complex task of translating Latin and Greek poetry into English. In his Latin-based works, as in the Greek ones, Prior's greatest talent is the ability to treat his subjects with mocking and easy domestic grace. In one of the best of his Latin imitations, "Daphne and Apollo (1715), Prior subheads his poem, "Faithfully translated from Ovids Metamorp. Book 1st: Nympha, Precor, Penei, mane: &ca." But if his pursuing Apollo tries to be faithful to Ovid, his taunting Daphne is jeeringly Neo-Augustan. If Apollo begs her to abate her speed, Daphne suspects that he is tiring: "Washy he is, perhaps not over Sound" (1. 10). If he tells her that he commends Claros and Tenedos, she retorts, "Thank you, I would not leave my Native Land" (1. 14). If he boasts that he can foretell the future, she replies, "Pish Partridge has as fair pretence as Thou" (1. 16). He flaunts his locks; she undercuts: "That may be counter-feit a Spanish Wigg./Who cares for all that Bush of curling hair/ Whilst your Smooth Chin is so extremely bare (11. 18-20). He tells her of his musical power; unimpressed, she retaliates that "Syphacio had an Admirable Voice" (1. 22). He vaunts of his healing powers; she replies "ours is a wholsom Air/You'd better go to Town and practice there . . ." (11. 25-26). He points out that he writes fine verses; she shrugs: "So do your Brother Quacks and Brother Beaux/Memorials only and Reviews write Prose" (11. 31-32). He exults in his prowess in archery; she directs him elsewhere: "Then leaving me whom sure you wou'dn't kill/In yonder Thicket exercise your skill/Shoot there at Beasts but for the Human Heart/Your Couzen Cupid has the only Dart" (11. 35-38). Daphne has reduced Apollo's every claim to nothing; finally he humbly asks "Oh let me woo thee as thou wou'd'st be woo'd" (1. 41). Then she informs him that, if he is to woo

her, he must behave like any other thoroughly domesticated
middle-class eighteenth-century rustic suitor in the presence of
her river-god father:

> First therefore don't be so extreamly rude
> Don't tear the Hedge down and tread the Clover
> Like a Hobgoblin rather than a Lover
> Next to my Fathers Grotto sometimes come.
> At ebbing Tyde He always is at home.
> Read the Courant with him and let him know ⎞
> A little Politicks how matters go   ⎬
> Upon his Brother Rivers Rhine and Po.   ⎠
> As any Maid or Footman comes or goes
> Pull off your Hatt and ask how Daphne does:
> These sort of Folks will to each other tell
> That you respect me, That you know looks well. (11. 42-53)

She also demands gifts from here and there, brought back from
his diurnal journeys, and a solid offer of marriage—"Make me
Your—Lord what Startles you—your wife" (1. 65)—for a few
settled years of domesticity that will close out her life but scarcely
mark his eternity: "what Signify/A Few odd years to you that
never Dye?" (11. 73-74). If these few years become boring to
him, he has his own amusements: "Or if a Winter Evening
Shou'd be long/E'en read your Physick Book or make a Song"
(11. 79-80). These are her final conditions; after her life he is
free to take another Daphne, but "Now Love or leave, my Dear,
retreat or follow./I Daphne, this premis'd, take Thee Apollo,/
And may I split into ten thousand Trees/If I give up on other
Terms than these" (11. 85-88). But rats eat the rest of the
manuscript, and we never learn Apollo's ultimate response.

I have stressed Prior's indebtedness to his Greek and Roman
sources—and the interest with which he paid back his debt—
because it is this emphasis upon classical languages and literature
that is still almost universally seen as a distinguishing trait of
the Renaissance. But if Prior is, in these multiple instances, a
Renaissance man, he is surely one of the last of the Renaissance
men, because for all his fascination with the literature of Greece
and Rome, he cannot take it seriously. Apollo is sadly out of
place courting an Augustan Daphne; gods and myth fit awkwardly
into Prior's humanistic world. Treat Cupid like a human boy and
he will wound you, laugh, and leave; treat Apollo like a human

beau and he will find all his powers unsuitable for the fine art of Augustan courtship. This insight is another facet of the mock-heroic, of the burlesque, whose humor is based upon the distance between the heroic age and language and devices and ideals, and the commonplaces of an unheroic age. When myth is domesticated, it is no longer godlike. If humanism leads inevitably into naturalism, then what is to become of the gods?

Prior also fits revealingly into those other patterns which literary critics still tend to see as "Renaissance": an uncritical and unskeptical nationalism and a critical and skeptical interest in religion. Combining as he did important political functions and a gift of poetry, Prior came to be thought of as an unofficial poet laureate. (In an age in which Thomas Shadwell and then Nahum Tate were the official poets laureate, there was room for more talent at the top.) Three of the poems of Prior's first poetic year (1685, when he was twenty-one) were poems on affairs of state—the coronation of James II and the Monmouth Rebellion. His role in the next decade became semi-official. When Queen Mary died and Prior did not immediately produce an elegy, others questioned his silence. He first designed a medal for the occasion; James Vernon wrote to him of it "if you think this will acquit you from the expectations people have of a poem from you, you will be mistaken, for they say you are not to come off with a posey and a shred of Horace; and they further desire, if you write anything in memory of the Queen, that you will take a little more notice of her than you do in your stamp . . . ."[4] Prior eventually capitulated and wrote "An Ode. Presented to the King, on his Majesty's Arrival in Holland, After the Queen's Death. 1695." He had built up this public expectation of his laureate performance by a number of laudatory odes upon King William, whom he regarded highly, as a great warrior-prince and leader of his people (though unable to control the political parties which plucked him bald). The earlier eulogies are high-flown, stiff, unbending—sound and dated laureate verse. With the death of William, Prior's laureate topics shift to the military exploits of the Duke of Marlborough—but there is soon a change in tone as well. Prior eventually served in the embassy in France, and in the peacetime interval between the wars (the War of the Grand Alliance and the War of the Spanish Succession) and in his secret negotiations at their ends, he came to know the enemy—

the French in general and Boileau, his parallel in France, in particular—for it was Boileau's function to celebrate the French military victories just as it was Prior's to celebrate the English ones. Even before he had met Boileau, Prior had been countering Boileau's panegyrics with his own in the eight-line "On the Taking of Huy" (1694): "Now Louis take Thy Titles from above,/Boileau shal Sing and We'll believe Thee Jove" (11. 3-4) and in "An English Ballad, On the Taking of Namur by the King of Great Britain, 1695":

> PINDAR, that Eagle, mounts the Skies;
>> While Virtue leads the noble Way:
> Too like a Vultur BOILEAU flies,
>> Where sordid Interest shows the Prey.
> When once the Poet's Honour ceases,
>> From Reason far his Transports rove:
> And BOILEAU for eight hundred Pieces,
>> Makes LOUIS take the Wall of JOVE. (11. 13-20)

In "An English Ballad" Prior wished so sharply to make the point that he was mocking Boileau that he printed "Ode Sur la Prise de Namur, Par les Armes du Roy, L'Année 1692. Par Monsieur BOILEAU DESPREAUX" beside his own poem. By the summer of 1699, Prior saw Boileau frequently, and he wrote to the Earl of Jersey, "Boileau says that I have more genius than all the Academy . . . ."[5] Slowly Prior's laureate verse changed in tone. True, the verses, though no longer Pindaric, continued to mock Boileau's previous eulogies. Prior celebrated Marlborough's victory at Blenheim in "A Letter to Monsieur Boileau Despreaux; Occasion'd by the Victory at Blenheim, 1704," again beginning with the conventional insult to Boileau—the enemy country's laureate is always a mere hireling, writing propaganda:

> SINCE hir'd for Life, thy Servile Muse must sing
> Successive Conquests, and a glorious King;
> Must of a Man Immortal vainly boast;
> And bring him Lawrels, whatsoe'er they cost . . . . (11. 1-4)

But this is a letter to Boileau, not just a panegyric on Marlborough's victory, and this time Prior does not entirely lose sight of the man in the enemy. He pauses, a quarter of the way through the poem, to discuss parenthetically the mutual difficulties which he and Boileau face in their roles as laureates:

> I grant, old Friend, old Foe (for such We are
> Alternate, as the Chance of Peace and War)
> That we Poetic Folks, who must restrain
> Our measur'd Sayings in an equal Chain,
> Have Troubles utterly unknown to Those,
> Who let their Fancy loose in rambling Prose. (11. 47-52)

And at the close of the poem, he inserts a rueful apology to his French competitor, a greater poet (though in the service of a worse monarch and a less efficient military machine):

> But We must change the Style.—Just now I said,
> I ne'er was Master of the tuneful Trade.
> Or the small Genius which my Youth could boast,
> In Prose and Business lies extinct and lost. (11. 182-185)

Here is laureate verse with a difference, the end of one kind of laureate verse. If the enemy is friend or foe by the chance of peace or war, then the chance wars and their victories are less Pindarically glorious than the young, untravelled Prior had originally believed. His unquestioning nationalism has been tempered by years and experience into a more complex, quietly witty, wry love of country.

In the Renaissance an unquestioning nationalism is supposed to be coupled with religious questioning and ferment. Prior's writings often deal with religious themes; frequently even their titles show that they are a reworking of a specific Biblical or theological topic, passage, or character: "On Exodus iii.14. I am that I am. An Ode. Written in 1688, as an Exercise at St. John's College, Cambridge," "There be Those that leave Their Names behind them. Ecc. 44.8" (1688), "Many Daughters have done well, but Thou Excellest them all. Prov. 31.29" (1688), "To Dr. "Sherlock, on his Practical Discourse Concerning Death" (1690), "Charity never faileth. 1 Cor: XIII.8" (1690), "Considerations on part of the Eighty Eighth Psalme" (1693), "Adriani Morientis ad Animam Suam. Imitated" (1703), "Charity. A Paraphrase on the Thirteenth Chapter of the First Epistle to the Corinthians" (1703), "Solomon on the Vanity of the World. A Poem in Three Books" (1708), "Alma: or, The Progress of the Mind. In Three Cantos" (1718), "Predestination, A Poem" (1721). From the time that he was twenty-four until the year of his death (at fifty-seven), Prior wrote poems on openly religious topics (while simultaneously

producing some of the liveliest bawdry of his period). These poems
included two of his three significant long poems—"Solomon"
and "Alma." Moreover, these poems show a remarkable consistency
of general attitude, of skepticism in the philosophical sense of
a distrust of human reason and a sharp awareness of its limits.
In the earliest of them all, "On Exodus iii.14," Prior wrote:

> MAN! Foolish Man!
> Scarce know'st thou how thy self began;
> Scarce hast thou Thought enough to prove Thou art;
> Yet steel'd with study'd Boldness, thou dar'st try
> To send thy doubting Reason's dazled Eye
> Through the mysterious Gulph of vast Immensity. (11. 1-6)

Twenty years later, in "Solomon," the long poem which he himself
considered his masterwork, Prior lets Solomon explore Knowledge,
Pleasure, and Power, only to be ultimately warned by an angel:

> Illustrious Wretch, repine not, nor reply:⟩
> View not, what Heav'n ordains, with Reason's Eye; ⟩
> Too bright the Object is: the Distance is too high. ⟩
> The Man who would resolve the Work of Fate,
> May limit Number, and make Crooked Strait:
> Stop Thy Enquiry then; and curb Thy Sense;
> Nor let Dust argue with Omnipotence. (III, 835-841)

"Alma: or, The Progress of the Mind," a decade later (1718), is
a hudibrastically irreverent investigation of the site of the human
soul, at the end of which Richard Shelton dismisses all Prior's
speculations by saying:

> Sir, if it be Your Wisdom's Aim,
> To make Me merrier than I am;
> I'll be all Night at Your Devotion—
> Come on, Friend; broach the pleasing Notion:
> But if You would depress my Thought;
> Your *System* is not worth a Groat— . . . . (II, 594-599)

Three years later, in "Predestination," a poem begun (August, 1721)
a month before his death, Prior still grapples reasonably with
problems he deems beyond the reason of man to explore, arriving
only at an ambiguous prayer invoking either a God of free will
or one of predestination:

O Soveraign! great Three One! O God and Man!
Who set those Measures which I dare not Scan;
If I have leave to chuse, I beg that choice
Guided at least by thy Assistant Voice.
If I must pursue a Destin'd way
Direct my Footsteps for thou can'st not stray.
From dangerous doubts my wandring Soul retrieve
I cannot Argue, grant me to believe!
Lifeless I lay, Thou wak'st me into Sense;
Frailty is mine, and Thine Omnipotence. (11. 267-276)

As a poet of the Age of Reason, Prior nevertheless maintains that
reason is insufficient, misleading, and unreliable in matters of
religion. He is a religious skeptic in the philosophical sense which
leads to fideism, not in the sense which attacks particular religious
dogmas or practices.

Thus, though Prior appears in a number of ways to be a
Renaissance man, he is always a Renaissance man with a difference.
His classicism repeatedly jests at the striking of heroic poses in
an unheroic and domesticated middle-class world; his nationalism
ends by recognizing that old friends are periodically old foes,
as chance dictates; his religious skepticism raises more doubts
about the efficacy of reason than about the tenets of traditional
Christianity. Perhaps he approaches most closely the Renaissance
ideal when he appears as the Renaissance man, the whole man,
the amateur, who can do many things well and easily, effortlessly,
with that sprezzatura quality of studied carelessness.

For Prior showed amazing versatility. An accomplished diplo-
mat, he was so instrumental in drawing up the Treaty of Utrecht
that it was popularly (and unpopularly) known as Matt's Peace.
He was Linacre Lecturer at St. John's College, Cambridge, and
Commissioner of Customs. And he was a writer of impressive
range, in content and form. In subject matter, he ranged from
fabliaux (like "Paulo Purganti and His Wife" and "The Ladle")
to long religious disquisitions, from lyrics (often set to music) and
odes to ballads and bitter satires. In form he wrote lucid prose
(especially in two essays "Heads for a Treatise upon Learning"
and "Opinion" and in the four Dialogues of the Dead—between
Charles V, the Holy Roman Emperor, and Clenard the Grammar-
ian, Locke and Montaigne, the Vicar of Bray and Sir Thomas

More, Cromwell and his Porter); occasional skillful blank verse (notably in "Frederic &ca: From Boccace"—1714); effective heroic couplets (as in "Solomon") which functioned so well that often they were lifted out and adapted by Pope (especially in his "Essay on Man"), and some of the best tetrameter and octasyllabics (in anapaests and iambs) of the Restoration-eighteenth-century periods, a form in which Prior excelled and from which Jonathan Swift learned much. And Prior did all these things while frequently professing, in the best sprezzatura fashion, to be surprised that he had done them and puzzled by their success. A conscious deprecation of the art which is concealing art is one of Prior's most winning poses, particularly in his lighter verse. In one of his most artless and charming (and ungrammatical) lyrics, Prior provides "A Better Answer" (1718) to Cloe, who has "blubber'd" her pretty face with jealous weeping because he has praised another woman in his verse:

> What I speak, my fair CLOE, and what I write, shews
>   The Diff'rence there is betwixt Nature and Art:
> I court others in Verse; but I love Thee in Prose:
>   And They have my Whimsies; but Thou hast my Heart.
>
> The God of us Verse-men (You know Child) the SUN,
>   How after his Journeys He sets up his Rest:
> If at Morning o'er Earth 'tis his Fancy to run;
>   At Night he reclines on his THETIS's Breast.
>
> So when I am weary'd with wand'ring all Day;
>   To Thee my Delight in the Evening I come:
> No Matter what Beauties I saw in my Way:
>   They were but my Visits; but Thou art my Home.
>
> Then finish, Dear CLOE, this Pastoral War;
>   And let us like HORACE and LYDIA agree:
> For Thou art a Girl as much brighter than Her,
>   As He was a Poet sublimer than Me. (11. 13-28)

Despite the studied carelessness of these lines and their closeness to the Cavalier tradition, Prior is not the Renaissance man in the sense that Sir Philip Sidney was. He is not the ideal courtier. Prior's father was a joiner (a carpenter) in Stephen's Alley, near Whitehall in London. When his father died, Prior dropped out of school at about eleven years of age and worked in his uncle's Rhenish Tavern on Channel Row, London. He was discovered there by the Earl of Dorset, who found him reading his Horace. The Earl asked him to translate one of the odes; Prior put it into English verse. The Earl was sufficiently impressed with the twelve-year-old to return him to Westminster School. From there Prior went to St. John's College, Cambridge. But the tavern interval continued to dog his political career; his political enemies referred to it frequently. Queen Anne felt that it was indecorous to put anyone of that low birth into a position of any conspicuous political prominence; an occasional high-born lord (e.g., the Earl of Strafford) refused to serve on a delegation if Prior were to hold equal rank on it. Prior was not born to easy aristocratic grace, however talented he might be, however sound his academic credentials were, however he might have risen. Moreover, the most notable use which he made of his poetry was to put it out by subscription (as the collected 1718 *Poems on Several Occasions*) and make a handsome profit on it of some four thousand guineas, thus becoming one of the few poets in England up to that time who had managed to support themselves well from their poetry, without the intervention of a patron. To have eliminated the patron was, in a sense, to have obliterated the prime mover of Renaissance art. Prior's life had begun with total dependence upon a patron (the Earl of Dorset); it ended by devising a means to make the patron superfluous.

Thus, to the list of those who have been designated by their admirers as "the last Renaissance man," it is well to append the name of Matthew Prior, who not only embodied in himself and in his writings many of the qualities which still seem to us peculiarly Renaissance in their emphases but also altered and metamorphosed those qualities in such ways that they could no longer be possessed in quite the same way as they had been during the height of the Renaissance. After Matthew Prior, the brave new world seemed a little foolhardy and considerably older.

BALL STATE UNIVERSITY

STUDIES IN

American

LITERATURE

Edgar Allan Poe's Last Bid for Fame

HALDEEN BRADDY

Winning belated praise in America and Europe first as both poet and storyteller, Edgar A. Poe near the end of his life sought to excel also as a literary critic. Anyone familiar with his goals, especially his grandiose, unrealized plans for *The Stylus* and *The Penn Magazine,* will remember how feveredly he labored to improve the standards of contemporary periodicals. There exists strong evidence in his essays, miscellaneous criticisms, and numerous book reviews to reveal that his deepest aspiration was to become the literary arbiter of his age. As one of his strong qualities, he possessed a religio-philosophic feeling for the sublime as his reviews show:

> To look upwards from any existence, material or immaterial, to its *design,* is, perhaps, the most direct, and the most unerring method of attaining a just notion of the nature of existence itself.
> ------Joseph Rodman Drake: *The Culprit Fay, and Other Poems* and Fitz-Greene Halleck: *Alnwick Castle, with Other Poems,* as reviewed by Poe in 1836.[1]

> An important condition of man's immortal nature is thus, plainly, the sense of the Beautiful. . . . It is a wild effort to reach the beauty above. It is a forethought of the loveliness to come.
> ------Henry Wadsworth Longfellow: *Ballads and Other Poems,* as reviewed by Poe in 1842 (XI, 71).

Poe developed as an essayist later than as either a poet or a storyteller; he composed the critical essays after he had ripened in experience as a creative artist. From about 1831 onwards, he wrote reviews intermittently, and then they appeared regularly after he began to work for the *Southern Literary Messenger* in 1835 and for such other periodicals as *Burton's Magazine* in 1839, *Graham's* in 1841, and the *Broadway Journal* in 1845. By this time he already enjoyed hard-earned renown as poet and storyteller; now he bent every effort to become recognized as a critic. Whereas he once held himself aloof from his fellows and apart from the world in the poems and tales, he now, in the role of a dictatorial critic, doffed his peacock plumage to don the chainmail fit for workaday criticism.

Poe immediately distinguished himself by the severity of his judgments. His reviews attacked both old and new writers, at least twice overindulging his talent until he lost the friendships of Lowell and Longfellow. He sometimes exhibited poor critical insight, his belittlement of James Fenimore Cooper being perhaps his most glaring miscalculation. At his worst he behaved somewhat pretentiously in his display of erudition. Sometimes he wasted time and space with small details; at others he indulged in aimless digressions on art in general.

Poe displayed several assets as a book reviewer. He was usually honest in his severity, his contempt for the shoddy helping to improve contemporary literary standards. The commentator did not ignore "unknown" authors, though erring occasionally in commending the "small fry" of his own circle. He labored even on book reviews, yet it was presumptuous of him in his review of 1836 to rewrite Halleck's verses. His methods nonetheless produced positive results. Such careful scrutiny of the smallest items of information served to establish respect for accuracy.

As for the quality of his book reviewing, Poe nowhere expressed his principles more effectively than in his remarks on Bryant's poems in 1837. The review is lucid and direct, unimpeded by superfluous literary quotations, qualities lacking in the majority of his other pieces. Throughout the discussion the reviewer commendably holds close to the meaning of Bryant's verses. In this critique Poe mastered his digressive tendencies, avoiding windy perorations on vague philosophical conceptions of beauty. All his statements resound with sincerity of idea and firmness of phrase. The review of Bryant's works might, in fact, serve as a model for the straightforward, short, and scientific book review. But the critic Poe did not habitually write with such directness. Surely few reviewers incorporate more extraneous matter than Poe, for he found it difficult to stick to the subject. The customary phrase used to return to the main discussion was "But to our sheep" (his literal translation of the French idiom, *"revenons a nos moutons,"* i.e., we return to the subject). He came to realize, evidently, that his digressions extended to undue length, because he later formed the habit of abbreviating personal names and literary titles. He further abbreviated Postscript (P.S.) and Opening Paragraph (O.P.). Seriousness of tone and objectivity of treatment rank among his highest virtues: at its best Poe's writing rises far above the general level of contemporary reviewing.

Poe's essays show a keen consciousness of America and its literary potentialities. At a period when his fellow writers paid homage to Old World fashions, this critic inveighed against imitating foreign models and urged the development of a native American culture. Commenting in his "Letter to B ----" (1831) on the difficulties of an American author before a public devoted only to European importations, the patriot assailed foreign competition.

> Besides, one might suppose that books, like their authors, improve by travel — their having crossed the sea is, with us, so great a distinction. Our antiquaries abandon time for distance; our very fops glance from the binding to the bottom of the title-page, where the mystic characters which spell London, Paris, or Genoa, are precisely so many letters of recommendation . . . . (VII, xxxv)

Remarking on "The American Drama" (1845), Poe spoke vigorously for the adoption in the United States of fresh departures in writing plays.

> The first thing necessary is to burn or bury the 'old models,' and to forget, as quickly as possible, that ever a play has been penned. The second thing is to consider *de novo* what are the capabilities of the drama — not merely what hitherto have been its conventional purposes. (XIII, 37)

The author's eight papers refer to about a dozen productions, of which six are briefly discussed: Sophocles' *Antigone*, Mrs. Cora Mowatt's *Fashion*, her *Faint Heart Never Won Fair Lady*, N. P. Willis's *Tortesa the Usurer*, Longfellow's *Spanish Student*, and the Shakesperean imitation *Katharine and Petruchio*. Strongly opposed to "closet drama," ill-constructed plots, and lifeless characters, Poe enunciated ideas a century in advance of their time.

To encourage more appreciation for the American short story, Poe in 1842 waxed enthusiastic about Hawthorne's *Twice-Told Tales*. The reviewer pronounced approval in a ringing tone: "As Americans, we feel proud of the book" (XI, 110). What Poe liked best about Nathaniel Hawthorne's treatment was his freshness in both style and plot.

Mr. Hawthorne's distinctive trait is invention, creation, imagination, originality — a trait which, in the literature of fiction, is positively worth all the rest. But the nature of the originality, so far as regards its manifestations in letters, is but imperfectly understood. The inventive or original mind as frequently displays itself in novelty of tone as in novelty of matter. Mr. Hawthorne is original in all points. (XI, 110)

In his book reviews Poe characteristically stated a good theory well. He sometimes wrote with persuasiveness even when his reasoning was illogical; that is, he could be accurate in his principles but incorrect in his examples. In his strictures on James Fenimore Cooper (1843), for instance, the review first introduced soundly reasoned differences between *popular* and *lasting* literature.

. . . there are two great classes of fictions — a popular and widely circulated class, read with pleasure, but without admiration — in which the author is lost or forgotten; or remembered, if at all, with something very nearly akin to contempt; and then, a class not so popular, nor so widely diffused, in which, at every paragraph, arises a distinctive and highly pleasurable interest, springing from our perception and appreciation of the skill employed, or the genius evinced in the composition. After perusal of the one class, we think solely of the book — after reading the other, chiefly of the author. The former class leads to popularity—the latter to fame. In the former case, the books sometimes live, while the authors usually die; in the latter, even when the works perish the man survives. Among American writers of the less generally circulated, but more worthy and more artistical fictions, we may mention Mr. Brockden Brown, Mr. John Neal, Mr. Simms, Mr. Hawthorne; at the head of the more popular division we may place Mr. Cooper. (XI, 206)

But this judgment here erred of course in its example, in his prognostication that the name of Cooper would be "lost or forgotten."

A critic rarely or never achieves accuracy in everything, and perhaps it is better to be right about generalities than particulars. Many of his critical judgments, however, revealed a positive flair for error in evaluating the lasting qualities of contemporary

authors. Although correctly stigmatizing Carlyle's stylistic extrava-
gances, Poe inaccurately predicted that in five or ten years
Carlyle "will be remembered only as a butt for sarcasm" (XVI, 99).
Another instance of the inspector's malice or short-sightedness
occurs in his review (1841) of Charles Dickens' *The Old Curiosity
Shop,* where Poe insinuates that Dickens was mad.

> We do not think it altogether impossible that the rumors
> in respect to the sanity of Mr. Dickens which were so
> prevalent during the first numbers of the work, had some
> slight — some very slight foundation in truth. (X, 143)

On safer grounds in generating critical formulas, Poe gained
attention and finally fame for his dictum about the indispensabili-
ty of brevity of expression. He launched his argument in a
review of Hawthorne's tales (1842). In this writing the reviewer
affirmed that a work of art, whether verse or prose, should not
be judged by its length.

> There has long existed in literature a fatal and un-
> founded prejudice, which it will be the office of this age
> to overthrow — the idea that the mere bulk of a work
> must enter largely into our estimate of its merit. I do
> not suppose even the weakest of the Quarterly reviewers
> weak enough to maintain that in a book's size or mass,
> abstractly considered, there is anything which especially calls
> for our admiration. A mountain, simply through the sensa-
> tion of physical magnitude which it conveys, does indeed,
> affect us with a sense of the sublime, but we cannot admit
> any such influence in the contemplation even of 'The
> Columbiad.' The Quarterlies themselves will not admit it.
> And yet, what else are we to understand by their continual
> prating about 'sustained effort'? Granted that this sustained
> effort has accomplished an epic — let us then admire the
> effort, (if this be a thing admirable,) but certainly not the
> epic on the effort's account. Common sense, in the time to
> come, may possibly insist upon measuring a work of art
> rather by the object it fulfils, by the impression it makes,
> than by the time it took to fulfil the object, or by the
> extent of 'sustained effort' which became necessary to
> produce the impression. The fact is, that perseverance is one
> thing and genius quite another; nor can all the trans-
> cendentalists in Heathendom confound them. (XIII, 150)

Later in his analysis of Hawthorne, he became more specific, asserting that a rhymed poem should not "exceed in length what might be perused in an hour. Within this limit alone can the highest order of true poetry exist" (XI, 106). As for a short story, the theorist held that "We may continue the reading of a prose composition . . . much longer than we can persevere . . . in the perusal of a poem" (XI, 106). Then the formula-maker endeavored to explain just how long a prose composition would require for its perusal. Obviously he must have had in mind short stories rather than long pieces like his own "Narrative of A. Gordon Pym" and "Journal of Julius Rodman" when limiting the reading time to an hour or so.

> We allude to the short prose narrative, requiring from a half-hour to one or two hours in its perusal. The ordinary novel is objectional, from its length, for reasons already stated in substance. As it cannot be read at one sitting, it deprives itself, of course, of the immense force derivable from *totality*. (XI, 106)

In both "The Philosophy of Composition" (1846) and "The Poetic Principle" (1850), Poe fully discusses his theories about brevity. The first essay claims that "a length of about one hundred lines" should be proper for a poem and notes that "The Raven" contains "a hundred and eight" (XIV, 197). The essayist failed to mention that most of his own poems run considerably shorter than one hundred lines or that a few others run considerably more. "The Bells" (1849) comprises one hundred and thirteen lines; "Tamerlane" (1827), two hundred and forty-three; and "Al Aaraaf" (1829), two hundred and sixty-four. But the inconsistency may be more apparent than real; both "Tamerlane" and "Al Aaraaf" manifest a variety of stanza forms that fall rationally into parts. Poe therefore could have defended himself on the basis that at least two of his three long poems represent "merely a succession of brief ones" (XIV, 196).

Poe's conception of a long poem as a composite of short poems contains some truth. Probably few readers, however, would agree with the idea that *Paradise Lost* is actually only "a series of minor poems" (XIV, 267). Students of *Paradise Lost* might admit that Milton's divisions into books and his introduction of successive speakers give variety to the epic; but such bold declarations as this one on Milton and a second one on the *Iliad*, in which "we have, if not positive proof, at least very good reasons, for believing it intended as a series of lyrics" (XIV, 267) overemphasize and strain Poe's point. He evidently derived his notion about the Greek epic from an imperfect understanding of the work of the celebrated German scholar Friedrich Wolf, whose *Prolegomena in Homerum* (1795) advanced the theory that the *Iliad* and *Odyssey* represent the blending of a number of separate hymns or poems. One cannot escape the further view that Poe's theory of brevity served in an important degree as a justification of his own methods of writing short lyrics and stories. Finally, the end in art which this inventor of artifices desired was not the inculcation of moral meaning but the achievement of emotional effect. Why? The reward of this effect, he probably reasoned, would provide the reader with one clear, tense, sharp impact, and obviously this end could be best achieved in a short composition.

Perhaps the most remarkable characteristic of the critical works is the diversity of the subject matter. The best known essays and criticisms amount to no more than forty in number, but the total of all the minor critical writings approaches three hundred. These minor works include journalism and book reviews, in which appear a myriad of topics. Poe wrote over a hundred reviews on literature alone, and it is this subject which stirred the author most deeply. Art was the end he sought. So much emerges from the facts of his biography. The ever-present trials of Poe, his imperative need to eke out a living, fill the pages of "Some Secrets of the Magazine Prison-House" (1845). The French saying *"La vie, c'est la femme que l'on a"* ("Life is the woman one has"); *"l'art, c'est la femme que l'on désire"* ("Art is the woman one desires") applies with unique force to Poe. Indeed, as a motto it might well have graced his editorial desk. He remained always conscious of the higher principles of art even when performing mean journalistic tasks.

Real life, and not the dream, came at times to waken the poet Poe and to stir him into action as journalist and critic.[2] Critical animus impelled him to think of collaborating on *The Conchologist's First Book* (1839); journalistic spirit led him to write about the laws governing International Copyright and to dream of such unattained projects as *The Penn Magazine* and *The Stylus*. Many of the minor essays he composed simply as a part of his job; such chores constituted his daily routine. In these often nondescript writings he commented on everything in the world about him — on aesthetics, diseases, drama, drinking, etiquette, furniture, games, literature, manners, poetry, politics, prejudice, religion, science, slavery, and even street paving. The writer who commented so broadly had to be of his own time and a man fully aware of his milieu.

Yet the permanent value of Poe's finest analyses endures beyond cavil. When compared with his stories and poems, the essays bespeak profound aspects of his character. They reveal him actively concerned with problems of his own age. They show him embroiled in questions of rigid decorum, discerning taste, or fair judgment. "The Philosophy of Composition" offers a singular account of the genesis and development of his poem "The Raven." "The Rationale of Verse" sets forth the rules a craftsman should observe in writing his works. "The Poetic Principle," published after his death, testifies to the loftiness of Poe's artistic standards. The body of his first-rate criticism, though modest in bulk, exhibits brilliance, artistry, and foresight.

Nowhere does Poe's longing for renown show through more clearly than in his criticism. He strove to leave a lasting imprint on American literature. Strong critical instincts impelled him to forsake the ivory tower where he had retired to write his unearthly stories and spiritualized verse in order to enter the world of his contemporaries. In the role of critic he engaged his fellows in scholarly controversies; there too he addressed them at seats of learning as a public lecturer. The first tokens of his fame came after 1845 from both at home and abroad, particularly from France. Since his temperament fitted him poorly for self-display, he came off badly in public appearances. Then success went to his head: the man who once lived as a recluse, a gloomy and forbidding raven, now strutted upon the stage, a bright and haughty peacock. With his startling critical essays, he made a last bid for literary immortality.

When posterity enters final judgment, Poe may well be acclaimed, not so much as storyteller and poet, but as an inventive critic.[3] As a major aim, the theorist sought to achieve the ideal of Art for Art's sake. This gifted man was one of the first authors in America to write for a living, to work as a professional writer. Much homage is his just due for not sinking to the level of becoming simply a journalist. He never brought his grandiose schemes to fruition, but he did enunciate admirable principles and he did exert serious efforts to follow them. Instead of meekly obeying contemporary trends in taste, the craftsman grew passionately dedicated to his art as something more than a means of livelihood. He dreamed his dream, his grand ambition. With mathematical precision, with the zeal of a scientist, his inventive mind endeavored to dictate for creative literature a set of inviolable rules. Art, pure and abstract, was the woman Edgar Allan Poe desired.

UNIVERSITY OF TEXAS AT EL PASO

"Very like a Whale":
Herman Melville and Shakespeare

Luther Stearns Mansfield

These words of Polonius to Hamlet, "Very like a whale," which figure in the title, Herman Melville included appropriately enough among the eighty-eight chronologically arranged extracts from the literature and lore about the whale from Genesis down which serve as a kind of prologue to *Moby-Dick* (1851). For Melville, however, there was possibly here a personal meaning undreamt of by Polonius, for, in 1849, less than a year before he began his epic of the white whale, Melville had remarked to a friend in a letter largely about Emerson and Shakespeare:

> I love all men who *dive*. Any fish can swim near the surface, but it takes a great whale to go down stairs five miles or more; & if he dont attain the bottom, why, all the lead in Galena can't fashion the plumet that will.[1]

Emerson's remark in his essay on "Shakespeare," in *Representative Men* (1850), is pertinent:

> Shakespeare is the only biographer of Shakespeare; and even he can tell nothing except to the Shakespeare in us, that is, to our most apprehensive and sympathetic hour.

Clearly Shakespeare spoke to the Shakespeare in Melville; it was the greatness in one that responded to the genius of the other. Both were men who dived, both were "very like a whale."

In 1839, just nineteen, Melville had published in the hometown newspaper, *The Democratic Press and Lansingburg Advertizer*, two juvenile articles called "Fragments from a Writing Desk," which are studded with quotations and allusions to many authors, including Shakespeare, used with an adolescent's sense of elegant adornment.[2]

Perhaps because the Puritans regarded the stage as wicked and Shakespeare primarily as a man of the stage, Americans in general had not until the middle-nineteenth century given Shakespeare the literary rank he now holds. There were frequent productions of the most popular plays in the major cities from the middle-eighteenth century on. And the major American actor of Melville's time, Edwin Forrest, frequently appeared in Shakespearean roles. From the time of Melville's coming to live regularly in New York after his marriage in August 1847, there were occasional evenings at the theatre, where sometimes the offering was one of Shakespeare's plays.

For the fusing of Shakespeare the dramatist and Shakespeare the poet and man of letters in the public's mind, to the great enhancement of Shakespeare's American reputation, much credit must go to Richard Henry Dana, Sr., himself a Cambridge poet and one-time editor of the *North American Review,* who from 1839 onward gave from time to time a series of eight lectures on Shakespeare in Boston, New York, Philadelphia, and other cities.[3] These lectures, repeated in New York in 1848, Melville almost certainly heard. And possibly Dana's influence combined with others led Melville to acquire the seven-volume edition of *The Dramatic Works of William Shakespeare* in February 1849 about which he wrote a friend from Boston:

> I have been passing my time very pleasurably here. But chiefly in lounging on a sofa (a la the poet Grey) & reading Shakespeare. It is an edition in glorious great type, every letter whereof is a soldier, and the top of every 't' like a musket barrel. Dolt & ass that I am I have lived more than 29 years, & until a few days ago, never made close acquaintance with the divine William. Ah, he's full of sermons-on-the-mount, and gentle, aye, almost as Jesus. I take such men to be inspired. I fancy that . . . Shakespeare in heaven ranks with Gabriel Raphael and Michael. And if another Messiah ever comes twill be in Shakespeare's person.[4]

About the time of his purchase of this edition of Shakespeare, Melville attended in Boston, 12 and 19 February 1849, the readings of *Macbeth* and *Othello* given by Fanny Kemble Butler, daughter of the English actor Charles Kemble, and herself a celebrated Shakespearean actress. For Melville, she made "a glorious Lady Macbeth," but he thought her Desdemona "like a boarding school miss."[5]

Melville's interest in Shakespearean performances in New York was heightened by his intensely critical and thoughtful reading of the plays, passages of which he sidelined, underscored, and annotated in his fine edition. He was back in New York in early May 1849 when on the 7th there were three performances of *Macbeth* at different theatres on the same evening—with Charles

Macready, Edwin Forrest, and Thomas S. Hamblin in the title role. This was probably a scheme of Forrest's to undermine Macready's American reputation, though certainly Forrest did not intend anything so bloody as the Astor Place Riot which occurred after the booing and rock, apple, and rotten egg pelting of Macready had stopped his performance early in Act III. In the large newspaper advertisements of May 9th appealing for decent behavior and respectful treatment of Macready, Melville's name was listed with forty-seven other prominent citizen signers, and it is likely that Melville attended the performance on May 10th by Macready, which continued to the end of the play though noise drowned out many of the words. That night the action outside the theatre, in which the police and militia intervened, brought the totals to twenty-two dead and thirty-six wounded.[6]

In London briefly in November and December 1849, Melville attended the theatre almost nightly, but apparently saw only one Shakespearean play—*Othello,* on which he commented: "Macready panted hideously. Didn't like him very much upon the whole— bad voice, it seemed. James Wallack, Iago, very good. Miss Reynolds, Desdemona, very pretty. Horrible Roderigo."[7]

In what was probably another intense reading of Shakespeare in the summer of 1850, in the midst of the composition of *Moby-Dick,* Melville paused to write his famous essay, "Hawthorne and his Mosses," in which he somewhat extravagantly compared Hawthorne with Shakespeare: Shakespeare had not been equaled but he had been approached. The essay, however, is perhaps more important for what it says about Shakespeare than for what it says about Melville's American contemporary.

In the earlier letter, Melville had found "the divine William . . . full of sermons-on-the-mount, and gentle, aye, almost as Jesus." And this gentle aspect of Shakespeare, Melville was never to overlook or obscure. But in discussing the "blackness in Hawthorne," Melville was more aptly concerned with

> the infinite obscure of . . . that background against which Shakespeare plays his grandest conceits, the things that have made for Shakespeare his loftiest but most circumscribed renown, as the profoundest of thinkers.[8]

Dismissing "those mistaken souls, who dream of Shakespeare as a mere man of Richard-the-Third humps, and Macbeth daggers," Melville insisted here that

it is those faraway things in him; those occasional flash-
ings-forth of the intuitive Truth in him; those short quick
probings at the very axis of reality; these are the things
that make Shakespeare Shakespeare. Through the mouths of
the dark characters of Hamlet, Timon, Lear, and Iago, he
craftily says, or sometimes insinuates, the things which we feel
to be so terrifically true that it were all but madness for
any good man, in his own proper character, to utter, or even
hint of them. Tormented into desperation, Lear the frantic
king tears off the mask, and speaks the sane madness of
vital truth.

Both the profound gentleness and "those short quick probings
at the very axis of reality" were the revelations of the whale-like
deep-diving thinker. Both were important in Melville's response
to Shakespeare and in the inspiration and, in the narrower sense,
the use of Shakespeare appearing in Melville's work.

In *The Confidence-Man* (1857) Melville was to name as the
three great "original characters in fiction" Hamlet, Don Quixote,
and Milton's Satan.[9] Much earlier than 1857, Hamlet had captured
Melville's imagination, and he had made Starbuck, Ahab's first
mate on the *Pequod*, a weaker Hamlet, who admits early in the
voyage after the white whale that "My soul is more than matched;
she's overmanned; and by a madman!"[10] Starbuck's fate Melville
foreshadows early as "the fall of valor in the soul."[11] And it is his
"miserable office,—to obey, rebelling; and worse yet, to hate with
touch of pity!"[12]

Hamlet's procrastination is heart and soul of the tormented
title character of *Pierre* (1852), whose meditation upon the
Shakespearean hero, with whom he identifies himself, affords
Melville the opportunity to comment:

> If . . . the pregnant tragedy of *Hamlet* convey any one
> particular moral at all fitted to the ordinary uses of man, it
> is this:—that all meditation is worthless, unless it prompt
> to action. . . .[13]

In the "plaintive fable" of Memnon, Melville found "embodied
the Hamletism of the antique world; the Hamletism of three
thousand years ago: 'The flower of virtue cropped by a too rare
mischance.' "[14] And for Melville, the English tragedy was "but
Egyptian Memnon, Montaignized and modernized. . . ." In his

copy of the play, Melville marked the comment of Hamlet that "there is nothing either good or bad, but thinking makes it so," and in the margin added the annotation, "Here is forcibly shown the great Montaignism of Hamlet."[15] On his visit to the British Museum in November 1849, Melville thought worthy of recording that he had seen Shakespeare's autograph in a copy of Montaigne.[16]

The soliloquies and the dramatic form of some chapters of *Moby-Dick* are obviously indebted to Shakespeare. The romantic rhetoric of Melville's style, its sweep and wide-ranging metaphor, is a heritage from the Renaissance writers, but not slavishly imitative. As Shakespeare was a man of his day, so was Melville of his. The railroad locomotive, "the mighty iron Leviathan" of Melville's day, could furnish an extended figure in one of Ahab's soliloquies:

> The path to my fixed purpose is laid with iron rails, whereon my soul is grooved to run. Over unsounded gorges, through the rifled hearts of mountains, under torrent's beds, unerringly I rush! Naught's an obstacle, naught's an angle to the iron way![17]

The general influence of Shakespeare, at least in *Moby-Dick,* is fairly obvious in the richness of language, the dramatic sweep of the plot, and the exaggerated stature of the characters. But there are also specific passages or devices that show more explicit indebtedness.

The prophecy of the witches to Macbeth with its seemingly unfulfillable conditions clearly inspired the terms of Fedallah's prediction of the only way Ahab could die.[18] "Hemp only can kill thee" meant for Ahab that he was safe from the whale and need fear only the gallows. The hearse "not made by mortal hands" and the hearse of wood grown in America he was to see before death, Ahab likewise dismissed, for he thought that one does not see hearses at sea. But Ahab did see Fedallah's body lashed to the body of the whale, the first hearse; and the splintered American wood of the *Pequod,* after Moby Dick had rammed and sunk the ship, served as the hearse of all the crew aboard, before Ahab himself was caught round the neck by the harpoon rope and strangled by the rushing whale in whom the harpoon was affixed.

Jaques' account of the seven ages of man in *As You Like It*[19] similarly would seem the likely inspiration of Stubb's finding in the twelve signs of the Zodiac "the life of man in one round chapter."[20]

Man by either Jaques' or Stubb's itinerary came to "mere oblivion." The zodiacal order in which Stubb rendered Capricornus, Aquarius, and Pisces as battering ram, deluge, and fishes, further forecast the *Pequod's* fate, and provided, like the harpoon rope, the appropriate maritime flavor.

One kind of reflection of Shakespeare appears in the chapter of *Moby-Dick* called "The Spirit-Spout," where the mood invoked by the initial phrase, "one serene and moonlight night," is re-enforced by echoes in "on such a silent night," or "the moonlight nights," or "herds of whales were heard by night," or "his turban and the moon, companions in one sky," or "that silvery, moon-lit jet," or "mysteriously jetted into the clear moonlight," on through long paragraphs, in much the same fashion as the repetitions of "In such a night" unify the dialogue of Lorenzo and Jessica in the opening of the final scene in *The Merchant of Venice*.[21]

Melville described "the sign-painters' whales seen in the streets hanging over the shops of oil dealers" as generally "Richard III whales, with dromedary humps, and very savage."[22] The chapter in which Stubb recounts his dream of being kicked by Ahab is entitled "Queen Mab," in obvious allusion to Mercutio's discourse to Romeo on dreams.[23]

Richard III. is unmarked in Melville's seven-volume edition of the plays, perhaps because in 1849 he was already thoroughly familiar with that tragedy. But it is clear that the characterization of Richard, as of Macbeth, strongly influenced Melville's conception of Ahab, in spite of the contemptuous remark about "Richard-the-Third humps and Macbeth daggers" in the article on Hawthorne. Indeed, Ahab has two distinguishing marks—the body-length lightning scar and the ivory leg—no less striking than Richard's hump.

Antony and Cleopatra, the most heavily marked play in Melville's edition, may have contributed something to the quality of Ahab indicated in his statement: "I'm demoniac, I am madness maddened! That wild madness that's only calm to comprehend itself!"[24] Of Antony after Actium, Enobarbus comments:

Now he'll outstare the lightning. To be furious,
Is to be frighted out of fear; and in that mood
The dove will peck the estridge; and I see still,

A diminution in our captain's brain
Restores his heart. When valor preys on reason,
It eats the sword it fights with.[25]

"The complete abasement of poor Starbuck's fortitude," as Melville
called it, before "an enraged and mighty man" such as Captain
Ahab, also referred to as "the incompetence of mere unaided
virtue or right-mindedness in Starbuck,"[26] also suggests the Soothsayer's words to Antony, which Melville sidelined in his copy:

Thy demon, that thy spirit which keeps thee, is
Noble, courageous, high, unmatchable,
Where Caesar's is not; but, near him, thy angel
Becomes a fear, as being o'erpower'd: therefore
Make space between you.[27]

The idea expressed in the Soothsayer's lines intrigued Melville's
imagination, so much that he sidelined in the final scene of *King
Lear* Edmund's defiant response to Albany's challenge,

What in the world he is
That names me traitor, villain-like he lies.
Call by the trumpet;—he that dares approach,
On him, on you, who not? I will maintain
My truth and honor firmly.[28]

And at the top of the page, Melville added a note: "The infernal
nature has a valor often denied to innocence."

In a variety of ways, *Lear,* the second most heavily marked and
annotated play in Melville's copy, contributed to *Moby-Dick.* When
he found it desirable to add a footnote to chapter 87 in the
English edition, to explain the term *gallied* as applied to a whale,
Melville wrote:

To gally, or *gallow,* is to frighten excessively—to confound
with fright. It is an old Saxon word. It occurs once in Shake-
speare:—
"The wrathful skies
Gallow the very wanderers of the dark,
And make them keep their caves."[29]

These words of Kent to Lear and the Fool during the storm
provided the pertinent illustration Melville needed.

Father Mapple's observation that "Virtue, if a pauper, is stopped

at all frontiers,"[30] is an idea akin to Melville's comment in the
"Mosses" article that "in this world of lies, Truth is forced to fly
like a scared white doe in the woodlands; and only by cunning
glimpses will she reveal herself, as in Shakespeare and other
masters of the great Art of Telling the Truth,—even though it be
covertly and by snatches."[31] The words of the Fool in *Lear*, "Truth's
a dog must to Kennel . . . ,"[32] Melville underlined in his copy, for
he regarded this play as an especially vivid illustration of the
difficulties Virtue and Truth encounter.

As he had sidelined Biron's words to King Ferdinand in *Love's
Labour's Lost* about "Necessity" and "special grace,"[33] and the
famous speech of Brutus in *Julius Caesar* about "a tide in the
affairs of men,"[34] so Melville, once again revealing his own fatal-
istic inclination, similarly marked the reflection of Kent on Lear's
daughters:

> It is the stars,
> The stars above us, govern our condition;
> Else one self mate and make could not beget
> Such different issues.[35]

The initial obsession of the King in dividing his kingdom
comes close to the captain's monomaniacal pursuit of the white
whale, and as time passes Ahab, like Lear, "tears off the mask,
and speaks the sane madness of vital truth." The Negro cabin boy
Pip, who in some ways resembles the Fool, especially after he has
been a castaway, is driven to idiocy when left adrift upon the
ocean for hours. As Melville explains,

> He saw God's foot upon the treadle of the loom, and spoke
> it; and therefore his shipmates called him mad. So man's
> insanity is heaven's sense; and wandering from all mortal
> reason, man comes at last to that celestial thought, which,
> to reason, is absurd and frantic; and weal or woe, feels then
> uncompromised, indifferent as his God.[36]

Charles Olson finds the association of Ahab and Pip after the
castaway experience "like the relations of Lear to both the Fool
and Edgar."[37] Although the Manxman of the *Pequod's* crew commented of the captain and the cabin boy, "One daft with strength,
the other daft with weakness,"[38] Pip seems hardly worthy of
comparison with the Shakespearean characters. He has very little

to say, for one thing; the reader must infer much from Ahab's reaction to him. The captain says to Pip:

> Lad, lad, I tell thee thou must not follow Ahab now. . . . There is that in thee, poor lad, which I feel too curing to my malady. Like cures like; and for this hunt, my malady becomes my most desired health.[39]

The analogy here is not so much to Lear in relation to the Fool or Edgar, as to the thoughts of Hubert on approaching young Arthur, in *King John,* with the intention of burning out the boy's eyes,

> If I talk to him, with his innocent prate
> He will awake my mercy which lies dead.
> Therefore I will be sudden and dispatch.[40]

Unlike Hubert, Ahab did not weaken.

Pip's gleaned wisdom smells of mortality and death and the uncertainty of all temporal things, as in his responding to the posted gold doubloon by merely conjugating the verb, "I look, you look, he looks; we look, ye look, they look,"[41] by way of illustrating that the consciousness alone is vital and things in themselves without substantiality. Pip is less like the Fool than like Hamlet contemplating the skull. But the clearest parallel to Hamlet's remarks in the grave is Ahab's address to the Sphinx-like head of the dead whale:

> Speak, thou vast and venerable head . . . which, though ungarnished with a beard, yet here and there lookest hoary with mosses; speak, mighty head, and tell us the secret thing that is in thee. Of all divers, thou hast dived the deepest.[42]

Melville had infinite pity and understanding for "a valor-ruined man"[43] like Starbuck, but his admiration went to the man who could make with Edgar the affirmation he sidelined in *King Lear:*

> Men must endure
> Their going hence, even as their coming hither;
> Ripeness is all.[44]

With his dying breath, Ahab made such an affirmation: "Oh, now I feel my topmost greatness lies in my topmost grief."[45] Keeping his integrity to the end, self-reliant, firm in his opposition to the incarnate evil which for him Moby Dick represented, Ahab—whatever else his faults—did not complain. He was content that his life-long struggle had brought his character to "ripeness."

For Ishmael the disastrous end of Ahab might also have some meaning, for it was the tragedy of Lear and Gloucester that brought Edgar to manhood, to the perception of "Reason in madness" in Lear's speech, to the assurance that taught him that "Ripeness is all," to the successful challenging of Edmund and the calm acceptance that "The gods are just."[46] Ishmael, spectator of the tragedy of Ahab and survivor, could learn from it. Despite the seeming skeptical despair of comprehension, Ishmael's Epilogue has much the same function as the final lines of the chorus in *Samson Agonistes:*

> His servants He, with new acquist
> Of true experience from this great event,
> With peace and consolation hath dismissed,
> And calm of mind, all passion spent.[47]

But Ishmael, "all passion spent," without as yet having fully reflected on the "true experience," was more the simple bearer of tidings, like the four messengers in Job: "And I only am escaped alone to tell thee."[48] Melville's myth—less dramatic than Shakespeare's, less didactic than Milton's—sought merely, like the book of Job, to propound the question and gave only the Biblical answer of the tidings of God's power.

In view of the notable differences between Ahab and Lear, and the relegation of Pip—the character most resembling the Fool—to a minor position, as well as in view of the differences in final outlook between Ishmael and Edgar, it would be most interesting to know precisely what Melville meant—whether possible agreement or disagreement—when he sidelined in his edition of Shakespeare a passage from Dr. Johnson's criticism of *Lear:*

> A play in which the wicked prosper, and the virtuous miscarry, may doubtless be good, because it is a just representation of the common events of life; but since all reasonable things naturally love justice, I can not easily be persuaded that the observation of justice makes a play worse. . . .[49]

The influence of Shakespeare in *Moby-Dick* is pervasive and of many kinds. Each reader of Melville's epic of the whale will probably have his own opinion of which evidences of influence are most significant and incontestable. Thus any account of what Shakespeare meant to Melville must be suggestive only, not exhaustive.

Melville's interest in other Renaissance dramatists followed soon upon his immersion in Shakespeare. In London in November 1849, he bought folios of Ben Jonson and Beaumont and Fletcher, *Fifty Comedies and Tragedies,* and the following month an edition of Christopher Marlowe. His journal of the voyage home in January 1850 testifies to his reading extensively from all three volumes.[50]

Of the non-dramatic Renaissance authors, Milton was clearly the most important for Melville, as even a casual reading of *Moby-Dick* makes clear. Indeed, Henry Pommer has done a book-length study.[51] Spenser's *Faerie* Queene provided the mottoes for the ten sections of *The Encantadas* (1854), with Melville making slight modifications in the texts.[52] The John Donne passage, which Ernest Hemingway was to make widely known by using part of it for his title, *For Whom the Bell Tolls* (1939), Melville had echoed in describing the crew in *Moby-Dick:*

> They were nearly all Islanders in the Pequod, *Isolatoes* too, I call such, not acknowledging the common continent of men, but each *Isolato* living on a separate continent of his own.[53]

But far outranking all other books in its all-pervading influence on *Moby-Dick* was the King James version of the Bible, which Melville read and reread, annotated and marked in more than one edition.

Shakespeare was probably the first to show Melville clearly that language was not merely a means of communication or a vehicle for thought, but could be literature appealing not only to the mind, but to the heart and soul as well—to the whole man in his profoundest moments. After his immersion in Shakespeare, Melville could read the King James version of the Bible in a new light, as he did, with numerous markings and annotations, in the spring of 1850.[54]

Melville regarded the authors and the King James translators of his favorite Bible passages, especially the writings of Solomon and the Book of Job, as, like Shakespeare, "very like a whale," for he loved "all men who *dive.*" The King James Bible was often his Holinshed and his Plutarch; he borrowed and adapted with the same inspired creativity with which Shakespeare had mined his sources. "Very like a whale," both authors went "down stairs five miles or more."

WILLIAMS COLLEGE

Functional Imagery in Simms's
"The Partisan"

L. MOFFITT CECIL

This study is an examination of the imagery in William Gilmore Simms's novel, *The Partisan*. It demonstrates that Simms could and did attain in his fiction a degree of artistry and a depth of meaning which scholars have been much too slow to recognize.

The Partisan (1835) was the first in a series of eight Revolutionary romances Simms published during his lifetime. Set in South Carolina, the novel describes events which occurred during a period of about two and a half months, from the middle of June to the end of August, 1780. The major historical episode, the Battle of Camden, falls suitably near the end of the novel. Simms presents detailed portraits of the principals in that engagement: General Gates, Baron DeKalb, Lord Cornwallis, Colonel Tarleton. The battle itself, which ended in a defeat for the Americans, he depicts graphically and well.

But the Battle of Camden was not Simms's primary interest in the novel. He saw that the really significant development in South Carolina in 1780, after the fall of Charleston to the British and before the Continental Congress could send adequate military aid, was the emergence of a native resistance corps, a group of loyal Carolinians he called the Partisans. The historical Francis Marion, the fictional Major Singleton, Colonel Walton, Lieutenant Porgy, Lieutenant Humphries, Lance Frampton and a host of other sandlappers and swampers are the true heroes of Simms's novel. They enact a sequence of fictional events which Simms has woven skillfully in and about the historical record and which carry the thematic burden of the book. The action ends not at Camden after the humiliating defeat, but deep within Cypress Swamp, where a small Partisan band, encouraged by its recent success in rescuing Colonel Walton from being hanged by the British, prepares to continue the desperate struggle against the powerful invaders.

Cypress Swamp, the hide-out of the Partisans, becomes a

dominant image in the novel. As the rebel Carolinians flee back time and again to the recesses of the swamp to regroup their forces and reshape their plans, so Simms returns in his descriptions, each time to enlarge and elaborate the image of the swamp. A reader's first glimpse of the secret campsite suggests the organic nature of the swamp metaphor which will eventually emerge:

> They stood upon an island in the very center of the swamp—one of those little islands, the tribute ooze of numerous minor water courses, hardening into solidity at last. These, beating their feeble tides upon a single point, in process of time create the barrier which is to usurp their own possessions. Here, the rank matter of the swamp, its slime and rubbish, resolving themselves by a natural but rapid decomposition into one mass, yield the thick luxuriance of soil from which springs up the overgrown tree, which throws out a thousand branches, and seems to have existed as many years—in whose bulk we behold an emblem of majesty, and, in whose term of life, standing in the utter defiance of the sweeping hurricane, we have an image of strength which compels our admiration, and sometimes the more elevated acknowledgment of our awe.*

The metaphorical implications of this passage are significant. The island after so long a time shored up within the swamps represents the heartland of the new American nation already emergent in 1780. From the flotsam and jetsam of England and western Europe has emerged at length a new civilization, firm and fertile, which like the mighty water oak can withstand even the hurricane.

In Simms's concept the land itself, the mysterious, fecund swamp, is the generating source and the sustaining power of the American rebellion. It is the original, native, vital principle which must triumph at last. The British are invaders alien to the new world; therefore they cannot thrive within the swamp, which inspires them with a distaste and fear amounting to revulsion. This fact is pungently illustrated in the jibe which British Sergeant Clough addresses to Huck, the Tory:

*William Gilmore Simms, *The Partisan* (New York, 1854), p. 72. Page references in this study are to this, the Redfield, edition.

"Well, thou dost promise largely, like an old debtor, but, to my mind, thou art just now where thou shouldst be—in the swamps; for, truth to speak, thou lovest them—thou lovest the wallow and the slough—the thick ooze which the alligator loves, and the dry fern-bank where he makes his nest, thou lovest the terrapin because of his home, not less than of the good soup which he gives us; and the ugly moccasin, and the toad, and the frog—the brown lizard and the green—the swamp-spider, with ropy house and bagging black body— all these are favorites with thee, because thy spirit craves for thee a home like that which they abide in." (p. 85)

Huck responds, "It is a goodly place," because though he is a Tory (Simms's most brutal characters are Tories) he is still a native American.

Simms's Partisans, on the other hand, are those who love the swamp, who turn to it for refuge, for instruction, and for sustenance. After each foray when, exhausted and discouraged, they regroup at their campsite, they are sure to find, Antaeus-like, their strength renewed and their fighting spirits revived.

The swamp is not merely passive in the support it renders to those who own it, who are at one with it. Active and creative, it evolves its own characteristic methods to insure survival and growth. The Partisans, then, must be schooled by the swamp if they are to prevail. They must look to the swamp's other creatures for instruction. Simms states this idea clearly when he describes the type of song his imaginary poet, George Dennison, would sing: "He would show us the rude forester, as, passing from his farmstead to the swamp, flying from the marauder, he became, in time, the adroit partisan, under the ablest leaders . . . . How he grew, in time, to practise all the arts of the natural inhabitants of the swamp and thicket: to imitate the cry of the bird, the stealth of the beast, the speed of the eagle, the fierce valour of the tiger" (p. 241). This concept explains the prevalence of animal imagery in *The Partisan* and shows why and how it is functional in the novel. Marion, the leader, is the Swamp Fox. Among his scouts are Crabstick, Red Possum, Fox Squirrel, and Slickfoot (p. 408). Sumter is the Gamecock. The cry of the owl is the signal of warning. The query "How are the owls?" is the code question for scouts and messengers (p. 407).

This significant kinship between the swamp creatures and the Partisans is most brilliantly realized in the persons of Dr. Oakenburg and Lieutenant Porgy. These two originals by Simms are truly children of the swamp. Dr. Oakenburg, tall and spare, is a naturalist of sorts, an amateur taxidermist, who catches birds and reptiles to stuff them. As a physician he is a gross pretender, knowing little more than how to concoct some beverages of dubious medicinal value. But he has a passion for snakes. A reader learns this fact very soon after meeting him: "The doctor turned his eyes to the designated point, and beheld the long and beautiful volumes of the beaded snake, as slowly crossing their path with his pack of linked jewels full in their view, he wound his way from one bush into another and gradually folded himself up out of sight. The doctor, however, was not to be alarmed by this survey. He had a passion for snakes; and admiration suspended all his fear, as he gazed upon the beautiful and not dangerous reptile" (p. 112). Later one sees him "sublimely employed stuffing with moss the skin of a monstrous 'coachwhip,' which, to his great delight, the morning before, he had been successful enough to take with a crotch stick" (p. 255).

Dr. Oakenburg himself has obvious ophidian characteristics. Tall, lank, and enigmatic, he suggests, not a reptile of the dangerous kind, but one of the more harmless inhabitants of the swamp. His contribution to the Partisan cause comes not from his efficiency as a fighter or a worker, but from his inarticulate loyalty and his bungling good humor. At once repellent and appealing, he is one of Simms's more interesting creations. Though not a major character, he makes an appearance in other of the Revolutionary romances.

Lieutenant Porgy, Simms's masterwork in the creation of character, suggests an animal of quite a different breed. Huge, ponderous, powerful, he is slow to get started, but once under way he is inexorable. Critics have erred in looking too exclusively to Shakespeare's Falstaff as Porgy's prototype; they should look rather to the great terrapin of the swamp.

One of the memorable scenes in the novel is that in which the obese and determined Porgy, grunting in imitation of a pig to beguile his intended prey, "coons the log" and captures three large alligator terrapins (Chapter XXX). Somewhat later, when the terrapins have been dressed and the stew so dear to the Partisans is under preparation, Porgy, in a contemplative mood, looks at the empty shells of the terrapins: "Musing thus, he grappled one of the shells, the largest of the three, and turning himself upon his back, with his head resting against a pine, he proceeded to adjust the back of the terrapin, as a sort of shield, to his own extensive abdominal domain. Large as was the shell, it furnished a very inadequate cover to the ample territory, at once so much exposed and so valuable. It was while engaged in this somewhat ludicrous experiment, that Lieutenant Porgy was surprised by Major Singleton" (p. 352). The conversation which follows this scene develops a jest about Porgy's bulk. But an identification has been made: Porgy is the possessor of the dependable virtues of the terrapin. Other animals lend their characteristic talents to the Partisan cause. The swamp fox is wily and quick, the snake is subtle, but the terrapin is indefatigable; it endures. When the unschooled John Davis asks Porgy if the Romans were "a kind of terrapins," Porgy replies: "Yes, indeed! a kind of terrapins that crawled over the whole earth, and claimed it for their own" (p. 322). It is significant that Porgy becomes a major center of interest as the Revolutionary romances progress. He emerges as the focal character in *Woodcraft* (1852), the post-war novel of the series.

Besides subserving the Partisans as a place of refuge and as primordial instructor, the swamp provides them also with food. The most definitive declaration of this fact is to be found in Porgy's description of the swamp as a land "flowing with milk and honey": "The phrase, milk and honey, simply means to convey the idea of a land full of all things that a man of taste can relish; or we may even go farther in this respect, and consider it a land teeming with all things for all tastes. Thus, yours, Doctor Oakenburg—even *your* vile taste for snakes and eels—has been consulted here not less than mine for terrapin" (p. 414). Porgy, in his prodigal manner of speaking, proceeds to enumerate such dubious edibles as the moccasin, the sly alligator, the summer duck, and the damned bodiless crane. Food is, of course, a passion with this philosophical gourmet.

What appears at casual reading to be the exaggerated emphasis upon food preparation and eating in *The Partisan* is not merely gratuitous burlesque. Rather it is a bold amplification of the image of the swamp. The philosophic basis for this development is whimsically phrased by Porgy:

> "Terrapin stew or pie seems to impart something of the
> sluggishness of the beast to him who feeds upon it. I must
> think of this; whether it is not the case with all animals
> to influence with their own nature, that of the person who
> feeds on them. It was certainly the notion of the ancients.
> A steak of the lion might reasonably be supposed to impart
> courage; wolf and tiger should make one thirst for blood;
> and"—seeing Oakenburg ride along at this moment—"who
> should wonder suddenly to behold that crane-bodied cormor-
> ant, after eating fried eel, suddenly twisting away from his
> nag, and, with squirm and wriggle, sliding off into the
> mud?" (p. 365)

The Partisans, the true children of the new world, are best nur-
tured by native foods. Alien nutriment is not sufficient for their
fullest needs. Therefore the preparation and eating of terrapin stew
become a ritual. Porgy, who presides on such occasions, is the high
priest. Only the true Partisan will eat, and only those who eat will
prevail. It should be remembered that Colonel Walton and his
men left the Cypress Swamp before the terrapin stew could be
served. This action was incredible to the zealous Porgy, who
exclaimed when he was told that Walton did not care for terrapin:
"Then no good can come of him; he's an infidel. I would not
march with him for the world" (p. 345). Walton was taken
prisoner at the Battle of Camden and later (as revealed in *Katherine
Walton*, 1851) was hanged by the British in Charleston. One should
remember too those delightfully grotesque chapters at the end of
The Forayers (1855) in which Porgy and his men prepare and
serve a sumptuous swamp repast of delicate frog, alligator, and
terrapin for General Greene, General Marion, Colonel Lee, Colonel
Horry, and others. These notables dine marvelously well, though
some of them are hardly aware of the true source of the viands
they enjoy. This sacrificial feast, this communion with the swamp,
stands them in good stead, for in a sequel volume they go up to
the Battle of Eutaw Springs and win a victory which proves to be
decisive.

Thus in *The Partisan*, through skillful and persistent shading
of setting, character, and incident, Simms elaborates the swamp
image to represent his concept of colonial organicism. The land,

its resources, and its inhabitants work together, drawing upon a a common, inherent, inexhaustible power to repudiate the alien invaders.

The antagonists in the novel, too, are figuratively represented. A second recurrent image in *The Partisan* is the hurricane. This alien destructive power represents the invader, and its impact upon the forests and the swamps represents war. In its wake follow desolation and suffering. But the mighty tree on the island in the swamp, Simms assures us, stands "in utter defiance of the sweeping hurricane" (p. 72).

The hurricane described in Chapter XV is suitably magnificent in its scope and its power.

> . . . then came the arrowy flight and form of the hurricane itself—its actual bulk—its embodied power, pressing along through the forest in a gyratory progress, not fifty yards wide, never distending in width, yet capriciously winding from right to left and left to right, in a zigzag direction, as if a playful spirit thus strove to mix with all the terrors of destruction the sportive mood of the most idle fancy. In this progress, the whole wood in its path underwent prostration—the tall, proud pine, the deep-rooted and unbending oak, the small cedar and the pliant shrub, torn, dismembered of their fine proportions; some, only by a timely yielding to the pressure, passed over with little injury, as if too much scorned by the assailant for his wrath . . . . Far and near, the moaning of the forest around them was strangely, but not unpleasantly, heightened in its effect upon their senses, by the distant and declining roar of the past and far traveling hurricane, as ploughing the deep woods and laying waste all in its progress, it rushed on to a meeting with the kindred storms that gather about the gloomy Cape Hatteras, and stir and foam along the waters of the Atlantic. (pp. 172, 173)

Simms is especially careful to point out the metaphorical nature of this devastating storm. The time of its occurrence is significant. The uneasy truce between the occupying British forces and the apparently subdued Carolinians has been dramatically presented. Sir Henry Clinton has just issued his harsh edict withdrawing the "protections" and ordering all loyalists to take up arms actively against the rebels. On the other side, it has been reported that a Continental Army is approaching from North Carolina. And the Partisan leaders have already, secretly, formed a band to offer resistance. Colonel Walton has just determined to "come out" for his rebel countrymen. In short, the contending forces have been estimated and placed in readiness. Then comes the hurricane. Lieutenant Humphries, in the pause, just before the onset, compares it to an invading army: "It's making ready for a charge, major: it's just like a good captain, sir, that calls in his scouts and sentries, and without beat of drum gets all fixed to spring out from the bush upon them that's coming. It won't be long now, sir, before we get it, but just now it's still as the grave. It's waiting for its outriders—them long streaky white clouds it sent out an hour ago, like so many scouts. They're a-coming up now, and when they all get up together—then look out for the squall" (p. 171).

Simms is not content with these somewhat indirect revelations of the meaning of the hurricane. He pictures Major Singleton as wondering how many "mighty pines were to be prostrated" and how many "beautiful vines . . . would share in their ruin." Then Simms asks rhetorically: "How could Singleton overlook the analogy between the fortune of his family and friends, and that which his imagination depicted as the probable destiny of the forest?" (p. 168) But if the onslaught of the hurricane presages death and destruction, its passing, marked by a returning light, promises surcease and restoration. "Such gleams in the natural, are like the assurances of hope in the moral world—they speak of tomorrow—they promise us that the clouds must pass away— they cheer, when there is little left to charm" (p. 174).

Though this hurricane blows itself out within a single chapter—out beyond Cape Hatteras into the foamy Atlantic—its image re-echoes throughout *The Partisan* and the other novels which comprise Simms's Revolutionary romances, as the British invaders bring aggressive warfare to the Carolinas. The opening sentence of Chapter XXI reads: "The clouds were gathering fast . . . and the approaching tumult and disquiet of all things in Carolina, clearly indicated the coming of that strife, so soon to overcast the scene—so long to keep it darkened—so deeply to empurple it with blood" (p. 233). And in his vivid portrayal of the battle of Camden, Simms evokes the hurricane image at crucial moments. Of General Gates's futile attempt to halt the panicky flight of

Steven's brigade, he writes: "He might as well have spoken to the winds, wild and headlong in the autumnal equinox. He might as well have spoken to the floods, loosed from the bonds of the deep, and mounting in foaming mountains above the shores" (p. 468). Just prior to Baron DeKalb's famous assault comes "one of those pauses of the storm that indicates the accumulation of the masses for new thunders" (p. 470). Soon afterwards "the opposing torrents were mingled together in the shock of battle" (p. 471). At the end of the novel one finds the Partisan band preparing for a long and desperate campaign. They are dedicated to fight until "step by step, beaten to the Atlantic shores, the invader" flees to his ships and leaves the country (p. 531). Like the hurricane, the invading British must be expelled, driven at length back into the sea.

A subtle extension of the storm imagery should be noted. Simms portrays the cataclysmic effects of the hurricane-invader not only in the physical realm, but in the world of mind as well. Mental storms, in the shape of madness and obsessive violence, are unleashed by the war. The extreme example of this effect upon man's mind is seen in the role of the elder Frampton, who, crazed by the brutal murder of his wife, returns at intervals throughout the story to wreak bloody vengeance upon the British.

It is in the character of young Lance Frampton, though, that Simms studies in detail the mental and moral effects of the war. Lance is timid, sensitive, somewhat effeminate when he joins the Partisan band. His indoctrination into violence comes during an ambuscade of a group of Tory marauders. The scene chosen for this bloody event is a peaceful vale containing a spring of which Simms declares: "War, in his violence, however destructive else, had spared, with a becoming reverence, the fountain and the little roof above it. . . . Yet was its sacred and sweet repose about to be invaded" (pp. 371, 372). Lance fires the initial shot in this encounter and kills the vicious Tory leader, Amos Gaskens. Afterwards, the youth must wrestle with his conscience. Like the peaceful, unsullied spring, his innocence has been defiled by the bloody deed. Strange, unnatural emotions awaken within the boy. Major Singleton, aware of what is taking place, speaks with Lance about man's moral responsibility in war. It is only, however, when Lance looks again into a clear stream and sees there a startling image of his new, fallen self that he is shocked into regaining his mental and moral equilibrium (pp. 402, 403).

Two dominant images, then, emerge in *The Partisan:* the swamp as heartland and the hurricane as invader. By depicting nature in violent conflict with itself, Simms enforces the concept of total war and makes more poignant the fratricidal struggle of the Revolutionary armies in the field.

The issue of the war is not resolved in *The Partisan.* Simms wrote seven additional novels to accomplish that end. Each book in the series attains a suitable degree of unity and completeness, and each makes its special thematic contribution to the whole. *The Partisan,* for instance, depicts dramatically the development of an effective native resistance to the British aggressors in Carolina. The novel is complete in the sense that at its end the Partisans are organized, have demonstrated their military prowess on several occasions, and are dedicated to the desperate task of earning their freedom. But in other important respects the novel presupposes the series, and herein it is truly a seminal work. It introduces characters and situations which demand treatment in other volumes: for example, the Blonay-Humphries feud in *Mellichampe* (1836) and the love story of Major Singleton and Katherine Walton in *Katherine Walton* (1851). And through its functional imagery it enunciates the theme of the entire series—the triumphant power of the mighty tree in the swamp to withstand the hurricane. The series celebrates the victory of young America, which, by insisting upon its own native strength and resourcefulness, established its sovereignty among the powers of the world.

TEXAS CHRISTIAN UNIVERSITY

The Regional Vision of
Laura Ingalls Wilder

FRED ERISMAN

The greatest strength of the best regional writings is the limitless range of their limited vision. They focus, like local color writing, on a specific locale—i.e., they reveal in some way the climatic, geographical, linguistic, and cultural peculiarities of a particular place and time. But, unlike local color writing, they go beyond these finite and idiosyncratic limits to deal with greater concerns. They integrate, for example, the setting with the lives of their characters, so that the reader can perceive how place, or locale, can force adjustments and adaptations in human life. They provide, moreover, a sense of local uniqueness: some experiences are common to all human life, but others are limited to a single place and time. These, too, are a part of regionalism. Ultimately, however, regional writings go still farther, involving their characters, their events, and their settings with the nation and the world. Local events do not take place in a vacuum; what affects them in some way eventually affects the nation, and conversely. Truly regional works, therefore, reflect their authors' awareness that the characters, places, and events are a part of a greater national culture, and the awareness that what affects the nation affects them. (Thus, for example, the Depression and Hitler's rise to power are essential parts of Harper Lee's *To Kill a Mockingbird;* the poignance of A. B. Guthrie's *The Big Sky* is intensified by the sense of irreversible change that permeates it.)

Most of the major documents of literary regionalism are well known. O. E. Rolvaag's *Giants in the Earth* comes immediately to mind, as do (in different times and locales) Sarah Orne Jewett's *The Country of the Pointed Firs* and Jack Schaefer's *Shane.* A comparatively little known expression of the regional vision, however, occurs in the eight "Little House" books of Laura Ingalls Wilder (1867-1957). First published in 1932 (and after), these books provide for American children a fictionalized version of the childhood and youth of young Laura Ingalls as she travels westward with her family. Almost from the first, the books were recognized as a distinguished addition to the genre of domestic and autobiographical fiction pioneered by Louisa May Alcott.

Neither was their description of the westward movement ignored;
a basic study of juvenile literature refers to them as "a dramatic
picture of intrepid pioneering."[1] Containing as they do, however,
the broader vision of the adult looking back (Mrs. Wilder was sixty-
five when the first book appeared), the books provide more than
autobiography. They provide, in addition, what one critic has
called a "compelling power of place"[2]; they reflect the ways in
which place, whether the Big Woods of Wisconsin or the plains
of Dakota Territory, makes its presence felt upon the Ingalls family;
and, finally, they provide a broad awareness of nineteenth-century
American culture, as they reflect the disparate and often conflicting
attitudes present in a nation undergoing radical change. They
provide, in short, a statement of literary regionalism that is un-
surpassed by many better-known "serious" works.

The places of which Mrs. Wilder writes are many, varied, and
real. As the Ingalls family moves from Wisconsin to the Indian
Territory to Minnesota to Dakota Territory, the changing locales
are made particular and unique, by specific references to specific
things. The reader is, for example, constantly made aware of the
changing landscape, from the Wisconsin forests to the virgin
prairie. "The great, dark trees of the Big Woods stood all around
. . . ," says Mrs. Wilder of Wisconsin, "and beyond them were
more trees. As far as a man could go to the north in a day, or
a week, or a whole month, there was nothing but woods. There
were no houses. There were no roads. There were no people.
There were only trees and the wild animals who had their homes
among them."[3] Then, contrasting with the dense, limitless woods
of Wisconsin, come the limitless plains of Kansas. "Kansas was
an endless flat land covered with tall grass blowing in the wind,"
Mrs. Wilder observes. "Day after day they traveled in Kansas, and
saw nothing but the rippling grass and the enormous sky. In a
perfect circle the sky curved down to the level land, and the
wagon was in the circle's exact middle" (*LHOP,* p. 13). Wherever
the place, and whatever the setting, it is quietly but effectively
characterized for the reader.

Mrs. Wilder's sense of place does not stop with simple descriptions of the landscape. Indeed, she acknowledges the changing of
the entire environment. As the books progress, the flora and
fauna change; the deer and black bears of Wisconsin give way
to the prairie chickens and jackrabbits of the Indian Territory.

Later on, the grasshoppers of the Minnesota plains, at first a
curiosity, wipe out a wheat crop and all the dreams that it was
to provide (*OBPC*, pp. 193-208). The people change, too, from
the closely knit family group of the Wisconsin woods to the
Indians of Oklahoma to the Scandinavians of Minnesota. And,
in the most subtle change of all, the weather changes. The weather,
so much a part of a farmer's or a settler's life, is as ubiquitous
a presence in the books as the geography. Sometimes its significance
is hidden from the family, as Pa Ingalls puzzles over the Scandinavian settlers' concern over "grasshopper weather," until the insects
that survived the mild winter ravish the family's crops (*OBPC*,
p. 66). More often, though, it is presented in matter-of-fact fashion,
as when Pa observes that Dakota winters somehow differ from
those in Minnesota (*BSSL*, pp. 153-54). However it is presented,
though, it contributes to the total sense of place that Mrs. Wilder
communicates. At the end of *Little House in the Big Woods*, five-
year-old Laura, warm and comfortable, thinks to herself: "This is
now" (p. 238). It is also, she might well have added, here.

The sense of place conveyed by the books, however, involves
more than merely local color. Mrs. Wilder is, to be sure, concerned
with the specific physical traits of each locale. She rounds out her
portrayal, though, by considering the effects of each place upon
the lives of her family. Sometimes the effect is bitterly comic,
as regional circumstances force the adaptation of a familiar legend:
" 'Didn't he have his reindeer?' Laura asked. 'You know he
couldn't,' Mary said. 'There isn't any snow.' Exactly, said Mr.
Edwards. Santa Claus traveled with a pack-mule in the southwest"
(*LHOP*, p. 247). Sometimes the effect of place is to bring about
a simple acceptance of things, different though they may be, as
they are. "I'd like to write to the folks in Wisconsin," says Ma in
Kansas. "If you mail a letter now [in early autumn], they can
write this winter, and then we can hear from them next spring"
(*LHOP*, p. 206). The distances of the Great Plains force the family
to accept, willy-nilly, a six-month delay in communications. And
sometimes Mrs. Wilder is concerned with the effect upon old
practices that the new life has. Pa Ingalls, for example, must
adapt his Wisconsin-formed plowing and planting habits to suit
the virgin sod of the prairie: "Where Pa had plowed, he didn't
have a plowed field. The long strips of grass-roots lay on top
of grass, and grass stuck out between them. . . . He said that

sod potatoes and sod corn would grow this year, and next year the roots and the dead grasses would be rotted. In two or three years he would have nicely plowed fields" (*LHOP,* p. 275). In a later book, the plow itself is modified, becoming a "breaking plow" developed specifically for the needs of prairie sod-busting (*LTOP,* p. 9). The implications are clear; the peculiar quality of the prairie earth has led an urban manufacturer to develop a specialized tool for a specialized task. That the manufacturer's motive was additional profit is immaterial. The region has affected even more than the Ingalls family.

Place and time can also affect matters more far reaching than family legends and farming habits. They can affect, as Mrs. Wilder amply documents, even the simple facts of survival. Pa returns from a hunt for food in the Dakota Territory with a commentary upon the effects of civilization: "Not a goose within gunshot. . . . The whole flock rose when it came to Silver Lake and kept on going north. They must have seen the new buildings and heard the noise. Looks like hunting's going to be slim around here from now on" (*BSSL,* p. 245). Farther-reaching still is the greater cost of civilization, as it is reflected in the family's gradual loss of their independence. Snowbound in DeSmet by the winter of 1881, the Ingalls come to realize that their welfare is no longer dependent upon Pa's skill with ax, trap, or rifle, but rather upon the railroad. If the trains cannot bring in food, the family will starve (*LW,* pp. 103, 119, 163). Whatever the episode that Mrs. Wilder relates, in short, it provides the sense that the characters involved are in a particular place at a particular time, and must, therefore, live in a particular way.

Of all of the qualities of regionalism present in the "Little House" books, perhaps the most striking is the pervasive sense of being a part of a larger, American culture. As William Jay Jacobs has argued, the entire "sense" of the series is American, as the books dramatize for their readers the American's fundamental faith in culture, moral certainty, and progress.[4] In addition to these general concerns, however, there is a particular, explicit Americanism to the stories. A frontier Fourth of July, for example, leads Pa to exclaim, simply, "Hurray! we're Americans!", and brings to the Ingalls girls a moment of almost religious intensity: "Laura and Carrie knew the Declaration by heart, of course, but it gave them a solemn, glorious feeling to hear the words. They took hold of hands and stood listening in the solemnly listening crowd. The Stars and Stripes were fluttering bright against the thin, clear blue overhead, and their minds were saying the words before their ears heard them" (*LTOP,* pp. 64, 73-74). At this moment, their American citizenship is a part of their being, overt and apparent.

In the same way, the increasingly inter-related nature of American life becomes apparent. Dependence involves more than the railroad. The Federal government becomes more than an abstraction when the family is forced to leave the Indian Territory, thanks to a change in government policy; their fiercely independent lives have been affected by a decision made two thousand miles away (*LHOP,* pp. 316-17). Even the use and misuse of law appear; underlying the last four books of the series is the Homestead Act of 1862, with its provision of free land after five years' residence. The prospect of free land leads the Ingalls family westward; it enables them to settle in DeSmet, Dakota Territory; and it lays the way open for exploitation, as Almanzo Wilder's experience suggests (*LW,* pp. 99-100). These people, the books seem to say, are unique individuals, but they are individuals subject to many pressures. Some pressures come from within—from the moral and cultural sense that is an almost innate part of their lives. Some come from without—from the demands made upon them by the place in which they live. And some come from still farther without—from the mere fact of their existence in the United States between 1871 and 1883. These were years of significant national change, and, inevitably, these changes were felt in the farthest reaches of the country. Mrs. Wilder, looking back to her childhood, sees how these changes touched her family, and conveys her awareness to her readers.

Children, Mary Austin has observed, are "at heart the most confirmed regionalists. What they like as background for a story is an explicit, well mapped strip of country, as intensively lived into as any healthy child lives into his own neighborhood."[5] Although this observation antedates even the first of the "Little House" books, it could easily have been based upon them. Mrs. Wilder does provide such a mapping. She records events and places with the authority that can come only from having been present. She makes the events and their settings as clear for her readers as they were for her.

Mrs. Wilder, however, does not stop with mere description. As Mary Austin's comment implies, there is more to the regional vision than portraying the mere surfaces of things; there is, in addition, an intense awareness of the quality of life that must appear. This, too, Mrs. Wilder provides. She gives her readers, for example, a clear-cut picture of life in another time and another place, a life as irrevocably lost in 1932 as the life of whaling was when Herman Melville described it in 1851. Moreover, like the regionalists who write for older audiences, she gives a picture of humanity in contact with the primal forces. She need not concern herself, as O. E. Rolvaag did, with such things as pathological guilt; for Mrs. Wilder, the problems of nature are enough. The modern child in his centrally heated, air-conditioned home may be virtually unaware of the storm blowing outside, but Mrs. Wilder reminds him that nature existed before man and may well dwarf man's technological achievements. If the reader happens to have had first-hand experience with a blizzard or a flood, all the better. If not, Mrs. Wilder's droughts, snows, floods, and freezes help him to restore man to his proper place in nature.

Of all of the qualities that Mary Austin invokes as important to children, the greatest is the sense of belonging. Children's reading must belong to its setting, as they belong to their own. It is here that Mrs. Wilder excels. Her characters belong to their surroundings, and both belong to the nation. Throughout the books, Mrs. Wilder gives her readers a sense of some of the indigenous themes of American thought, quietly transmitting the foundations of American life. She is concerned with the relationship of the white man and the Indian. She is concerned with the pioneer spirit and its part in the settling of the West. And she is concerned with the same attitude toward the land that leads a midwestern real estate agency specializing in farm properties to describe its Spring, 1971, offerings as "The American Dream." The frontier may well have closed in 1890, but its appeal is no less strong eighty years later. Mrs. Wilder helps the urban child to understand why.

In this is the justification for calling the "Little House" books regional literature. They are excellent juvenile literature; of that there has been little question. They are, however, also worthy of standing alongside the major works of literary regionalism. Like these works, they are written in particulars—a particular family, a particular time, and a particular place. Like these works, in addition, they possess a vision that transcends the particular. By focusing upon what is closest to her childhood, while still retaining the awareness of the nation and the world derived from sixty years of experience, Mrs. Wilder is able to look beyond the limits of the nineteenth-century Midwest, and to say something of value to Americans of all times and all regions. She writes in her books of the family and its role in society. She writes of the relationship of man to man. She writes of the use and misuse of nature. Within her limits, she writes of these and other topics in timeless terms. Many more serious authors never achieve as much.

TEXAS CHRISTIAN UNIVERSITY

Nature and Grace
in Caroline Gordon

LOUISE COWAN

In her short story, "Emmanuele! Emmanuele!" Caroline Gordon
has seized upon the Claudel-Gide contrast as a vehicle for an
exploration of two opposite attitudes toward the artist's function.
A young admirer of the celebrated Guillaume Fäy is discussing
Fäy's journals with the poet Raoul Pleyol:

> "In his journals he dares face himself. It is more than
> most of us can do. . . ."
>
> Pleyol said heavily: "It is a more than any of us can do
> . . . Do you think that a man sees himself when he looks
> into a mirror? He sees only the pose he has assumed. If you
> want to see yourself look into the eyes of your friends—or
> your enemies — who are made in the image of God."
>
> Heyward said stubbornly: "An artist's first duty is to
> confront himself."
>
> Pleyol brought his big hand down on the desk. "An
> artist's first duty is the same as any other man's — to serve,
> praise, and worship God."

Pleyol's is the orthodox Christian position, one which Miss
Gordon has displayed with increasing boldness in the last few
years — in her anthology *The House of Fiction* (edited jointly
with Allen Tate), in her critical essays on various writers, in
several short stories, and in the novels *The Strange Children* and
The Malefactors. The position reveals a Christian concept of the
artist deriving at least in part from the Southern culture in which
Miss Gordon was steeped.

In that it is concerned with a young man's struggle to as-
similate his heritage, Faulkner's *Absalom, Absalom!* may be taken
as representative of the Southern conception of the artist. On the
basis of this interpretation, it is instructive to contrast it with
Joyce's *Portrait of the Artist as a Young Man,* in which, as the
maturing Stephen Dedalus becomes more dedicated to his art,
he finds he must progressively sever the ties that bind him to
humanity. Finally, at the end of the work, it is "to forge the
uncreated conscience" of his race that he sets out. His purpose
is to bring into being a kind of truth that has not existed in
life itself, and he is fully cognizant of the dangers inherent in
such a task. In Faulkner's novel, on the contrary, Quentin Compson
finds himself increasingly bound to a way of life, a group of people,

and even a certain set of events — unwilling though he may be — as he is placed ever more surely in the position of viewer. His task has been to uncover what is already in existence, to uncover it and place it in the proper position to be recognized and known. His painful identification with the truth he sees and his suffering acceptance of his role are revealed in his cry, "I don't hate the South! I don't hate it!" — the antithesis of Stephen's cold rejection of his native land.

The difference in the two attitudes may be traced to the artist's conception of himself as subject to the creator and the laws of his creation or as artificer of an independent order. Modern Southern writers in general have regarded their task as the discovery of an already existent pattern in actual experience rather than as the imposition of an ideal pattern upon experience. Their unanimity of attitude is not traceable to a conscious aesthetic (for there has been no traditional Southern theory of art), but to an instinctively coherent way of dealing with the world, a way inherited from their culture and underlying their own personal vision of life. This world view can best be described, I think, by the word *sacramental,* since it is a way of looking at the physical universe as existing both in its own right and as a sign. But, to the Southerner, matter is not in any simple fashion an embodiment of spirit. Objects and creatures are real in themselves, and yet they are also mysteries, reflecting God and each other in a network of resemblances which at times illumine and at times veil the relationship between the creator and his creation. The mode of thought resulting from this attitude is analogical, and, though it is of course far older than the American South, it is not encountered consistently elsewhere in literature written in English since the seventeenth century.

What I have termed the sacramental attitude Caroline Gordon has described in an article ("Some Readings and Misreadings," *Sewanee Review,* Summer, 1953) as a "patient, passionate portrayal of natural objects" which, in being based on "a recognition of the natural order," she can only consider Christian, at least "in hope." She finds this kind of writing in Yeats and in the nineteenth-century masters of the art of fiction, from whom she learned her techniques. But many of the great nineteenth-century novels she finds to have a more direct indebtedness to Christianity, one grounded in revelation rather than immanence, for they embody unconsciously "the strange   and   original plot" of the

Christian scheme of redemption. From the study of her masters—
Flaubert, Turgenev, Chekhov, James, and the early Joyce — she
gained not only her distinguished technical competence but an
architecture basically Christian, one consistent "in hope" with
her heritage. Moreover, her own creative imagination has given
a remarkable integrity to the two traditions within which she
has worked; and, though the surface of her novels (before *The
Strange Children,* in 1951) moves toward destruction and despair,
the "current in their depths" moves in a strongly different direction.

"My stories, I think, are all one story, and as yet I hardly know
what the plot is," Caroline Gordon has written. "Like most
fiction writers, I seem to spend my life contemplating the same
set of events. Each novel is what I make of those events." It is
perhaps her short stories that provide the key to what is "the
same set of events," since they are of necessity more tightly
constructed than the novels and less involved in an expansive
enveloping action. Of the stories published in *The Forest of the
South* (1945), more than half deal with the special betrayal
involved in the man-woman relationship. In his admirable article
"Caroline Gordon and the Historic Image" *(Sewanee Review,*
Fall, 1949), Andrew Lytle has remarked in Miss Gordon's writings
the theme of man's inadequacy to woman and has given as demonstration a detailed analysis of the short story "The Brilliant
Leaves." This inadequacy of man is truly one of Miss Gordon's
persistent themes and the consequent turning away of the woman
one of the principal events in her stories. But there is another
betrayal in "The Brilliant Leaves," another event, so that I may
perhaps be forgiven if I consider the story further, taking advantage of Mr. Lytle's perceptive criticism. In this brief narrative,
a boy watches helpless while the girl he loves falls to her death
from a rocky ledge that she has wilfully insisted upon their
climbing. The account would be one of unmitigated and senseless
horror without the modifying and enlarging effect of the recurrent imagery which informs the story and, in reality, carries its
meaning. At the beginning, when the boy goes to keep an innocent assignation with the girl in the woods, he must pass his
mother and his aunt, who are sitting on the gallery, gossiping
about the people who live in the white houses — the little white
houses which, in the boy's eyes, cluster on the hill in all the
solidarity of the featureless but encompassing world which cups

his life. It is the boy who listens to the women on the porch
recount the tale which is at once the prelude to and the recapitula-
tion of the main story, and it is the boy who carries to the girl
the tale of betrayal by inadequacy — the story of an old maid,
Miss Sally Mainwaring, who, when a girl, descended a ladder
to find her father, shotgun in hand, and her lover disappearing
into the bushes. The woman's fate begins to be seen as an ironic
parallel to the young couple's when the boy proposes marriage
to the girl and is answered, "They wouldn't let us; we're too
young." By the time the pair comes to the falls, the reader has
been prepared for the powerful extensions of meaning in Miss
Gordon's careful description:

> They came out of the hollow and were on the brow of
> the mountain again. In front of them was a series of limestone
> ledges that came down one after another like steps. Gushing
> out from one of them, filling the whole air with the sound of
> its rushing, was the white waterfall they called the Bridal Veil.

This is the "ladder" the girl is to descend when her foot slips
and she falls backward; and like Miss Sally Mainwaring, she is
to find no human lover waiting for her below. But, before the
accident, standing over the precipice, her face moist from the
spray, she urges the boy to attempt the climb behind the falls.
"I like doing things with you," she confides, and, his cheeks
burning, he consents against his better judgment. Later, we know
from her failure to see the boy when he finally reaches her—
though her eyes are open — and from her screams when he
tries to lift her up that she feels herself bitterly betrayed.

But though the girl is betrayed, so too is the boy, albeit in
a less simple manner — by his trust in the benevolence of the
surrounding world. When he first leaves the chatting women on
the porch to follow a path into the woods, he halts once and
looks back, seeing the women and unconsciously knowing them
for what they are: the women for whom life — that inner life of
joy and adventure — has stopped. They are "on the shelf," viewing
experience from the outside, and their concern is with the civilized
and conventional white houses. As the boy enters the woods,
he sees under his feet the "brilliant, fallen leaves" and remembers
his aunt's comment about them the day before, when she had
returned from a walk; the entrance to the woods was "positively
spectacular," she had said; but she had gone no further into the

woods. The dazzling colors of the autumnal leaves were, like everything else for her, a matter for conversation. But in the boy's mind they are connected with the passion and excitement of the ripened moment, now when the two young people stand on the threshold of maturity, when their adolescent love has changed in its character. "It's different, isn't it?" the girl comments and, when she is questioned, replies, "Last time we were here the woods were just turning green." But after she has fallen from the ledge, the full comprehension of the plight of the leaves is left to the boy, who, running for help, understands them now, though only on the periphery of his own extremity:

> He ran slower now, lurching sometimes from side to side, but he ran on. He ran and the brilliant, the wine-colored leaves crackled and broke under his feet. His mouth, a taut square, drew in, released whining breaths. His starting eyes fixed the ground, but he did not see the leaves that he ran over. He saw only the white houses that no matter how fast he ran kept always just ahead of him. If he did not hurry they would slide off the hill, slide off and leave him running forever through these woods, over these dead leaves.

Time has frozen for the boy, and, with a nightmare-like clarity, he sees into the depths of his relationship with nature. He is engaged in an efforted and painful flight that takes him nowhere, with help from society beyond his reach. He is ineffectual and alone, and he sees that eternity could be like this one suspended moment. The fallen, brilliant leaves now are known for what they are: dead and dry bits of vegetation, cut off from their source; and likewise the boy must recognize the life of innocent joy and delight (the green leaves) irrecoverably gone and the dazzling and exciting life of adventure and passion (the brilliant leaves) heartbreakingly deceptive.

It has been written of Turgenev, whom out of the whole world of novelists Miss Gordon most resembles, that his women are strong, his men weak, and chance all-powerful. One might be tempted to substitute death (or time) for the word *chance* and to let the statement stand for Caroline Gordon's chief theme, particularly after a reading of "The Brilliant Leaves." But, though, as Mr. Lytle has suggested, the boy is inadequate to the girl in the grim drama, his inadequacy derives from his strength. Both are defeated by the conditions of human life — by being committed to nature, which carries within itself the principle of its own dissolution. The defeat is more painful in being of necessity solitary.

"The Brilliant Leaves" is almost parabolic, so clear, hard, and precise are its analogical formulations. And when we look back over Miss Gordon's novels, we realize that indeed it is a kind of parable, or — perhaps more properly — a dumb-show in which the events of the novels are acted out in shortened and pantomimic version. The constant set of events in all the novels revolves around man and woman, caught in mortality and seeking self-realization. Woman attempts to find fulfillment in love, whereas man looks outward to some aspect of "the world." Both become aware of their defeat at about the same time: a crisis may precipitate its sudden discovery, or it may lie hidden under the surface of an increasingly meaningless life. Two paths are open to the woman: to fall over the precipice into utter destruction, as does the girl in "The Brilliant Leaves," or to become one of the women on the porch, as does Miss Sally Mainwaring in the same story. But the men must engage themselves in perpetual flight. And for both sexes, the common enemy Death is constantly at hand, and, as time wears on, increasingly more bold in revealing himself.

"This slow, intricate dance" (a phrase Miss Gordon has used to describe the action of the man and woman in Chekhov's "On the Road") is performed against so many backgrounds and is seen from so many perspectives that it is not at first apparent as her chief situation. Her first novel, *Penhally* (1931), for instance, has as its central action the attempt by Nicholas Llewelleyn to hold intact the ancestral homeplace, established when the family came to Kentucky from Virginia. This principle, passed on by Nicholas to his nephew John, finds its final betrayal in the twentieth century, when John's elder grandson sells Penhally and is murdered by his outraged younger brother. But the mutual betrayal of lovers is a motif occurring throughout the book, coming more sharply into focus in John Llewelleyn's life, however, than in any of the others. John's betrayal of his cousin Alice Blair is made clear in an important scene: the pair are caught out in a storm, and Alice willingly rides back with him through a flooded stream; she is almost swept away when her horse is stricken by panic, and yet the experience, for her, is the triumphant

surrender of self to the man she trusts in love. But John never
"speaks to her," never seizes from the flood of time that moment
of commitment which, by open declaration, can be held against
eternity. In his own mind he has yielded her to his cousin Charley;
and after Charley is dead, when John has a second chance — and
this event we see only through John's reconstruction of incidents—
he lets her be swept from him toward the precipice, lost in a stream
she cannot cross without help. And Lucy, whom he has won
without opposition, without volition, chooses eventually to become
one of the women on the gallery:

> It was when the boy, Frank, was three years old that
> Lucy turned against him — as quietly and as surely as the
> bough that you have drawn aside swings back into place.
> He knew the very day, the hour, the minute even. A rainy
> day in early April. Coming by the woodpile in late afternoon
> he had filled a basket with chips and kindling and had
> taken them into the chamber, intending to make a blaze on
> the hearth. Lucy was there, the child in her arms. A cold
> grey light, filtered through dripping boughs, filled the room.
> Kneeling on the hearth, arranging his kindling, he had
> anticipated the way the blaze would in a minute start up
> and light all the room.

According to John's account, he knows the cause of her withdrawal; he analyzes it as pride, as the desire to be desired. He
does not see that pride is Lucy's last tool, seized in desperation,
to protect herself from the anguish of further vulnerability. An
action on his part would have changed reality, it seems to him;
but he is too tired: "There was always somewhere in his mind a
very deep pool of weariness." There are Alice, Penhally, the War
— all these things have so fatigued him that he cannot raise his
hands to halt Lucy's turning away.

John Llewelleyn's defeat may conceivably be laid to the decline
of a way of life to which he is loyal and from which he derives
his strength (though I think not), but *Aleck Maury, Sportsman*
(1934) provides a more detailed examination of man's commitment to the world and shows that it is *per se* foredoomed to failure,
regardless of social or economic corruptions. Aleck Maury's commitment is to nature; at eight years he falls prey to the delusion
that he can learn her secrets if he approaches her with loving
and reverent service. His life is spent in a progressively more

frantic pursuit which, at the end of the work, shows itself for what it is: a flight, in which he has become the hunted rather than the hunter.

Aleck Maury's passion for nature insulates him even from the decline of the Southern culture. He accommodates himself easily to the diminished interest in the study of the classics; and he views his real interest less as an inherited ritual than as a personal quest. His inability to face with equanimity the people he has known in the past does not stem from a nostalgia for an old way of life, but from a perception of the mutability inherent in the human condition. All Maury's memories are connected with the unbearable poignancy of the passage of time and the impending awareness of death: there is his first possum hunt, where he is brought face to face with the quarry and looks into "those burning eyes" for, it seems, an eternity before he hears the gunshot and sees the gray ball drop at his feet; there is Old Red, the fleet and cunning fox, who is at last caught by Old Whiskey, the champion foxhound. He sees death as an inexorable law of nature, not only between different kinds but within a species, when the quail cocks, shut up in a room together, kill each other in mass destruction. And, in the tragi-comic scene where the mare sinks slowly to the ground under Uncle Jack, who has with age become too fat to ride, Maury sees that death is inflicted not only from outside man, but also slowly and certainly from within. Time itself is death. And with this understanding comes an increased desire to spend his time in "the life of adventure and deep, secret excitement" that hunting and fishing bring to him.

Since the novel assumes the form of Maury's memories, we know nothing of Molly's feelings after their marriage, though they can be assumed from her reproach once when Maury showed himself more concerned over the prospect of losing Gyges, his dog, than Dick, their son. The death of the son several years later is the crisis destroying finally the unity of the two and causing in Molly the same turning away that was observed in Lucy. Molly lives through her grief essentially alone, and Maury is forced to record the barrier that exists between them from then on. "Yet I believe I loved him in my own way as much as Molly did," he writes. But hereafter Molly's inner life is no longer shared with him. She withholds from him the knowledge of her illness and dies with no word to him. Left alone and in possession, finally, of the freedom he has long sought, he finds it tasteless; he must scheme and plan to eke out his furtive glimmers of delight, but he finds only the hollowness of death waiting for him at every turn. Yet his defeat and betrayal are not the result of his changed methods in approaching nature; the planning and scheming are implicit from the first in Maury's passion. There is no ending possible for his drama except the cunning and flight of the hunted animal; Maury's merging of himself with the fox in the short story "Old Red" is an unconscious admission that he knows himself trapped in nature.

The "same set of events" is encountered again in Miss Gordon's Civil War novel *None Shall Look Back* (1937), although in it the marriage of Lucy Churchill and Rives Allard is of such short duration before Rives is killed at the Battle of Franklin that the ultimate "turning" is implied rather than realized. But in her dedication to her husband's love Lucy's daily portion is death, just as, in his commitment to the defeated South, it is death itself that he serves. Rives dies a hero's death — a fate which throughout history has been considered a means of self-tran- scendence. Yet for Rives there is no triumph in giving himself, and this lack is not attributable to the defeat of his cause. At the time of his death Rives is in flight from life. Abstracted in his single-minded pursuit, he has cut himself off from Lucy's love and has looked too deeply into the natural order, where he has discovered the vanity of man's existence. A brief scene which he recalls later becomes an epiphany, revealing to him the nature of human life. Once, when his regiment had been forced to pass over a field of wounded soldiers, one man who had kindled a small fire turned his eyes for a moment on Rives' face:

> The dark glance had been enigmatic but there had been in it a flicker of the hostility with which men look on at un- bearable suffering. It was as if the man dying in the circle of the firelight could not endure the spectacle of the living, who were only riding toward death.

At the news of Rives' death, Lucy in amazement watches his mother weep. "She has never seen him die before," she thinks; and though she knows she should comfort the old woman, she cannot pull herself away from the window, where she stands looking out over the landscape (as did Lucy Llewelleyn and Molly Maury before her):

The sun dropped behind the pines. She watched the light go from the sky and knew that when she saw the green fields of Kentucky again they would be as alien as the gullied pine-clad slopes outside the window.

Because she is a woman, she does not run, as Aleck Maury does, from time and nothingness; where he seeks frantically to justify himself in nature, she rejects the physical world and is alienated, actually, from the mortal condition.

Technically less proficient than her other novels — perhaps because it is her first full-length attempt in the modern idiom — *The Garden of Adonis* (1937) is nevertheless instructive of further aspects of Miss Gordon's central situation. Persistently present in it is the motif of woman's betrayal in love. In one plot, Idelle Sheeler, the daughter of shiftless poor whites, is like Alice Blair in *Penhally* in choosing security rather than uncertain love. In the other plot of the novel, Letty Allard, a descendant of the Allard clan of *None Shall Look Back,* pursues a passionate affair with a married man, Jim Carter, to the inevitable flight together into the abyss of selfishness and sensuality. Letty is betrayed by herself, perhaps, as much as by Jim, but there are others he has known and injured in passing. In particular, with Sara, his wife, there has been that same moment of turning, when in her hurt and pride she refuses to admit her need for Jim and takes the path instead of withdrawal. The real cause of his elopement with Letty, however, is indicated in a comment made by his dentist:

> "Nature," Ogden had said. "You see up to the time you're forty she's on your side. Everything is for building up . . . But after you pass forty or forty-five, after you get on the wrong side of the slope, it's different. Everything's giving way then. It's slow, so slow you can hardly notice what's happened from year to year, but it's going on all the time. It takes almost as long as the first building-up process and when it's finished you're old — or dead."

Miss Gordon has prefaced *The Garden of Adonis* with a passage from *The Golden Bough* explaining her title. The gardens of Adonis were baskets of earth in which the plants, tended by women, grew rapidly: "but having no root they withered as rapidly away, and at the end of eight days were carried out with the images of the dead Adonis and flung with them into the sea or into springs." The Southern land itself, of course, is a garden of Adonis: held by Ben Allard, Letty's father, against the mounting debt, it can supply no sustenance for the love between Ote Mortimer and Idelle Sheeler but can only provide a temporary nuptial couch for Letty and Jim. But since the defeat and destruction of these characters are attributable to causes in no way peculiar to a specific locale — nor even generically to a declining society — the idea is suggested to us that nature itself is the inadequate garden ,since it cannot sustain and nourish man, the essentially rootless plant.

Green Centuries (1941) has as its enveloping action the westward movement into Kentucky just before the American Revolution. Miss Gordon quotes on one of the section pages of this novel a passage from a letter of Flaubert mentioning "the innate loathing of life which compelled [barbarian tribes] to abandon their country as if abandoning themselves." It is this flight to which Orion Outlaw is committed, lured on by the kind of dream that only men such as he and Daniel Boone can have. But by the last chapter, though American settlers have established and held a new community in Indian territory, Rion, "the mighty hunter," reflects on the futility of man's conquests:

> His father had come west across the ocean, leaving all that he cared about behind. And he himself as soon as he had grown to manhood had looked at the mountains and could not rest until he knew what lay beyond them. But it seemed that a man had to flee farther each time and leave more behind him and when he got to the new place he looked up and saw Orion fixed upon his burning wheel, always pursuing the bull but never making the kill . . . Were not men raised into the westward turning stars only after they had destroyed themselves?

Of all the women in Miss Gordon's novels, Cassy is most pathetic. She loves her husband with the terrible certainty of the pure-hearted, yet her courage, endurance, and unselfishness bring her nothing but bitter annihilation in the new country, at her husband's side. Before she leaves Virginia, after surrendering herself to Rion, a visit to her father's grave gives her an insight into the implications of mortality: bemused, gazing down at the grave, she sees the red earth and the vegetation as a thin veil, hiding the white bones at the bottom of the pit. Years

later, when she "turns" against her husband, screaming as Rion
had once seen a horse scream when it was trapped by high water,
he accepts the inevitablity of the event: "It had come then. He
had always known it would, when he stopped to think about it,
and yet he had always felt safe minute by minute." Love such
as Cassy's is a gift, he recognizes, and since it is not in the order
of nature, it can be withdrawn. But nothing short of hurtling
over the precipice would have made Cassy withdraw her love.

In *The Women on the Porch* (1944) can be seen for the
first time the proper order and arrangement of the events to
form the complete pattern of Caroline Gordon's "plot." Marriage
itself — in its idea and its actuality — is the subject of this
novel; the enveloping action and the other characters are shaped
around the drama of Catherine and Jim Chapman. The same
set of events occurs, but the temporal pattern — which in her
other works Miss Gordon has shown as ending in the observable
motifs of withdrawal, flight, and death — is seen in this novel
to have its roots in eternity .

The two alternatives which Miss Gordon's women choose
— the cliff or the gallery — face Catherine Chapman when she
discovers her husband's infidelity: fleeing New York, she is
directed by her intellect to the desperate waters of the Mississippi
but by her unconscious will to Swan Quarter, her family home in
Tennessee, where, fighting her way through the brambles, she
faces the women on the porch. They who have turned aside
sit there in their despair, in their courage, and in their fear. Cousin
Daphne, insulted and injured by the desertion of her husband
on her wedding night, wanders the woodland to pluck with
esoteric craft the benevolent mushroom from its fatal counterfeit.
Miss Willy, whose life is one of immolation without joy,
endures for the purpose of enduring. And Old Miss Kit,
recognizing that death is at hand — "has been all along" — faces
only the horror of ceaseless wandering without identity. And
behind them, like a black shadow, is old Aunt Maria, a sort of
inverse Virgin Mary, with her husband Uncle Joe and her martyred
son Jesse. (Aunt Maria's love of her son and participation in
his "crucifixion" bring her only bitterness; and her second sight
is into sin, not grace.) A new possibility comes to Catherine,
however, out of the land of her ancestors: the life of fertility
and meaning which first bursts upon her in the presence of
a beautiful red stallion, virgin yet but ready to stand, seeming

both the product and the progenitor of nature. In the prospect
of marrying Tom Manigault, her cousin and the owner of the
neighboring quarter, Catherine recognizes her chance for the
simple earthy pleasures: "It is the life I was made for," she
thinks, "the life which I have always missed."

It is part of the workings of the novel to show that both
Tom and the stallion are flawed: the horse, stepped on by his
mother soon after his birth, was nursed back to health and
apparent soundness by Miss Willy and Mr. Shannon, who is for
Miss Willy the counterpart of Tom Manigault; Tom, injured by
his mother's rejection when he was young, is unable to love the
land or a woman without constraint. Tom and the stallion represent
nature, which in its fallen and wounded state turns in upon
itself instead of reflecting its creator. And Catherine, caught up
in that nature, repudiates it, arising from the sylvan couch she
thought to call her wedding bed to find herself lost in the
wods: "I have made a mistake," she thinks; "I have taken the
wrong road . . . "

The husband she has left in New York, Jim Chapman, a
professor of history, has been misled — by middle age, by
fatigue, by rootlessness — into a half-hearted love affair. At
Catherine's turning away from him — an actual geographical
movement, dramatizing her withdrawal, which the women in
Miss Gordon's novels set in the past would have found socially
castigable — Jim is cut off and isolated, and like the boy in "The
Brilliant Leaves" he can only run toward the white houses seeking
for help. The first page of the *Divine Comedy*, however, viewed
in a discussion with college students, is his first step toward
self-knowledge:

> In the middle of the journey of our life I came to myself
> in a dark wood where the straight way way lost.

Seeking Catherine, he comes to Swan Quarter fatigued and ineffectual, and confronted with his wife's unfaithfulness, he attempts
to strangle her in an attempt to prevent his total engulfment in
nothingness. His hands seem to have a life of their own, a
fact indicating the almost total separation in him of body and
spirit, and without Catherine's urgency to save him (not herself)
he would have killed her.

That their marriage cannot be destroyed is the one overwhelming
reality with which Jim and Catherine are left: not his adultery

nor hers, nor the desire of either, nor physical violence can destroy the ties that bind them together. Both have had inklings of this indissolubility apart; the knowledge has come to them in dreams and images. An unconscious perception that one has committed oneself for eternity in marriage comes to Chapman when he recalls a friend's dream that she and her husband had mounted an elevated railway to find the rails extending into infinity. In one of Catherine's dreams, in which she must conduct a dead man safely through a dark tunnel to a grave, "from which, it was hoped, he would rise," she is told that she must be careful, that the safety of the man depends on her alone. But the actuality of their bond is revealed to them in the simple ceremony of making coffee together after their storm of self-concern has passed. By her humbling of pride in not turning away irrevocably and by his refusal to take flight, they destroy the natural barriers which time throws up to isolate man in a finite world.

Mr. Lytle has spoken of Miss Gordon's failure to make us believe in the reconciliation of Jim Chapman and his wife, designating this one flaw as a crack in her otherwise faultless structure. This apparent lack of motive does seem indeed a crack, though perhaps it would be better to call it an aperture, through which something supernatural enters into the dramatic framework of the novel. We do not need to believe in the vitality of Catherine's and Jim's love for each other, since it is not the strength of their love which brings them back together but something which results from the sacrament of their bond. And since Miss Gordon does not desert her naturalistic method, this supernatural intrusion can be surmised only from the apparently powerful mutual change of heart and from the controlling symbols within the whole work.

The symbol of water as both destruction and salvation permeates the novel. By the healing effect of water Jim Chapman is saved in his crisis: both aspects of water are at hand for him to choose — the black, still pool in which to fling himself, or the fresh, clear spring. It is death by water Catherine seeks, on her way to Swan Quarter, coming with a surfeit of pain and loss and an unrecognized thirst for salvation. She intends to drive past Swan Quarter through Nashville to Atlanta, to New Orleans and on into the muddy water:

But it would not stay yellow. Swirling over your head, it
would change, to blue, to green, to purple laced with foam.
Where'er thy bones are hurled.

Here is expressed her unconscious insight into the transformation
worked by water. And though both Jim and Catherine picture
Time as a flood which engulfs and destroys them, they are
aware too of the gentle, healing power of water. Both are
attracted to "the lady tree" (symbol of the Mediatrix of grace)
standing by the spring at Swan Quarter, out of which Catherine
herself has swept the debris — the spring that can convert
destruction into balm.

The vanquishing of Jim's brutal hands is a foreshadowing of
the death of the stallion, the carnal element that must be shattered
before grace may grow. The last words of the novel, "We'll bury him
when it's light, and then we'll go," are profoundly reverberatory,
revealing the events of the novel as the agonies of childbirth
rather than of death. The characters are looking toward dawn
now, whereas when Catherine first came to Swan Quarter,
everything was seen "under a western light." Emphasized also in
this last sentence is the idea that though conversion may have
taken place, the process of enlightenment is not yet accomplished;
action and growth will occur after "it's light" and the old, sinful self
is buried.

The Women on the Porch, then, completes the sequence of
events inchoate in the other novels so that one can perceive the
"one story" Miss Gordon has been writing about all along: man's
search for grace in a fallen world. According to orthodox Christian
theology, grace is the supernatural life of the soul, the more
abundant life of which Christ spoke, the participation in the
life of God. It is this plenitude which Adam lost in the fall,
and it is the lack of the plenitude which nature suffers in its
present wounded state. The life everlasting for which the soul
yearns is not to be found in mere human love, nor in nature,
nor in the pursuit of new horizons but in the life with Christ
in God. Nature, though not entirely cut off from God, because
of its ambiguity cannot without grace afford man a path to
salvation. As Jean Mouroux has written (in *The Meaning of
Man),* "Nature will always set before us both the Dionysian
and the Christian lesson, because she is big with both possibilities
and because it is for man to actualize the one or the other, saving

or submerging the creation in the act of fulfilling himself."

In the writings preceding *The Women on the Porch* Miss Gordon's characters are defeated in their attempts to fulfill themselves (and to redeem creation) because they flee from their finiteness and thus do not prepare by utter self-immolation the ground into which the gratuitous gift of grace can enter. The last three novels, however, include in their scope the operations of grace, as opposed to nature alone and unaided. *The Strange Children* and *The Malefactors,* much more overtly than *The Women on the Porch,* delineate the workings of grace in the soul, since since in them the religious theme is apparent and undisguised. This change rather than any subsidiary one indicates that at the time of her conversion to Catholicism Caroline Gordon entered upon a stage of artistic productivity in which she examined openly and clearly those concerns which in her earlier work she had treated obscurely though powerfully. If one is to judge from the published chapter of her new novel (*The Sewanee Review,* Autumn, 1969), Miss Gordon has begun a further extension of her range; and though it would be arrant presumption to predict what any subsequent writing will be like, one can now with some feeling of completeness survey the work leading up to this point.

University of Dallas

NOTES

"The Polylithic Romance: With Pages of Illustrations"

*The topics here developed have been considered since the mid-fifties in graduate and undergraduate classes at Texas Technological College and Texas Christian University and in papers read at the University of Kentucky Foreign Language Conference, April 25-27, 1963, and at the Work in Progress Forum of the English Department of North Texas State University on November 19, 1969. It is a pleasure to express again to my students and to my hosts in Lexington and in Denton my gratitude for fruitful stimulus and multiple kindnesses. The illustrative citations which follow record a further indebtedness, one extending indeed to all students of medieval letters, whether named or unnamed, from Ker and Kittredge to Frye and Bloomfield and beyond to the younger scholars of our declining century.

[1]Morton W. Bloomfield, "Sir Gawain and the Green Knight: An Appraisal," PMLA, LXXVI (1961), 17. Quoted by permission of the author.

[2]Northrop Frye, Anatomy of Criticism (Princeton, 1957), p. 50.

[3]Verses 1512-1513, as translated by M. R. Ridley in his Story of Sir Gawain and the Green Knight in Modern English (Leicester, Eng., 1944), p. 63.

[4]Anatomy of Criticism, pp. 33-35. 42-43, 48-50, 65, 147-150, 239, and passim.

[5]The traditional classifications of medieval romance are based chiefly on subject matter and geographical provenance. In the published part of the 1967 Manual of the Writings in Middle English, 1050-1500 (Fascicule I: Romances; J. B. Severs, general editor — [New Haven: Connecticut Academy of Arts and Sciences]), the classification follows that of the Wells 1916 Manual: native English, Arthurian, romances of Charlemagne and of the Crusades, legends of antiquity, Breton lays, and miscellaneous romances. Laura Hibbard Loomis's Medieval Romance in England (New York, 1960; first ed., 1924) includes native English romances and others designated as "romances of trial and faith" and "romances of love and adventure." See also W. P. Ker, Epic and Romance (London, 1896); N. E. Griffin, "The Definition of Romance," PMLA, XXXVIII (1923), 50-70; Dorothy Everett, Essays on Middle English Literature (Oxford, 1955), pp. 1-22; D. M. Hill, "Romance as Epic," English Studies, XLIV (1963), 95-107; Frye, Anatomy of Criticism; A. C. Gibbs, Middle English Romances (York Medieval Texts; Evanston, Illinois, 1966), pp. 1-27; and especially Dieter Mehl, The Middle English Romances of the Thirteenth and Fourteenth Centuries (New York, 1969, pp. 13-39 and passim). Mehl classifies Middle English romances as "shorter," "longer," "homiletic," and "novels in verse." His awareness of the variety and complexity of these romances is more perceptive and sophisticated than such an elementary taxonomy may suggest.

[6]P. 63.

[7]On Jean de Meun's part of the Roman de la Rose as a "philosophical romance," see the present writer's The Mirror of Love: A Reinterpretation of "The Romance of the Rose" (Lubbock, Texas, 1951, 1952), esp. pp. 199-314.

[8]J. A. Burrow, A Reading of Sir Gawain and the Green Knight (London, 1965), pp. 180-181; and Frye, pp. 49-51. The passage from pp. 50-51 is here quoted again by permission of the Princeton University Press.

[9]See Vinaver's discussion on pp. lxv-lxx of the introduction of his Works of Sir Thomas Malory, (2nd ed., Oxford, 1967).

[10]See Judith Weiss's recent study, "Structure and Characterization in Havelok the Dane," Speculum, XLIV (April, 1969), 247-257. See also Mehl, pp. 161-172, for an even more illuminating analysis.

[11]See J. Burke Severs, "The Antecedents of Sir Orfeo," in Studies in Medieval Literature in Honor of Professor A. C. Baugh (Philadelphia, 1961); G. V. Smithers, "Story-Patterns in Some Breton Lays," Medium Aevum, XXII (1953), 61-91; Donald

B. Sands, *Middle English Verse Romances* (New York, 1966), pp. 185-187; Mortimer J. Donovan, *The Breton Lay: A Guide to Varieties* (Notre Dame, Ind., 1969); Mehl, pp. 40-44; and A. J. Bliss's treatment of the literary qualities of *Sir Orfeo* on pp. xli-xiv of his second edition of the romance (Oxford, 1966).

[12]See Kemp Malone, *Chapters on Chaucer* (Baltimore, 1951), pp. 105-108.

[13]See R. K. Root's edition of *Troilus and Criseyde* (Princeton, 1916), pp. xvi-xviii, xxxiii-xxxiv.

[14]Root, passages cited.

[15]A listing of *Troilus* scholarship and criticism is available in A. C. Baugh, *Chaucer* (Goldentree Bibliographies, New York, 1968), pp. 38-46. See esp. D. C. Boughner, "Elements of Epic Grandeur in the *Troilus*," *ELH*, VI (1939), 200-210; and Elizabeth Salter, "*Troilus and Criseyde:* A Reconsideration," in *Patterns of Love and Courtesy: Essays in Memory of C. S. Lewis,* ed. John Lawlor (London, 1966), pp. 86-106.

[16]More recently in exegetical criticism the emphasis has been upon the three levels of *littera, sensus,* and *sententia.* See D. W. Robertson, Jr., *A Preface to Chaucer: Studies in Medieval Perspectives* (Princeton, 1962); B. F. Huppé and D. W. Robertson, Jr., *Fruyt and Chaf: Studies in Chaucer's Allegories* (Princeton, 1963), esp. pp. 3-31.

[17]Cf. the essay by Elizabeth Salter cited above.

[18]See Baugh, pp. 67-70. Key studies are those by Edward B. Ham, "Knight's Tale 38," *ELH*, XVII (1950), 252-261; and Charles Muscatine, "Form, Texture, and Meaning in Chaucer's *Knight's Tale*," *PMLA, LXV* (1950), 911-929.

[19]See Stuart Robertson, "Elements of Realism in the *Knight's Tale*," *Journal of English and Germanic Philology,* XIV (1915), 226-255.

[20]On the intensity and recurrence of the mood of pathos in Chaucer's poetry, see G. H. Gerould's *Chaucerian Essays* (Princeton, 1952), pp. 81-92; and in John Lawlor's *Chaucer* (London, 1968), p. 67 and *passim.*

[21]Chaucer's awareness of modes and genres is expressed in these familiar passages: *Troilus and Criseyde,* V, 1786-1792; *Legend of Good Women* (F version), 414-430; and in the *Canterbury Tales* in the *General Prologue,* 725-798, the "Introduction" to the *Man of Law's Tale,* 46-96, in the links before and after the *Monk's Tale,* 1991-1998, 2777-2805, and in the poet's *Retractions.* Yet these are only the most explicit and the most personal expressions of his consciousness of the nature and the variety of the types, modes, and styles of poetry; a multitude of others, some hardly less explicit, witness to his continuing fascination with the protean art of verse.

[22]G. L. Kittredge, *Chaucer and His Poetry* (Cambridge, Mass., 1915), *passim* but esp. pp. 45 ff.

[23]G. V. Smithers has argued in his article on "Story-Patterns in Some Breton Lays" (pp. 89-92) that the poet designated his romance by his use of the term *laye,* and that "the immediate antecedent of *GGK* was a literary Breton lay" (p. 91). Cf. Laura Hibbard Loomis, "Gawain and the Green Knight," in *Arthurian Literature in the Middle Ages,* ed. R. S. Loomis (Oxford, 1959), p. 537.

[24]Cf. Charles Moorman, "Myth and Mediaeval Literature: *Sir Gawain and the Green Knight*," *Mediaeval Studies,* XVIII (1956), 158-172, esp. pp. 164-165.

[25]See Hans Schnyder, *Sir Gawain and the Green Knight: An Essay in Interpretation* (Bern, 1961). Cf. D. W. Robertson, cited in note 16.

[26]On the elements of ambiguity and mystery in *Sir Gawain and the Green Knight,* see the article by Bloomfield cited above, esp. p. 19. His survey has now been supplemented by R. W. Ackerman's "*Sir Gawain and the Green Knight* and Its Interpreters," included in *On Stage and Off: Eight Essays in English Literature* (Pullman, Wash., 1968); see pp. 66-73.

[27]Cf. again Bloomfield, p. 17.

[28]See John Speirs, *Medieval English Poetry: The Non-Chaucerian Tradition* (London, 1957); J. L. Weston, *From Ritual to Romance* (London, 1920); Heinrich

Zimmer, *The King and the Corpse* (New York, 1948); W. A. Nitze, "Is the Green Knight Story a Vegetation Myth?" *Modern Phiology*, XXXIII (1956), 158-172; Charles Moorman, "Myth and Medieval Literature," and *The Pearl Poet* (New York, 1968), esp. pp. 101-102, 104-107. Cf. Gibbs, pp. 10-11.

[29]See, e.g., C. S. Lewis, "The Anthropological Approach," in *English and Medieval Studies Presented to J.R.R. Tolkien* (London, 1962), pp. 219-230.

[30]Cf. John Sturrock, *The French New Novel* (London, 1969), esp. pp. 5-8.

"A Metrical and Stylistic Study of 'The Tale of Gamelyn' "

[1]The poem is available in several anthologies, the most available of which are Walter French and Charles Hale, eds., *Middle English Metrical Romances* (New York, 1930), and Donald B. Sands, ed., *Middle English Verse Romances* (New York, 1966). The only scholarly edition is Walter W. Skeat, ed., *The Tale of Gamelyn* (Oxford, 1884, 2nd ed., 1893). *Gamelyn* is also included in Skeat's edition of *The Complete Works of Geoffrey Chaucer* (Oxford, 1894).

[2]Skeat, *The Tale of Gamelyn*, pp. xxiii-xxvii.

[3]Skeat's italics. P. xxvi.

[4]William Ellery Leonard, "The Scansion of Middle English Alliterative Verse," *University of Wisconsin Studies in Language and Literature*, II (Madison, 1920), 58-104.

[5]Laura Hibbard Loomis, *Medieval Romance in England*, 2nd ed. (New York, 1960), p. 158; John Edwin Wells, *A Manual of the Writings in Middle English, 1050-1500* (New Haven, Conn., 1916), p. 27.

[6]Donald B. Sands, *Middle English Verse Romances*, p. 156.

[7]F. Lindner, *Englische Studien*, II (1879), 101-108.

[8]Skeat, pp. xxvi-xxvii.

[9]Sands, p. 156.

[10]For reasons which will be clear later in the paper, lines quoted from *Gamelyn* are taken from MS. Corpus Christi 198 rather than from the more readily available edition by Skeat. The Corpus MS. is available in Frederick J. Furnivall, ed., *A Six-Text Print of Chaucer's Canterbury Tales* (The Chaucer Society, London, 1868).

[11]Skeat, p. xxvi.

[12]Leonard, p. 67.

[13]Marie Borroff, *Sir Gawain and the Green Knight: A Stylistic and Metrical Study* (New Haven, Conn., 1962), p. 174.

[14]George R. Stewart, Jr., "The Meter of Piers Plowman," *PMLA*, XLII (1927), 113-128.

[15]Leonard, p. 73.

[16]Borroff, p. 182.

[17]Borroff, p. 178.

[18]Albert B. Lord, *The Singer of Tales* (Cambridge, Mass., 1960). For treatment of the Middle English tradition see Albert C. Baugh, "Improvisation in the Middle English Romance," *Proceedings of the American Philosophical Society*, LIII (1957), 418-54; or Ronald A. Waldron, "Oral-Formulaic Technique and Middle English Alliterative Poetry," *Speculum*, XXXII (1957), 792-804.

[19]Lindner, p. 98.

[20]See C. S. Lewis, "The Fifteenth Century Heroic Line," *Essays and Studies by Members of the English Association*, XXIV (1938), 28-41, and Northrop Frye, *Anatomy of Criticism* (Princeton, N. J., 1957), pp. 251-262. It is of some interest that whereas Stewart and Borroff use Meredith's *Love in the Valley* as an example of a clearly dipodic or compound meter, Frye uses Meredith's poem to illustrate the four-stress line.

[21]Sands, p. 156.

[22]Borroff, p. 182.

[23]Presented to Indiana University, 1967.

[24]Eleanor P. Hammond, *English Verse Between Chaucer and Surrey* (1927; reprinted, New York, 1965), pp. ix-x.

[25]Alan Swallow, "The Pentameter Lines in Skelton and Wyatt," *Modern Philology,* XXVIII (1950), 1-11, holds this view of fifteenth century prosody along with Lewis and Frye.

[26]Frye, p. 251.

[27]Seymour Chatman, in *A Theory of Meter* (The Hague, 1965), demonstrates that there is no objective or scientifically measurable component of speech which can be equated with ictus (metrical stress).

"John of Angoulême and His Chaucer Manuscript"

*Reprinted from *Speculum,* XVII (1942), 86-99. Some revisions have been made throughout, mainly bibliographical.

[1]Cf. the description of *Ps* in J. M. Manly and Edith Rickert's *The Text of the Canterbury Tales* (Chicago, 1940), I, 399-405. For other descriptions of *Ps,* see Gustave Dupont-Ferrier, 'Jean l'Orléans, comte l'Angoulême, d'apres sa bibliothèque', *Bibliothèque de la faculté des lettres de Paris,* III (1897), 64; Johann Halfmann, *Das auf der Bibliothèque zu Paris befindliche Manuscript der Canterbury Tales* (Kiel, 1898); Gaston Raynaud, 'Catalogue des manuscrits anglais de la Bibliothèque Nationale,' *Cabinet historique,* XXIX (1883), 582-583; William McCormick, *Manuscripts of Chaucer's Canterbury Tales* (Oxford, 1933), pp. 379-386.

[2] Cf. C. Johnson and H. Jenkinson, *English Court Hand,* A.D. *1066-1500* (Oxford, 1915), p.xxi; also plates xxxiv and xxxviii.

[3]See below, n. 11.

[4]Dupont-Ferrier, pp. 41-42, 64.—Angoulême's manuscript of Petrarch's *Division and Profit of Prayer* also has on the first page his coat of arms, but here it is the second pendant which is charged with a crescent (*ibid.,* p. 77). According to A. C. Fox-Davies, *The Art of Heraldry* (London, 1904), p. 344, and according to Charles Grandmaison, *Dictionnaire héraldique* (Paris, 1852), col. 92, Angoulême added for brisure a crescent gules on each point of the lambel of the arms of the dukes of Orléans. Also, the coat of arms on Angoulême's portrait in A. Thevet's *Protraits et vies des hommes illustres* (Paris, 1584), reproduced by Pierre Champion in his *Vie de Charles d'Orléans* (Paris, 1911), plate VII, opposite p. 353, shows the lambel charged with three crescents. Leopold Delisle, in his *Cabinet des manuscrits de la Bibliothèque Impériale* (Paris, 1868-81), I, 148, says the second pendant was charged with a crescent gules. Dupont-Ferrier, pp. 41-42, corroborates Delisle in a note which shows evidence of careful research. The attachment of the crescent to the first pendant on the coat of arms in *Ps* is heraldically wrong, according to Dupont-Ferrier, p. 64; though the arms are of course Angoulême's, the crescent should appear on the second pendant.

[5]Cf. Dupont-Ferrier, p. 64.

[6]Champion, p. 450. — An account of the life of John of Angoulême is contained in *Dictionnaire de Biographie Francaise* (Paris, 1935), fascicule XI, cols. 1219-21. See also Charles Lafon, "Louis d'Orléans et Jean d'Angoulême, comtes de Périgord (1400-1437)," *Bulletin de la Société historique et archéologique du Périgord,* LXXXIV (1957), part 4, pp. 165-9; *Nouveau Dictionnaire des Biographies francaises at étrangéres* (Paris, 1964), I, 541. The five hundredth anniversary of the death of Jean d'Angoulême was commemorated at Angoulême on April 30, 1967. An account of his 'saintly and heroic' life was prepared by Patrick Esclafer and a summary published in *Mémoires,* Société archéologique et historique de la Charente (Angouléme, 1967), No. 4. p. 55.

[7] Dupont-Ferrier states that the duke of Clarence on his own authority added 60,000 crowns to the 150,000 agreed upon in the treaty of Buzancais ('La captivité de Jean d'Orléans, comte d'Angoulême,' *Revue historique,* LXII [September-December, 1896], 44). It appears, however, that this statement is erroneous. The duke of

Orléans and his party, having asked the English to aid them in their struggle with the duke of Burgundy, had agreed to pay the English 150,000 crowns in cash. Finding themselves unable to raise this sum at once, the French agreed in the treaty of Buzancais to give 210,000 crowns in deferred payments, security for the payments being offered in the form of hostages, one of whom was John of Angoulême (J. H. Wylie, *History of England under Henry IV* [London, 1898], IV, 81). Dupont-Ferrier bases his statement on original documents in the British Museum and the Bibliothèque Nationale which I have not yet been able to examine. However, C. P. Cooper, in appendix D of his *Report on Rymer's Foedera* (London, 1835?), p. 147, furnishes proof that the French agreed to pay the sum of 210,000 crowns on November 14, 1412, the date of the treaty of Buzancais. The 60,000 crowns could not, therefore, have been added by Clarence on his own authority after the treaty had been signed. This conclusion derives further support from Monstrelet, who states that the duke of Orléans paid the duke of Clarence all that he could, but, as he could not then advance the whole sum owed the duke of Clarence, he gave, as a pledge for the due fulfillment of his engagement, his youngest brother and six others as hostages (Enguerrand de Monstrelet, *Chronicles, 1400-1467*, trans. Thomas Johnes [London, 1877], I, 228).

[8] The date commonly given for the birth of John of Angoulême is June 26, 1404 (cf. L. Mas-Latrie, *Tresor de chronologie et de géographie* [Paris, 1889], p. 1538). The only authority for this date is Jean du Port's biography of Angoulême, published in 1589, a work proved to be inaccurate in many respects. E. Jarry was the first to set an earlier date for Angoulême's birth. He presents evidence based on a study of documents relating to the Orléans family to show that John, the third son of Louis de France, was born between October 30, 1399, and May 5, 1400 (*La vie politique de Louis de France, duc d'Orléans* [Paris, 1889], p. 231). Later Dupont-Ferrier made a study of the subject and concluded that the count was born between May 1 and August 7, 1399 ('La date de la naissance de Jean d'Orléans, comte d'Angoulême,' *Bibliothèque de l'école des chartes,* LVI [1895], 518-527). Dupont-Ferrier's argument rests on two statements found in documents in the Bibliothèque Nationale (*MS. fr. 20379* and the testament of Louis de France, dated August 7, 1399), in the Doat collection). The first statement is that on May 1, 1399, Louis de France received from the king 'houppelandes' for his *two* sons; the second is that on August 7, 1399, in his testament of that date, Louis de France names John as one of his *three* sons.

[9]Dupont-Ferrier, *Revue historique,* LXII (1896), 47.

[10]Dupont-Ferrier, p. 57.

[11]Dupont-Ferrier, pp. 59-60.—During the years of quiet immediately following the disastrous failure of 1422 I think it probable that Angoulême had his Chaucer manuscript made. The date of the making of the manuscript must not be placed too near 1412, because we must allow time for Angoulême, who was just a boy when he first arrived in England, to learn English and to develop an interest in Chaucer. Nor must the date be placed too near 1445, because in the last years of Angoulême's captivity he was making such great efforts to free himself that he would have had little leisure for working with manuscripts. Between 1422 and 1430 there was a lull in his efforts to escape; within these years I should place the making of *Ps.*

[12] This Suffolk is the same of whose unhappy end Shakespeare gives an unjust account in *2 Henry VI.*

Suffolk's marriage to Alice Chaucer, his close friendship for John and Charles of Orléans, his interest in poetry as shown by the French love lyrics which he wrote while a prisoner in France, just as Charles wrote English love lyrics while a prisoner in England, the possible love affair between Charles and Alice (see Pierre Champion, 'La dame anglaise de Charles d'Orléans,' *Romania,* XLIX [1923], 580)—all these circumstances lead to interesting speculations as to whether William de la Pole or his wife did not lend Charles of Orléans or his brother John a manuscript of the *Canterbury Tales* for the scribe Duxworth to copy, or more probably to use in correcting the copy already made; for *Ps* was probably made before the brothers knew Suffolk and was made from a poor exemplar, while the one it was corrected by was evidently very good, such as Alice Chaucer no doubt would have had. (For further discussion of the corrections, see below; also, M. M. Crow, 'Corrections in the Paris Manuscript of Chaucer's *Canterbury Tales,'* Texas *Studies in English,* XV [1935], 5-18).

[13]Dupont-Ferrier, *Revue historique,* LXII (1896), 61.

[14]Dupont-Ferrier, pp. 62-64.

[15]Dupont-Ferrier, p. 56.

[16]Cf. John Fox, *The Lyric Poetry of Charles d'Orleans* (Oxford, 1969), p. 23. In chapter I ('The poet and His Age') Fox gives an account of Charles' imprisonment in England, 1415-1440.

[17] After the death in 1444 of Angoulême's master, the duke of Somerset, the duke of Suffolk had charge of Angoulême, acting as agent for the duchess of Somerset. Among the Arundel manuscripts is a collection of historical tracts and state papers of William Botoner and John Fastolf, in which are preserved two warrants of 'Guill'e de la Pole Conte de Suffolk to Thomas Gower lieuten' de Chièrebourgh for the release of Jean d'Angoulême from his custody.' The first is dated August 22, 1444, and the second March 29, 1445. The delay of seven months was due to Somerset's death. (See *Catalogue of the Arundel Manuscripts in the Library of the College of Arms* [London, 1829], pp. 85-86).

The close relationship between Angoulême and Suffolk is attested also by two of Angoulême's own letters to the Bastard of Orléans, one dated June 11, 1444, and the other June 28, 1444. Both of these letters, which are printed by E. Charavay *(Revue des documents historiques* [Paris, 1877], pp. 22-23), speak of the negotiations for Angoulême's release conducted by the Bastard and Suffolk, to whom Angoulême refers affectionately as 'mon cousin Southfolk.'

[18] Margaret, when she married the duke of Clarence in 1411, was the widow of John Beaufort I, marquis of Somerset (see G. E. Cokayne, *The Complete Peerage of England* [London, 1913], III, 259).—She died in 1439.

[19] The duchess of Somerset, widow of John Beaufort II, and the executors of the duke's will were granted a pardon on July 19, 1445, 'of all trespasses, misprisions, and offenses committed by them or the duke on the occasion of the escape of John, count of Angoulême, and of all impeachments, actions, suits, quarrels, and demands' *(Calendar of the Patent Rolls Preserved in the Public Record Office,* IV [A.D. 1441-1446], 349).

[20]Dupont-Ferrier, *Revue historique,* LXII (1896), 49.

[21]We have Duxworth's signature to the manuscript of the *Canterbury Tales (Ps)* and to the manuscript of the *Dialogue of St Anselm,* which was begun by Duxworth and finished by Angoulême *(Ms. Lat. 3436,* Bib. Nat.).

Probably both of these manuscripts were made for the count during his captivity in England. That the Chaucer manuscript was made there rests upon the following evidence: (1) It contains the work of an English poet. (2) The scribe bears an English name. Angoulême had other scribes in France —Georges le Maalot, his chaplain and confessor, and Guillaume Arbalêtrier (see Delisle, I, 147). (3) The count added corrections and a table of contents in English. (4) The manuscript bears on the first page the coat of arms of the house of Angoulême alone, not the arms of Angoulême parted with those of Rohan, which Angoulême caused to be drawn upon his manuscripts after his marriage to Marguerite of Rohan shortly after his return to France (Champion, *La librairie de Charles d'Orléans* [Paris, 1910], p. 120).

[22]Dupont-Ferrier, *Revue historique,* LXII (1896), 52.

[23]Delisle, p. 147.

[24]Delisle, p. 147.

[25]Delisle, pp. 148-149.

[26]Champion, *Vie de Charles d'Orléans,* p. 355.

[27]Thevet, in Champion's *Vie*, plate VII. — Angoulême's heart was buried in the church of the Celestines and was religiously guarded there until the revolutionists threw its dust to the winds in 1792 (P. Paris, *Les manuscrits francois de la bibliothèque du roi* [Paris, 1841], IV, 103). According to Esclafer, the Count was buried, after his funeral on May 5, 1467, in the cathedral of Angoulême. In 1562, when the Protestants sacked the cathedral, they threw the remains of the Count out of his tomb. These were recovered by the canons and, at the time of the restoration of the cathedral in 1634, were enclosed in a little lead coffin and deposited in a vault within the choir *(Mémoires*, 1967, p. 55).

[28]Charles of Valois, count of Angoulême, father of Francis I. — According to Jean du Port, *La vie de tres illustre et vertueux prince Jean, conte d'Angoulême*, (Angoulême, 1589), quoted by Champion, Angoulême was a man chaste to the point of never in his life having known any woman but his wife. However, Mas-Latrie, p. 1538, states that Angoulême had a natural son named John, whom Charles VII legitimized. As the biography written by Jean du. Port was based on the inquiry for canonization of Angoulême, it emphasized the saintly qualities of his character.

[29]Champion, *Histoire poétique du quinzième siècle* (Paris, 1923), I, 379.

[30]Dupont-Ferrier, *Bibliothèque de la faculté des lettres de Paris*, III (1897), 39, 92.

[31]Dupont-Ferrier, p. 86.

[32]Dupont-Ferrier, See p. 40 and ff.

[33]The fact that Angoulême read and liked especially the *Somme des vices et des vertus* is of much interest, for it makes probable an important inference concerning the exemplar of *Ps, viz.*, that it lacked the *Parson's Tale*. If the count liked Friar Lorens' work, which is so much like the *Parson's Tale* that it was long regarded as a source, certainly he would not have failed to have this tale, had it been available, copied into his manuscript of the *Canterbury Tales*.

[34]Dupont-Ferrier, *Bibliothèque de la faculté des lettres de Paris*, III (1897), 47-49.

[35]Dupont-Ferrier, p. 50.

[36]Charavay, pp. 19-20.

[37]Dupont-Ferrier, *Bibliothèque de la faculté des lettres de Paris*, III (1897), 53-54.

[38]Champion, *Vie de Charles d'Orléans*, pp. 440, 451.

[39]A humorous account of the last judgment. The manuscript is reproduced in photostate by Champion, *Histoire poétique du quinzième siècle*, I, 382 (plate xxxvi).

[40]Champion, p. 381.

[41]Delisle, I, 147.

[42]Champion, *Vie de Charles d'Orléans*, p. 450.

[43]Dupont-Ferrier, *Bibliothèque de la faculté des lettres de Paris*, III (1897), 54.

[44]One would suppose that the manuscript descended to John of Angoulême's son, Charles of Valois, count of Angoulême, who formed in his chateau at Cognac a fine collection of manuscripts and printed books, and from him to his son, Francis I. But the inventory of Charles' library, made, in 1496, lists among its 180 items no Chaucer (see inventory prepared by Francois Corlieu and published first by Samuel Bentley, *Excerpta Historica, or, Illustrations of English History* [London, 1831], pp. 345-352, and second by E. Sénemaud, *La bibliothèque de Charles d'Orléans, comte d'Angoulême, au chateau de Cognac en* 1496 [Paris, 1861]). Champion ('Librairie du comte d'Angoulême, appendix II of *La librairie de Charles d'Orléans*, p. 120) states that the books of the count of Angoulême formed the most ancient collection of the library which Francis I reunited at Fontainebleau in 1544 (cf. P. Arnauldet, 'Inventaire de la librairie du chateau de Blois en 1518,' *Le bibliographe moderne*, VI [1902], 148-149).

[45]Aside from the facts that Johannes Duxworth (Duxwurth) was an Englishman whose dialect was Northern or North Midland, that he made two manuscripts for John of Angoulême, and that he was a neat and painstaking copyist, we know but little of the *Ps* scribe. He accompanies his signature in both *Ms. anglais 39 (Ps)* and

Ms. Lat. 3436 with the figure *XII* and with a motto, 'a elle magre.' Just above the motto in *Ps* is a drawing of a small deltoid leaf with serrated edges and reticulate venation. The motto, the leaf, the numeral no doubt would all, if rightly explained, tell us much about the man John Duxworth; but they all present problems for which I can offer no very satisfactory solutions.

For the numeral I shall attempt no explanation. That a man might accompany his signature with a numeral having some special significance is illustrated in Charles of Orléans' use of *XL* on his signet, supposed to refer to the year of his delivery from captivity, 1440 (Champion, *La librairie de Charles d'Orléans*, p. xliii).

The motto is not as clear in *Ps* as it is in *Ms Lat. 3436*. McCormick, p. 386, questions the reading 'magre' in *Ps;* Halfmann, p. 57, reads 'a elle uiagre.' In the Latin manuscript the reading 'magre' is unmistakable. 'A elle ma gré' might be translated 'to her my favor,' were *gré* only a feminine noun. There is a feminine form, spelled *grée*. Both *gré* and *grée* are defined by Godefroy as meaning 'volonte' — an interesting fact in that Charles of Orléans bore on his signet the motto 'ma voulenté' (see Champion, *La librarie de Charles d'Orléans*, p. xliii). The motto might be one of the enigmatic variety popular in the days of chivalry. Ancient mottoes, according to Oswald Barron (see article 'Heraldry,' *Enc. Brit.*, 14th ed.), were often cryptic phrases whose meanings were known only to the user and perchance to his mistress; e.g., 'Plus est en vous' of Louis de Bruges, and 'Till then thus' of an English gentleman.

The leaf might have some connection with the cult of the Flower and the Leaf, which was at its height in France and England at the time the Orléans brothers were prisoners in England and Duxworth was making manuscripts for John. Charles wrote two ballads on the subject, presenting the leaf as his choice. It would not be impossible that John as well as Charles was devoted to the cult of the leaf, and that Duxworth adopted it in honor of his patron.

The leaf in the manuscript, however, although it is not drawn with enough detail to permit accurate identification, seems to be none of those usually mentioned for their lasting quality in poetry on the Flower and the Leaf — laurel, woodbine, hawthorne, oak, and agnus castus (cf. G. L. Marsh, 'Sources and Analogues of "The Flower and the Leaf," ' *Modern Philolgy*, IV [1906-07], 131-133, 154-155). I suggest that the leaf is a dock, a pun on Duxworth, or Dokesworth, being intended. Examples of the spelling 'Dokesworth' may be found in the *Calendar of Wills Proved and Enrolled in the Court of Husting, London, A.D. 1258 — A.D. 1688*, ed. R. R. Sharpe (London, 1889), I, 334, 359-360, 390, etc. The spelling 'dok' for *dock* is common in Middle English (see *N.E.D.*). Dock (burdock) leaves were used in the fourteenth century arms of Sir John de Lisle (see Barron) and in the arms of Hepburn (see A. C. Fox-Davies, p. 194).

[46]Cf. Richard Jordan, *Handbuch der Mittelenglischen Grammatik*, rev. H. C. Matthes (Heidelberg, 1934), pp. 17, 48-49 and *passim;* Samuel Moore, Sanford B. Meech, and Harold Whitehall, "Middle English Dialect Characteristics and Dialect Boundaries," *University of Michigan Publications in Language and Literature*, XIII (1935), 1-60; Samuel Moore, *Historical Outlines of English Sounds and Inflections*, rev. A. H. Marckwardt (Ann Arbor, 1951), pp. 110-129; Hans Kurath and Sherman M. Kuhn, "The Dialect Areas of England, 1400-1450," *Middle English Dictionary, Plan and Bibliography* (Ann Arbor, 1954), pp. 8-12; Fernand Mossé, *A Handbook of Middle English*, trans. J. A. Walker (Baltimore, 1952), pp. 16-86 *passim;* G. L. Brook, *English Dialects* (New York, 1963), pp. 61-78; Gillis Kristensson, *A Survey of Middle English Dialects, 1290-1350. (The Six Northern Counties and Lincolnshire)*, Lund, 1967. For a more detailed analysis of the Northern elements in *Ps*, see Crow, Texas *Studies in English*, July, 1938, pp. 16-19.

[47]In trying to determine the identity of the corrector manuscript used by Angoulême and Duxworth, I have made a study of all corrections in *Ps* that are erroneous and that show agreement in error with other manuscripts. There are forty-two such corrections. There is some evidence that the manuscript used in

making corrections was related to *Harley 7335, B. M.* But because the corrections are unimportant in character and might occur independently to different scribes, and because they show agreement with widely scattering manuscripts, no sound conclusion can be drawn.

[48]For a detailed study of the corrections, see Crow, Texas *Studies in English,* XV (1935), 5-18.

[49]For examples of other unique spurious lines, probably composed by Duxworth or Angoulême, see Crow, 'Unique Variants in the Paris Manuscript of the *Canterbury Tales,*' Texas *Studies in English,* XVI (1936), 26.

[50]For other incipits and explicits, see *ibid.,* pp. 18-19.

[51]See p. 34.

[52]*Monk's Tale,* B 2399-2406. Cf. F. N. Robinson, ed., *The Works of Geoffrey Chaucer,* 2nd ed. (Boston, 1957), p. 749.

[53]For numerous other examples of editorial variants, see Crow, Texas *Studies in English,* XVI, 23-25.

[54]For the evidence upon which these statements are based, see Manly and Rickert, *Text of the Canterbury Tales,* I, 401; II, 81, 130-131, 144-145, 160-161, 181-182, 196-197, 212, 223-224, 231-232, 240, 250, 267, 269-270, 276-277, 290-291, 298, 310, 319, 333, 343, 357, 366, 401-402, 416, 430-431, 443-444, 449, 453. See also chapter X, pp. 99-118 ('Textual Relationships') of my unpublished doctoral dissertation, *Scribal Habits in the Paris Manuscript of Chaucer's Canterbury Tales,* The University of Chicago, 1934. Although my dissertation shows divergence of opinion as to the classification of *Ps* in some tales, it illustrates fully the highly variable nature of *Ps* textual relationships.

[55]*Harley 1239* contains, of the *Canterbury Tales,* only the *Knight's Tale, Man of Law's Tale, Clerk's Tale, Wife of Bath's Tale,* and *Franklin's Tale.*

[56]See Manly and Rickert, II, 76-77.

[57]Manly and Rickert, II, 24-27, 41; see also Eleanor P. Hammond, *Chaucer: A Bibliographical Manual* (New York, 1908), p. 112.

[58]See Champion, *Vie,* pp. 668-70.

"An Easter Play in Finland"

[1]Toivo Haapanen, *Verzeichnis der mittelalterlichen Handschriftenfragmente in der Universitätsbibliothek zu Helsingfors,* III, *Breviaria,* Helsinki, 1932, pp. 19-20.

[2]Matt. xxviii.5-10; Mark xvi.5-7; Luke xxiv.4-6 as reprinted from the Vulgate in Karl Young, *The Drama of the Medieval Church,* 2 vols. (Oxford, 1933), I, 202.

[3]O. B. Hardison, Jr., *Christian Rite and Christian Drama in the Middle Ages* (Baltimore, 1965); Helmut de Boor, *Die Textgeschichte der lateinischem Osterfeiern* (Tubingen, 1967). De Boor includes in his study plays from Spain and Hungary as well, but he states specifically that he knows of no Easter plays from the Scandinavian countries (p. 18).

[4]Dr. Toni Schmid, "Das Osterspiel in Schweden," *Kyrkohistorisk Arsskrift,* 1952, pp. 1-14.

[5]Translation:

Chorus: Mary Magdalene and the other Mary bore spices at daybreak, seeking the Lord in the tomb.
Women: Who will remove for us from the door the stone that we see covering the holy tomb?
Angel: Whom seek you, O fearful women, in this tomb, weeping?
Women: We seek Jesus of Nazareth who was crucified.
Angel: He whom you seek is not here; but go swiftly and announce to the disciples and Peter that Jesus has arisen.
Women: We came to the tomb lamenting, we saw the angel of the Lord sitting and saying that Jesus has arisen.
Two a(postles) (?): Two ran together, and the other disciple ran before faster

than Peter and came first to the tomb.

Two elders (?):   Perceive, O comrades, behold the graveclothes and sudary, and
                    the body of Jesus is not found in the tomb.

Chorus: The Lord has risen from the tomb, who for us hung on the cross,
                    alleluia.

[6]Reprinted from Young, I, 201. From the content and from other versions of
the trope we infer that the third sentence, the announcement of the Resurrection,
was spoken by the speaker(s) of the first. Translation:

Question: Whom seek you in the tomb, followers of Christ?

Answer: Jesus of Nazareth who was crucified, O Heaven-Dwellers. He is
                    not here, he has risen, as he foretold; go, announce that he has risen
                    from the tomb.

[7]Die lateinischen Osterfeiern, (Munich, 1887).

[8]Young, I, 308-13.

[9]Hardison, 220.

[10]Hardison, p. 182 ff.

[11]De Boor, p. 148, "Er [Typus II] is nicht nur im formalen Aufbau eine
geschlossene Neuschöpfung, er ist aus einer neuen inneren Konzeption gestaltet."
Convinced that earlier critics, especially Lange and Young, missed the significance
of the difference, De Boor emphasizes the point repeatedly—pp. 131-32, 147-49,
155-58.

[12]Hardison, p. 231.

[13]De Boor, pp. 137, 148.

[14]Hardison, p. 232.

[15]De Boor, p. 133.

[16]De Boor, pp. 207, 219.

[17]Discussed by De Boor, pp. 137-47.

[18]Young, I, 232, 315.

[19]Young, I, 631.

[20]Hardison, p. 236.

[21]The lone Finnish bishopric, centered in Turku, was functioning at least as early
as 1902 (John H. Wuorinen, A History of Finland [New York, 1965], p. 35),
and the earliest monastery in Finland appears to date from 1249 (Wuorinen,
p. 42). The considerable influence of this Dominican house on the Finnish Church
and liturgy was wholly French (H. Holma and A. Maliniemi, Les Etudiants Fin-
landais a Paris au Moyen Age [Helsinki, 1937], p. 6 ff.). Since the Stage II play was
a German innovation and no extant texts of it are from France, it seems unlikely
that the play was brought to Finland by these Dominicans.

[22]Wuorinen, pp. 38-41.

" 'Everyman': The Way to Life"

[1]For the customary view of the play, see for example Albert C. Baugh, "The
Middle English Period," in A Literary History of England, edited by Albert C. Baugh
(New York, 1948), p. 286; Arnold Williams, The Drama of Medieval England
(East Lansing, Michigan, 1961), p. 161; and A. P. Rossiter, English Drama from
Early Times to the Elizabethans (New York, 1950), p. 95.

[2]David Kaula, "Time and the Timeless in Everyman and Dr. Faustus," College
English, XXII (October, 1960), 12.

" 'Haf owre to Aberdour': A Note on
'Sir Patrick Spens' "

[1]Sir Patrick Spens is balled No. 58 in Volume II of the Child collection (Boston,
1882-1898), with notes and texts on pp. 17-20, 32, and 20-32 respectively. More

recent ballad editors have followed Child's identification of Aberdour without question; e.g., MacEdward Leach, ed., *The Ballad Book* (New York, 1955), p. 179: "The ship was lost off the Scotch coast of Aberdeenshire."

[2]II, 20.

[3]II, 19.

[4]"Kean-Gorn" in version R is surely a phonetic corruption of "Kinghorn."

"The Ingenious Compliment: A Consideration of Some Devices and Episodes in 'The Merry Wives of Windsor' "

[1]William Green, *Shakespeare's "Merry Wives of Windsor"* (Princeton, 1962), pp. 21-50. The second chapter of this work contains a summary of earlier scholarship on this point.

[2]Green, pp. 195-197.

[3]Allan Gilbert, *The Principles and Practice of Criticism* (Detroit, 1950), pp. 71-73. See also Green, pp. 195-198, especially the footnotes dealing with Professor O. J. Campbell's latest opinion on the subject, and also William Bracy, *"The Merry Wives of Windsor," The History and Transmission of Shakespeare's Text* (Columbia, 1952), pp. 11-12.

[4]Gilbert, pp. 70-71.

[5]Green, p. 49.

[6]Ruth Kelso, *The Doctrine of the English Gentleman in the Sixteenth Century* ("University of Illinois Studies in Language and Literature," XIV, Urbana, 1929), p. 13.

[7]William Garrard, *The Art of Warre* (London, 1591), sig. L1[V]. See also the account of the elaborate retinues used by Lord Hunsdon and Sir Henry Lee in E. K. Chambers, *Sir Henry Lee, An Elizabethan Portrait* (Oxford, 1936), pp. 172-173.

[8]Citations from Shakespeare in this essay are to William Shakespeare, *The Merry Wives of Windsor,* ed. George Van Santvoord (New Haven, 1955).

[9]William Shakespeare, *The Merry Wives of Windsor,* ed. George Van Santvoord, "Notes of Act II, scene iii," p. 114.

[10]Sir William Segar, *The Booke of Honor and Armes* (London, 1590), sig. F2[R] See also Vincentio Saviolo, *Of Honor and Honorable Quarrels* (London, 1595), sig. Gg2[R].

[11]*Cal. State Papers, Eliz. Dom.,* III, 477: Sir John Burgh arranges to meet John Gilbert with "only one gentleman of good quality or Alone." See also Edward Herbert, *Autobiography of Edward, Lord Herbert of Cherbury,* ed. Sidney Lee (London, 1892), p. 131.

[12]The Folio text does not include the words "Give me thy hand, terrestrial; so." These words do appear in the Quarto text, however. Recent textual criticism of the play suggests that the Quarto is a memorial reconstruction by the actor who played the Host. His necessary familiarity with his own part suggests the Quarto's version of this speech is the correct one. See William Green, pp. 73-120, for a summary of the scholarship on this point.

[13]Green, pp. 39, 40.

" 'By Shallow Riuers': A Study of Marlowe's Dido Queen of Carthage' "

[1]See H. J. Oliver, ed., *"Dido Queen of Carthage" and "The Massacre at Paris"* (Cambridge, 1968) in *The Revels Plays* with Clifford Leech as general editor, p. xli: "the Jupiter-Ganymede part is minor and quickly forgotten"; and my own *"Dido, Queen of Carthage,'* N&Q, n.s., 9 (1958), 371-373.

[2]All quotations and line numberings from Marlowe's plays are taken from the

following text: C. F. Tucker Brooke, ed., *The Works of Christopher Marlowe* (Oxford, 1910; reprinted 1953). In this essay line numberings are included parenthetically following the quotation.

[3]The 1594Q text has "Alcion, a Musition," which is usually interpreted as the result of Marlowe not referring to known legends but to be inventing. I suggest that it is a form of "Halcyon" and refers to the legend of Ceyx and Halcyon (Ovid's *Metamorphoses*, Book XI) in which Halcyon and Halcyon days represent "peace and tranquillitie" after the storms and tempests that severed husband and wife. See George Sandys, *Ovids Metamorphosis* (London, 1632, 1640), commentary on Book XI, Sig.Gg2-3. Sandys' information basically stems, of course, from Natalis Comes' *Mythologiae* (Venice, 1568), *Liber Octauus, Cap.* XVI *De Halcyonibus.*

[4]See Clifford Leech. "Marlowe's Humor," in *Essays on Shakespeare and Elizabethan Drama in Honor of Hardin Craig,* ed. R. Hosley (London, 1963), p. 73, and Oliver, p. 67, nn. 29, 30.

[5]The story of Pigmalion in the *Metamorphoses,* Book X, occurs in Orpheus' song of "inordinate affections"—Cyparissus, Hyacinthus, Ganymede, etc.

[6]Compare the use of Sinon throughout Shakespearian drama for instance, especially in *Cymbeline,* III.iv; *3 Henry VI,* III.ii; *Titus Andronicus,* V.iii, and in "The Rape of Lucrece."

[16]Oliver, p. 34, nn. 272-288, though Oliver does not show its dramatic relevance.

[8]Compare " 'as fierce *Achilles* was' *Tamburlaine*" (478) and "Tamburlaine 'as fierce *Achilles* was'," *Comparative Drama,* I, 2 (Spring, 1967), 105-109.

[9]T. S. Eliot, *Selected Essays* (New York, 1932).

[10]Compare the beginning lines of Book II of *The Aeneid.*

[11]See Sandys, p. 247.

[12]Compare Gonzalo in *The Tempest*—"It is foul weather in us all, good sir,/When you are cloudy" (II.i.137-138) with "Our hint of woe/Is common . . . . then wisely, good sir, weigh/Our sorrow with our comfort" (II.i.3-4; 8-9) where deference is tempered with common sense. The many correspondences between *The Tempest* and *The Tragedie of Dido* make this reference particularly appropriate. See J. M. Nosworthy, "The Narrative Sources of *The Tempest*," *RES,* XXIV (1948), 281-294, and my " 'How came that wido in, widow Dido? A Note on *The Tempest*," *American Notes & Queries,* I, 9 (May, 1963), 134-136; I, 10 (June, 1963), 150-152.

[13]Oliver, p. xlii.

[14]C. F. Tucker Brooke, ed., *The Works of Christopher Marlowe* (Oxford, 1910; rep. 1953), p. 567.

[15]Oliver, p. xlii, accepts this rather naively at surface level.

[16]Oliver, p. 34 nn. 272-288, though Oliver does not show its dramatic relevance.

[17]Compare *Titus Andronicus,* I.i.136-138, where Shakespeare emphasizes Hecuba's revenge on Polymnestor.

[18]Oliver, p. 35, nn. 297-299, calls this inconsistent!

[19]Arthur Golding, trans., *The xv. Bookes of P. Ouidius Naso, entytuled Metamorphosis . . . .* (London, 1567), The Preface, Sig. Aiii[v].

[20]Compare the beginning lines of *Faustus:* "Not marching now in fields of Thracimene,/Where Mars did mate the Carthaginians" and my suggestion iñ "The Marlowe Canon," *N&Q,* n.s. VI, 2 (February, 1959), 71-74, that a play by Marlowe on Hannibal may have been lost.

[21]Compare Iago's threat that Brabantio shall have "gennets for germans" in a context of "Barbary horse" and sexual prowess, *Othello,* I.i.

"Peele's 'Old Wives' Tale' and
Tale-Type 425 A"

[1]Line 196. The phrase is repeated in ll. 203, 205, 480. These and subsequent line references to the play, which has no act or scene divisions, are to the modernized

text of C. F. Tucker Brooke and Nathaniel B. Paradise, *English Drama, 1580-1642* (Boston, 1933).

[2]L1. 220-21.

[3]That is, insofar as the text shows. As a popular attraction, evidently live bears appeared on the stage in *Mucedorus* and Shakespeare's *Winter's Tale;* and of course bears are easily personated by actors. But since Erestus becomes a bear only at night, Peele would have been handicapped in exploiting the attraction.

[4]Joseph Jacobs, *English Fairy Tales* (New York, n.d. [preface d. 1895]), p. 280.

[5]For a third suggestion see n. 21 below.

[6]*Representative English Comedies,* ed. Charles M. Gayley (New York, 1903), I, 345.

[7]Univ. of Texas *Studies in English,* No. 6 (1926); see pp. 146, 148.

[8]Jacobs, pp. 137-45, 279-85.

[9]Ruth L. Tongue, co-ed, (Chicago, 1965), pp. xxv-xxvi.

[10]*The Folktale* (New York, 1946), p. 100.

[11]The wife is sometimes reunited with her husband through her ability to wash his shirt clean after others have failed. Recitation of the charm is, however, far more prevalent in variants examined for this study. The Aarne-Thompson index is somewhat vague in specifying the charm; see plot-division V. under Type 425.

[12]See Leland L. Duncan, "Folk-Lore Gleanings from County Leitrim," *Folk-Lore,* IV (1893), 190-94, and Mabel Peacock, "The Glass Mountain," *Folk-Lore,* IV, 322-27.

[13]Vance Randolph with Herbert Halpert, *Who Blowed up the Church House?* (New York, 1952), p. 174.

[14]Stith Thompson, ed., *One Hundred Favorite Folktales* (Bloomington, 1968), p. 114.

[15]Richard Chase, ed., *Grandfather Tales* (Boston, 1948), pp. 55-56.

[16]Martha W. Beckwith, *Jamaica Anansi Stories* (New York, 1924), p. 130.

[17]Emelyn E. Gardner, *Folklore from the Schoharie Hills, New York* (Ann Arbor, 1937), p. 112.

[18]See Patrick Kennedy, *Legendary Fictions of the Irish Celts* (London, 1866) pp. 57-67.

[19]Called "King Henry" in Jamaican variants (see nn. 16, 35 above and below), the bridegroom appears to have become confused with a monarch real or legendary. The suggestion of a werewolf in the Gardner variant is particularly interesting. *The ancient English romance of William and the Werewolf,* ed. F. Maddan (London, 1832), was not examined in the preparation of this study, but the title remains intriguing. Further, one of Marie's *Lays* concerns a nobleman who is a werewolf.

[20]Noted in *Backwoods to Border* (Pubs. of the Texas Folklore So., No. XVIII), ed. Mody C. Boatright and Donald Day (Dallas, 1943), pp. 76-77.

[21]In *Milton's Poems on Several Occasions* (1785). Gummere indicates that Warton also would trace the man-bear motif to Apuleius; but he rightly concludes that Apuleius's spectacle of a thief masquerading as a bear (Book IV) offers little similarity. Warton discussed Peele's play in connection with *Comus,* believed to have been influenced by the play.

[22]L1. 104-107.

[23]Line 115.

[24]David H. Horne, *The Life and Minor Works of George Peele* (New Haven, 1952), pp. 132 ff., discusses the possibility.

[25]*The Golden Asse* (New York, 1931), pp. 123, 124.

[26]L1. 430-33.

[27]Thompson, *Favorite Folktales,* p. 114.

[28]*The Golden Asse,* p. 107.

[29]L1. 489, 651.

[30]Line 659; see also 11. 494-95.

[31]See Randolph, p. 174; Thompson, *Favorite Folktales,* p. 121; Chase, p. 61; Beckwith, p. 130; Gardner, pp. 113, 115, 116. In Apuleius it is Psyche who, having

opened a small chest given her by Proserpina, is overcome with forgetful sleep.

[32]Randolph, p. 174.

[33]Ll. 980-95.

[34]*Life and Complete Works . . . of Robert Greene,* ed. Alexander B. Grosart (London, 1881-83), XIII, 120.

[35]In *Singers and Storytellers* (Pubs. of the Texas Folklore So., No. XXX), ed. Mody C. Boatright *et al.* (Dallas, 1961), p. 42. Whereas Leach's Jamaican informant knew only the "song" or incantation, Beckwith, however, collected the tale in its entirety from islanders.

[36]Briefly discussed, though not in connection with Peele's play, in Arthur K. Moore, *The Secular Lyric in Middle English* (Lexington, Ky., 1951), p. 7. See 11. 295-99, and especially 11. 625-26, of the play (see also the following footnote).

[37]The more significant of these, along with "Childe Roland" and (now) "The Monster Bridegroom," are "The Good Gal and the Bad Gal" and the motif of "the grateful dead." The clerical satire arising from the "grateful dead" element is reinforced, it is worth noting, by the enchanted carolers, Peele's "Harvest-men." They enter immediately following the churchyard scene (11. 525-618), at the conclusion of which Corebus says: "Well, we'll to the church-stile and have a pot, and so trill-lill." The church-stile, as a boundary, coincides with the fable of the carolers, who had been doomed to rove, dance, and sing for a twelvemonth for having danced within a churchyard.

"Maia's Son: Milton and the

Renaissance Virgil"

[1]*Milton and the Renaissance Ovid* (Urbana, Illinois, 1946).

[2]An edition of Bernard's manuscript (parts of which are almost undecipherable) is being prepared by Professor J. W. Jones of William and Mary.

[3]*Auctores Mythographi Latini* (London, 1742). Citations from Fulgentius are taken from this edition, to which references will subsequently be made in the text of the paper by page number.

[4]*Paradise Lost,* IV, 297. All citations from this poem are taken from H. C. Beeching, ed., *The Poetical Works of John Milton* (Oxford, 1904, reprinted 1952). References to book and line will be made in the text of the paper.

[5]For a discussion of Bernard, see Henry Osborn Taylor, *The Medieval Mind* (New York, 1902), II, 142-143.

[6]The copy of Landino that I consulted is an incunabulum in the Rare Books Room of the University of North Carolina Library. There is no title page for the whole work. The title page for Book I identifies it as follows: "Christophori Landini Florentini ad Il. Federicum Principem Urbinatum Disputationum Camaldulensium Liber Primus de vita contemplativa et activa feliciter incipit." "Florence, 1475" has been added in pencil. The title page for the third book reads: "Liber III In P. Virgilii Maronis Allegorias incipit feliciter." Pagination has been added in pencil in such a way that it is necessary in references to specify *recto* or *verso* for each page. Reference to the work will be made in this way in the text of the paper.

[7]Edgar Wind, *Pagan Mysteries in the Renaissance* (New Haven, 1958), p. 119.

[8]Wind, p. 118.

[9]*Areopagitica,* ed. Henry G. Bohn, *The Prose Works of John Milton* (London, 1848), II, 68. Merritt Y. Hughes discusses parallels between the allegorical treatment of the *Aeneid* and Spenser's *Faerie Queene* in *Virgil and Spenser, Publications in English, University of California,* II (1928-9). Considering it probable, though incapable of being definitively proved, that Spenser knew Landino's commentary on the *Aeneid,* Hughes suggests a parallel between Redcrosse and Contemplation

and the allegorized Aeneas and Sibyl, though he acknowledges that Guyon's descent to the Cave of Mammon parallels the allegorical descent of Aeneas (pp. 402-403). The Palmer did not accompany Guyon to the Cave of Mammon (*pace* Milton), but Milton could have been thinking of the likeness between Guyon and the allegorized Aeneas.

[10]George Ferguson, *Signs and Symbols in Christian Art* (New York, 1954), p. 171.

[11]In addition to the commentaries of Landino and Fulgentius on the *Aeneid* there were allegorical versions of Ovid, such as that of Sandys, and of Homer, for which one should see Harding (Note 1 above) and George Lord, *Homeric Renaissance: The Odyssey of George Chapman* (New Haven, 1956), pp. 111-112.

[12]Giovanni Pico Della Mirandola, *Oration on the Dignity of Man,* trans. Elizabeth Forbes, *The Renaissance Philosophy of Man,* eds. Ernst Cassirer, Paul Kristeller, and John Randall, Jr. (Chicago, 1945), pp. 230-237. The equation of Raphael and Hermes occurs frequently.

[13]Wind, pp. 107-108, cites other passages of Ficino's works to explain the Hermes of Botticelli's *Primavera* as a "divine mystagogue."

"Matthew Prior as the Last Renaissance Man"

[1]The present article is in part an outgrowth of a book-length study of Matthew Prior which I was enabled to make by the assistance of a McClintock Research Grant and a Ball State University Faculty Research Grant. I therefore wish to express my appreciation to Dr. James McClintock and to the Ball State University Research Committee for the time and the funds which they made available to me.

[2]Published by Karl J. Trübner.

[3]"The Third Ode of Anacreon, Translated." All quotations throughout this paper from poems written by Matthew Prior and the chronology attributed to these poems are taken from H. Bunker Wright and Monroe K. Spears, eds., *The Literary Works of Matthew Prior,* 2 vols. (Oxford, 1959).

[4]MSS. of the Marquess of Bath at Longleat, Wiltshire, III, 50, April 19/29, 1695.

[5]Middleton Park Papers, Oxford, no. 19, Paris, June 21/July 1, 1699, as quoted by L. G. Wickham Legg, *Matthew Prior: A Study of His Public Career and Correspondence* (Cambridge, 1921), p. 84 n.

"Edgar Allan Poe's Last Bid for Fame"

[1]Edgar Allan Joe, *Works,* ed. James A. Harrison (New York, 1902), VII, 281. The Harrison work runs to seventeen volumes and is known as the Virginia Edition. The late T. O. Nabbott (1898-1968) contracted with the Harvard University Press to do a new full edition, but his death prevented its completion. Parenthetical notes in this essay are to the Virginia Edition.

[2]Poe drew attention to his name and literary reputation when he spunkily filed a lawsuit for libel against T. D. English in 1846; see Sidney P. Moss, *Poe's Major Crisis* (Durham, N. C., 1970), p. 77.

[3]Two recent books emphasize Poe's repute as a critic: see Louis Broussard, *The Measure of Poe* (Norman, Oklahoma, 1969), pp. 27-43; Robert D. Jacobs, *Poe Journalist & Critic* (Baton Rouge, Louisiana, 1969), pp. 376-401.

" 'Very like a Whale': Herman Melville and Shakespeare"

[1]Melville to Evert A. Duyckinck, Boston, 3 March 1849, in Merrill R. Davis and William H. Gilman, eds., *The Letters of Herman Melville* (New Haven, 1960), p. 79. Subsequent references to this edition will be cited as *Letters.*

[2]14 and 18 May 1839; quoted Raymond M. Weaver, *Herman Melville, Mariner and Mystic* (New York, 1921), pp. 114-21.

[3]*D.A.B.*, V. 60.

[4]Melville to Evert A. Duyckinck, 24 February 1849, in *Letters*, p. 77. Melville's Shakespeare was published Boston: Hilliard and Gray, 1837. It is now in the Houghton Library of Harvard University.

[5]*Letters*, p. 77.

[6]George C. D. Odell, *Annals of the New York Stage* (New York, 1931), V, 481-84. See also New York *Herald*, 9 May 1849.

[7]Herman Melville, *Journal of a Visit to London and the Continent*, ed. Eleanor Melville Metcalf (*Cambridge*, 1948), p. 38-entry for 19 Nov. 1949.

[8]*Literary World*, VII (17 August 1850), 127.

[9]*The Confidence-Man*, ed. Elizabeth S. Foster (New York, 1954), pp. 270-71.

[10]*Moby-Dick*, eds. Luther S. Mansfield and Howard P. Vincent (New York, 1952), p. 166. All references to *Moby-Dick* are to this edition.

[11]*Moby-Dick*, p. 113.

[12]*Moby-Dick*, p. 167.

[13]*Pierre or, The Ambiguities*, ed. Henry A. Murray (New York, 1949), pp. 198-99.

[14]*Pierre*, p. 199.

[15]*Hamlet*, II.ii.255-57. The line numbering for all plays cited is that of William Allan Neilson and C. J. Hill, eds., *The Complete Plays and Poems of William Shakespeare* (Cambridge, 1942).

[16]*Journal*, ed. Metcalf, p. 51-entry for 26 Nov. 18-49.

[17]*Moby-Dick*, p. 166.

[18]*Moby-Dick*, p. 492. Compare *Macbeth*, IV.i.

[19]*As You Like It*, II.vii,139-163.

[20]*Moby-Dick*, p. 430.

[21]*Moby-Dick*, pp. 230-231. Compare *Merchant of Venice*, V.i.1-25.

[22]*Moby-Dick*, p. 264.

[23]*Moby-Dick*, pp. 127-129. See *Romeo and Juliet*, I.iv.53-94.

[24]*Moby-Dick*, p. 166.

[25]*Antony and Cleopatra*, III.xi.195-200.

[26]*Moby-Dick*, p. 113, p. 184.

[27]*Antony and Cleopatra*, II.iii.19-23.

[28]*King Lear*, V.iii.97-101.

[29]*Moby-Dick*, p. 382. *King Lear*, III,ii,43-45.

[30]*Moby-Dick*, p. 43.

[31]*Literary World*, VII (17 Aug. 1850), 127.

[32]*King Lear*, I.iv.124.

[33]*Love's Labour's Lost*, I.i.150-153.

[34]*Julius Caesar*, IV.iii.218-224.

[35]*King Lear*, IV.iii.34-37.

[36]*Moby-Dick*, p. 413.

[37]*Call Me Ishmael* (New York, 1947), pp. 59-63. Olson also discusses, pp. 47-51, other aspects of Melville's relation to Shakespeare, but generally in terms somewhat different from those used here.

[38]*Moby-Dick*, p. 515.

[39]*Moby-Dick*, p. 525.

[40]*King John*, IV.i.25-27.

[41]*Moby-Dick*, p. 432.

[42]*Moby-Dick*, pp. 309-10. Compare *Hamlet*, V.i.104-121, 202-216.

[43]*Moby-Dick*, p. 114.

[44]*King Lear*, V.ii.9-11.

[45]*Moby-Dick*, p. 565.

[46]*King Lear*, IV.vi.179; V.ii.11; V.iii.170.

[47]*Samson Agonistes*, ll.1755-58.

[48]*Moby-Dick,* p. 567; see also notes on Job, pp. 699-703, p. 831. Job I: 15, 16, 17, 19.

[49]*The Dramatic Works of William Shakespeare* (Boston, 1837), VII, 134.

[50]*Journal,* ed. Metcalf, p. 31, p. 84, p. 114, pp. 171-172-entry for 14 Nov. 1849, list of books purchased, notes made at sea. See also Jay Leyda, *The Melville Log* (New York, 1951), I, 359-60 and 363, for annotations of Beaumont and Fletcher and of Ben Jonson.

[51]Henry Pommer, *Milton and Melville* (Pittsburgh, 1950).

[52]See Russell Thomas, "Melville's Use of Some Sources in *The Encantadas,*" *American Literature,* III (January 1932), 432-56. *The Faerie Queene,* Book 6, Canto 10, 11. 5-9, also served as one of the extracts at the beginning of *Moby-Dick.*

[53]*Moby-Dick,* p. 118. Compare "Meditation" section of John Donne's *Devotion* XVII.

[54]*The Holy Bible . . . Together with the Apocrypha* (Philadelphia: Butler, 1846; 2 vols. in 1) is inscribed "Herman Melville March 23^d 1850," and is heavily marked. With some forty verses checked, sidelined, or underscored, Job is the most heavily marked book, with Ecclesiastes next. Now in the New York Public Library. Nathalia Wright, *Melville's Use of the Bible* (Durham, N.C., 1949), pp. 9-10, gives some account of frequencies of marking in this and other Melville editions of the Bible, and p. 5, comments on Melville's tendency to associate Shakespeare and the King James Bible: "The thought of both was couched in the early seventeenth century idiom, the metaphysical strain of which is echoed in his most characteristic style."

"The Regional Vision of Laura Ingalls Wilder"

[1]Cornelia Meigs, *et al., A Critical History of Children's Literature* (New York 1953), p. 505.

[2]Eleanor Cameron, *The Green and Burning Tree* (Boston, 1969), p. 171.

[3]Laura Ingalls Wilder, *Little House in the Big Woods* (New York and Evanston, 1953), pp. 1-2. All references to the "Little House" books are to the uniform edition of the series published by Harper & Row in 1953. Further citations will be given in the text. The titles of the books, with dates of original publication and abbreviation, are as follows: *Little House in the Big Woods* (1932), *LHBW; Farmer Boy* (1933), *FB; The Little House on the Prairie* (1935), *LHOP; On the Banks of Plum Creek* (1937), *OBPC; By the Shores of Silver Lake* (1939), *BSSL; The Long Winter* (1940), *LW; The Little Town on the Prairie* (1941), *LTOP;* and *These Happy Golden Years* (1943), *HGY.*

[4]William Jay Jacobs, "Frontier Faith Revisited: The Little House Books of Laura Ingalls Wilder," *Horn Book Magazine,* XLI (October, 1965), 464-473.

[5]Mary Austin, "Regionalism in American Fiction," *English Journal,* XXI (February, 1932), 102.